BANKERS' TRUST

A volume in the series

Cornell Studies in Money
Edited by Eric Helleiner and Jonathan Kirshner

A list of titles in this series is available at cornellpress.cornell.edu.

BANKERS' TRUST

How Social Relations Avert Global Financial Collapse

Aditi Sahasrabuddhe

CORNELL UNIVERSITY PRESS   ITHACA AND LONDON

Visit our website at cornellpress.cornell.edu.

First published 2025 by Cornell University Press

Library of Congress Cataloging-in-Publication Data

Names: Sahasrabuddhe, Aditi, author.
Title: Bankers' trust : how social relations avert global financial collapse / Aditi Sahasrabuddhe.
Description: Ithaca : Cornell University Press, 2025. | Series: Cornell studies in money | Includes bibliographical references and index.
Identifiers: LCCN 2024049553 (print) | LCCN 2024049554 (ebook) | ISBN 9781501782589 (hardcover) | ISBN 9781501782602 (ebook) | ISBN 9781501782596 (pdf)
Subjects: LCSH: International finance—Social aspects. | Financial crises—Prevention—International cooperation. | Banks and banking, Central—Political aspects. | Institutional cooperation.
Classification: LCC HG3881 .S1544 2025 (print) | LCC HG3881 (ebook) | DDC 332.1/1—dc23/eng/20250218
LC record available at https://lccn.loc.gov/2024049553
LC ebook record available at https://lccn.loc.gov/2024049554

Contents

Acknowledgments

This book is about the personal relations that facilitate cooperation and experimentation in times of crisis. In the spirit of the argument, I cannot overlook the people and personal relationships without which this project could ever have been completed, even if not in crisis situations (most of the time, at least).

I'm especially thankful to my advisers, Jonathan Kirshner, Peter Katzenstein, Tom Pepinsky, and Eswar Prasad, at Cornell University, where I started this project. Together, they helped me realize and streamline a very nebulous idea. In their own ways, they each kept me on track with an abundance of support and encouragement, while also providing the necessary but healthy skepticism that helped me sharpen my arguments.

In addition to all his advice, time, and conversations, Jonathan understood, even before I did, what I was trying to say, and reminded me to stop and regroup every time I got lost in the details. Most importantly, he encouraged me to be me, especially when I doubted myself and my work. His guidance gave me the confidence to pursue unconventional ideas and challenge the conventional ones. Tom, Peter, and Eswar pushed me to think big and, when necessary, small and precise to clarify my arguments. Their support and guidance helped me frame my work to engage a wider audience. Christopher Way was an invaluable external reader and mentor during my time at Cornell. They all remain a constant source of support, and I continue to learn from all of them.

No historical work can be undertaken without the tireless efforts of the archivists who manage the files and records that scholars consult. I am especially thankful to Hannah Cleal and Margharita Orlando at the Bank of England, as well as Marcia Cavalinhos, Mihaiela Donisa, Lazaros Filis, and Joanne Ruff at the Bank for International Settlements, the numerous archivists at Columbia University's Rare Book and Manuscript Library, for all their assistance, kindness, and patience during my visits to the archives. To whoever has digitized all the records in the Federal Reserve Archival System for Economic Research, thank you. None of this research would have been possible without support from the Cornell Graduate School, the Social Science Research Council, the Einaudi Center Dissertation Proposal Development Fellowship, the Hayek Fund for Scholars, the Adam Smith Fellowship, the Mario Einaudi Center for International Studies, the Carpenter Fellowship, the Sage Fellowship, and the Global Political Economy Project Pre-Doctoral Fellowship at Georgetown University.

Chapter 4 could not have been written without the willingness and enthusiasm of my interviewees. I am especially thankful to Charlie Bean, Benjamin Bernanke, Forrest Capie, Stephen Cecchetti, Piet Clement, Tim Fogarty, Charles Goodhart, Mervyn King, Donald Kohn, Masaaki Shirakawa, Patricia Mosser, Adam Posen, Simon Potter, Duvvuri Subbarao, Jean-Claude Trichet, Ted Truman, Paul Tucker, and David Wessel, as well as the many other central bankers and journalists who remain anonymous, for their time, valuable insights, and willingness to be interviewed or to meet for conversations. I learned an extraordinary amount of technical and historical detail about the subject and the connections they shared that gave me the opportunity to interview policymakers from across the world.

I would not have even considered a PhD were it not for the inspiration and encouragement of former advisers-turned-friends. James Morrison and Sandy Hager have helped me assimilate into the academic world, kept me engaged in their academic communities, and introduced me to so many peers in the field. They are some of my earliest cheerleaders and their influence is reflected throughout my work.

While at Georgetown, I was lucky to find advisers in Kate McNamara and Abe Newman, who, along with Siyao Li and Nicky Bell, shared thoughtful and constructive feedback on key parts of this book. Kate, along with Juliet Johnson and Steve Nelson, spent an extraordinary amount of time engaging carefully and critically with the manuscript. I cannot thank them enough for their advice and guidance. During my time at Wellesley College, Stacie Goddard provided invaluable support and feedback as I worked through my muddled ideas. Mark Blyth has been an unwavering source of encouragement since I arrived at Brown, and his suggestions as I revised the manuscript have strengthened the book immensely.

I'm very grateful to the guidance and developmental editing from Tom Mowle, who helped me find my voice in this book. Liz Acorn was a great teammate to go through the book writing process together. Nina Obermeier has been a steadfast friend and a fellow finance nerd who has provided support, feedback, and encouragement from beginning to end. I also thank Isabella Bellezza, Julie George, Eun A. Jo, Mike Kriner, and Julius Lagodny for their friendship and generosity, for reading and commenting on drafts chapters, and sharing words of encouragement. My Cornell community, Michael Allen, Colin Chia, Debak Das, David de Micheli, Alex Dyzenhaus, Naomi Egel, Lincoln Hines, Nazli Konya, Cameron Mailhot, Pauliina Patana, Lindsey Pruett, Jake Swanson, Whitney Taylor, and Jess Zarkin, provided helpful critiques and suggestions, which helped get this project off the ground.

A countless number of scholars gave up their valuable time to read my work. I presented parts of the manuscript at Brown University, Johns Hopkins SAIS, the Balsillie School of International Affairs at the University of Waterloo, and the London School of Economics, as well as at annual meetings of the International Political Economy Society and the International Studies Association. I thank all participants for their helpful critiques and suggestions. From the large list of scholars who provided helpful suggestions, feedback, support, and guidance through various phases of writing, revision, and the publication process, I will single out a few: Bill Allen, Faisal Ahmed, Sheri Berman, Benjamin Braun, Jeff Colgan, Seb Diessner, Daniel Driscoll, Derek Hall, Nikhil Kalyanpur, Paul MacDonald, Jamie Martin, Matthias Matthijs, Daniel McDowell, Richhild Moessner, Yumi Park, Reid Pauly, David Steinberg, Abigail Vaughn, Kate Weaver, and Will Winecoff. Oksana Levkovych provided excellent research assistance at the Bank of England Archives. Victoria von Stein provided an immense amount of support in arranging a manuscript workshop and taking notes on a whole day of discussion. Betty Qian provided excellent research assistance for key parts of this book. I thank them all for their invaluable and enthusiastic work on this project.

Sections of the introduction and chapter 4 originally appeared in Aditi Sahasrabuddhe, "Central Bankers in Crisis: Interpersonal Trust, Cooperation, and the Creation of the Fed Swap Network during the 2008 Global Financial Crisis," *International Studies Quarterly* 68 (2). I thank Oxford University Press for granting me permission to reuse this material.

I am especially thankful to Eric Helleiner and Jackie Teoh, who were immensely supportive in navigating the publication process and the final stages of carrying this book through Cornell University Press. I am indebted to them and to two anonymous reviewers for their critical feedback, generosity, and time in helping me take this over the finish line.

My life outside academia has helped me through this project, right from when this book first began at Cornell, to the final stretch. In particular, I am grateful to Fiona Goldizen, Sara Keen, and Alisha Pinto whose unwavering friendship means more to me than I can express.

Finally, I would not be where I am today without the support of my parents, Anuradha and Atul Sahasrabuddhe, my brother, Kunal, and my sister, Divya. I could not possibly do what I do without the support and opportunities my parents gave me and my siblings. For that, I dedicate this book to them.

Abbreviations

Banxico	Banco de Mexico, or Bank of Mexico
BEA	Bank of England Archives
BIS	Bank for International Settlements
BISA	Bank for International Settlements Archive
BoE	Bank of England
BoJ	Bank of Japan
BSA	Bilateral Swap Agreement
ECB	European Central Bank
EME	Emerging Market Economy
EPU	European Payments Union
ESF	Exchange Stabilization Fund
FIMA	Foreign and International Monetary Authorities
FOMC	Federal Open Market Committee
FRASER	Federal Reserve Archival System for Economic Research
FRB	Federal Reserve Board
FRBNY	Federal Reserve Bank of New York (also New York Fed)
G7	Group of 7
G10	Group of 10
G20	Group of 20
GAB	General Agreements to Borrow
GFC	Global Financial Crisis
GFSN	Global Financial Safety Net
HBOS	Halifax plc and Bank of Scotland
HSBC	Hong Kong and Shanghai Banking Corporation
IFI	International Financial Institution
ILLR	International Lender of Last Resort
IMF	International Monetary Fund
NAFA	North American Framework Agreement
NAFTA	North Atlantic Free Trade Agreement
OEEC	Organisation for European Economic Co-operation
PBoC	People's Bank of China
RBI	Reserve Bank of India
RBML	Columbia University Rare Book and Manuscript Library
RCA	Reciprocal Currency Arrangement

Repo Repurchase facility
SNB Swiss National Bank
TAF Term Auction Facility
WEC World Economic Conference

Cast of Characters

Ansiaux, Hubert, Governor of the National Bank of Belgium (1957–1971).

Avenol, Joseph, Deputy Secretary-General (1923–1933) and Secretary-General of the League of Nations (1933–1940).

Baring, George Rowland Stanley, Lord Cromer, the Third Earl of Cromer, Governor of the Bank of England (1961–1966).

Bean, Charles R., Deputy Governor for Monetary Policy of the Bank of England (2008–2014).

Bernanke, Benjamin S., Chair of the Federal Reserve Board of the United States (2006–2014).

Blessing, Karl, President of the Deutsche Bundesbank (1958–1969); assistant to the Reichsbank President (1929–1934); at the Reich Ministry of Economics (1934–1939).

Bradbury, John S., Joint Permanent Secretary to the Treasury (1913–1919); and Principal British Delegate to the Reparations Committee in Paris (1919–1925).

Bradbury, Sir John (later Lord), with British Treasury (1913–1919); and British Delegate, Reparation Commission (1919–1925).

Bridge, Roy Arthur Odell, joined the Bank of England in 1929; later UK alternate director to the European Payments Union (1950–1952); Deputy Chief Cashier (1957–1963), Adviser to the Governors (1963–1965), and Assistant to the Governors (1965–1969) at the Bank of England.

Brunet, Jacques, Governor of the Bank of France (1960–1969).

Bruning, Heinrich, German Chancellor (1930–1932).

Bullard, James Brian, President and Chief Executive Officer of the Federal Reserve Bank of St. Louis (2008–2011).

Carli, Guido, Director General (1959–1960) and Governor (1960–1975) of the Bank of Italy; later Italian Minister of the Treasury (1989–1992); and President of the LUISS University of Rome, now LUISS Guido Carli (1978–1993).

Case, James Herbert, Deputy Governor (1917–1930) and Chairman of the Board, and Federal Reserve Agent (1930–1936) of the Federal Reserve Bank of New York.

Churchill, Winston (later the British Prime Minister), First Lord of the Admiralty (1911–1915); and Chancellor of the Exchequer (1924–1929).

Ciechanowski, Jan, Polish Minister to the United States (1925–1929).

Clemenceau, Georges, Prime Minister of France (1917–1920).

Cobbold, Cameron Fromanteel, Governor of the Bank of England (1949–1961).

Coombs, Charles, Vice President in Charge of the Foreign Department and Special Manager of the Federal Open Markets Committee, Federal Reserve Bank of New York.

Crane, Jay E., Manager, Foreign Department (1919–1927), Assistant Deputy Governor (1928–1929), and Deputy Governor (1929–1935), Federal Reserve Bank of New York.

Cunliffe, Walter, Governor of the Bank of England (1913–1918).

Dawes, Charles G., President (1902–1921) and Chairman (1921–1925), Central Trust Co. of Illinois; American Member and Chairman, First Committee of Experts on Reparations (1924); Vice President of the United States (1925–1929); and American Ambassador to Great Britain (1929–1932).

de Rothschild, Édouard Alphonse James (Baron), French aristocrat and financier, Regent of the Bank of France (during the Great Depression).

de Wendel, François, French industrialist and politician; Regent of the Bank of France (1913–1936).

Dewey, Charles, Assistant Secretary to the United States Treasury (1924–2917); and Financial Adviser to the Polish government (1927).

Dillon, Douglas, United States Secretary of the Treasury (1961–1965); and US Under Secretary of State (1959–1961).

Ferguson Jr., Roger W., Member of the Federal Reserve Board of Governors (1997–1999); and Vice Chair of the Federal Reserve (1999–2006).

Fisher, Richard W., President and Chief Executive Officer of the Federal Reserve Bank of Dallas (2005–2015).

Fowler, Henry Hammill, US Secretary of the Treasury (1965–1968).

Franck, Louis, Governor of the National Bank of Belgium (1926–1937).

Franks, Sir Oliver Shewell, British Ambassador to the United States (1948–1952).

Fraser, Leon, Director and Alternate President (1930–1933), and President (1933–1935) of the Bank for International Settlements.

Fukai, Eigo, Deputy Governor (1928–1935) and Governor (1935–1937), Bank of Japan; and previously Secretary to the Minister of Finance and Financial Adviser to the Japanese delegation at the Paris Peace Conference in 1919.

Geithner, Timothy F., President and Chief Executive Officer of the Federal Reserve Bank of New York (2003–2009).

George, David Lloyd, Prime Minister of the United Kingdom (1916–1922).

Harrison, George L., Deputy Governor (1920–1929) and Governor (1928–1936); and President of the Federal Reserve Bank of New York (1936–1940).

Harvey, Ernest Musgrave, Chief Cashier of the Bank of England (1918 to 1925), Comptroller (1925–1928), Director (1928–1929), and Deputy Governor (1929–1936), Bank of England.

Hautain, Fernand, Governor of the National Bank of Belgium (1923–1926).

Havenstein, Rudolf, President of the Reichsbank (1908–1928).

Hayes, Alfred, President of the Federal Reserve Bank of New York, and Vice Chairman of the Federal Open Markets Committee (1956–1975).

Holtrop, Dr. Marius, President of De Nederlandsche Bank (1946–1967).

Hoover, Herbert, Director of the United States relief program in Europe (1914–1919); Secretary of Commerce of the United States (1921–1928); and President of the United States (1929–1933).

Hull, Cordell, Congressional Representative (1923–1931) and Senator (1931–1933), Tennessee; and US Secretary of State (1933–1944).

Iklé, Max, Head of Department III, Swiss National Bank (1956–1968).

Ingves, Stefan Nils Magnus, Governor of the Sveriges Riksbank (2006–2022).

Inoue, Junnosuke, Governor of the Bank of Japan (1919–1923 and 1927–1928); and Minister of Finance (1923–1924 and 1929–1931).

Jacobsson, Per, Chief Economist at the Bank for International Settlements (1931–1956); and Managing Director of the International Monetary Fund (1956–1963).

Jay, Pierre, Chairman of the Federal Reserve Bank of New York (1913–1927).

Johnson, Lyndon B., Vice President of the United States (1961–1963); and President of the United States (1963–1969).

Kemmerer, Edwin W., Economics Professor at Princeton University (1912–1943); and adviser to many foreign governments (1917–1934).

Kennedy, John F., Congressional Representative (1947–1953) and Senator (1953–1960), Massachusetts; and President of the United States (1961–1963).

Keynes, John Maynard, Economist and Fellow at King's College, Cambridge University; Member of the Macmillan Committee (1919–1931); and author of *The Economic Consequences of the Peace* (1919), *A Tract of Monetary Reform* (1932), *The Economic Consequences of Mr. Churchill* (1925), and *The General Theory of Employment, Interest, and Money* (1936).

King, Lord Mervyn, Governor of the Bank of England (2003–2013).

Kohn, Donald L., Vice Chair of the Federal Reserve Board of the United States (2006–2010); later Senior Fellow at Brookings Institution and member of the Financial Policy Committee for the Bank of England.

Lacour-Gayet, Robert, Financial Attaché at the French Embassy in Washington (1924–1930); and Director of Economic Research, Bank of France (1930–1936).

Lamont Jr., Thomas William, Partner at J. P. Morgan & Co. (1911–1947).

Layton, Walter, Member of the British Liberal Party, Editor of *The Economist* (1922–1938).

Logan, James A., Unofficial American Delegate, Reparation Commission (1923–1925).

Luther, Hans, German Minister of Finance (1923–1925); German Chancellor (1925–1926); and President of the Reichsbank (1930–1933).

MacDonald, J. Ramsey, British Prime Minister (1924, 1929–1935).

Martin Jr., Willian McChesney, Chairman of the US Federal Reserve and Member of the Board of Governors (1951–1970).

McGarrah, Gates W., American Member, General Counsel of the Reichsbank (1924–1927); Chairman and Federal Reserve Agent at the Federal Reserve Bank of New York (1927–1930); and President of the Bank for International Settlements (1930–1933).

Mereilles, Henrique de Campos, Chair of the Central Bank of Brazil (2003–2010); and Minister of Finance (2016–2018).

Mishima, Yatarō, Governor of the Bank of Japan (1913–1919).

Mlynarski, Felix, Vice President of PKO Bank Polski (1924).

Moley, Raymond, American lawyer; and Adviser to President F. D. Roosevelt (1932–1933).

Moll, Victor, Governor and First Deputy of the Sveriges Riksbank (1912–1929).

Monnet, Jean, Deputy Secretary-General of the League of Nations (1919–1923); partner at Bancamerica-Blair (1925–1929); and President of the High Authority of the European Coal and Steel Community (1952–1955).

Moreau, Émile, Governor of the Bank of France (1926–1930).

Moret, Clement, French Ministry of Finance (1908–1928); Deputy Governor (1928–1930) and Governor (1930–1935), Bank of France.

Morgan, J. P., Partner (1891–1940) and Senior Partner (1913–1940) at J. P. Morgan & Co.; Chairman of J. P. Morgan & Co., Inc. (1940–1943); and American Member, Committee of Experts on Reparations (1929).

Mynors, Humphrey Charles Baskerville, Deputy Secretary (1938–1949), Director (1949–1954), and Deputy Governor (1954–1964), Bank of England.

Norman, Montagu Collet (later Lord), Director (1907–1944), Deputy Governor (1918–1920), and Governor (1920–1944), Bank of England.

O'Brien, Leslie Kenneth, Governor of the Bank of England (1966–1973).

Oddsson, Davíð, Governor of the Central Bank of Iceland (2005–2009).

Ortiz Martínez, Guillermo, Governor of the Bank of Mexico (1998–2009).

Pallain, Georges, Governor of the Bank of France (1897–1920).

Parsons, Maurice Henry, joined the Bank of England in 1928, Private Secretary to the Governor of the Bank of England (1939–1943); Director of Operations at the International Monetary Fund (1947–1950); Deputy Cashier and Assistant to the Governors (1950–1957), Executive Director (1957–1966), and Deputy Governor (1966–1970), Bank of England.

Pierre-Koszul, Julien, Head of the Foreign Department at the Bank of France.

Plosser, Charles Irving, President of the Federal Reserve Bank of Philadelphia (2006–2015).

Pöhl, Karl Otto, President of the Bundesbank and Chairman of its Central Bank Council (1980–1991).

Quesnay, Pierre, General Manager and Head of the Economic Analysis Department of the Bank of France (1926–1929); and first General Manager of the BIS (1930–1937).

Raminsky, Louis, Governor of the Bank of Canada (1961–1973).

Reuff, Jacques Leon, French economist and adviser to the French government.

Rist, Charles, Professor at the University of Paris (1914–1926); Deputy Governor of the Bank of France (1926–1929); Financial Counselor of the National Bank of Rumania (1929).

Robineau, Georges, Governor of the Bank of France (1920–1926).

Roosa, Robert, Federal Reserve Bank of New York (1946–1961); Under Secretary for Monetary Affairs at the US Treasury (1961–1964); General Partner at Brown Brothers Harriman & Company (1965–1991).

Roosevelt, Franklin Delano, Governor of New York (1929–1932); and President of the United States (1933–1945).

Rooth, Ivar, Governor of the Sveriges Riksbank (1929–1948).

Rosengren, Eric S., President and Chief Executive Officer of the Federal Reserve Bank of Boston (2007–2021).

Sayers, Richard Sidney, Economist and historian specialized in the history of banking; Lecturer at the LSE and Oxford; and author of *Bank of England, 1891–1944* (1976).

Schacht, Horace Greeley Hjalmar, President of the Reichsbank (1923–1930 and 1933–1939).

Schwegler, Walter, Head of Department III (1954–1956), Chairman and Head of Department I (1956–1966) of the Swiss National Bank, and Member of the Board of the Bank for International Settlements (1956–1966).

Sheets, Nathan, Director of the Division of International Finance at the Federal Reserve (2007–2011), and Under Secretary of the Treasury for International Affairs (2014–2017).

Shirakawa, Masaaki, Deputy Governor (2008) and Governor (2008–2013) of the Bank of Japan; previously General Manager for the Americas for the Bank of Japan, and Professor at Kyoto University.

Siepmann, Harry A., Assistant to Finance Member, Executive Council of the Governor General of India (1922–1926); Head of the Central Banking Section (1926–1936) and Director (1945–1954), Bank of England.

Skinner, Ernest, Private secretary to Montagu Norman.

Sproul, Allan, President of the Federal Reserve Bank of New York (1941–1956).

Stewart, Walter W., Director of the Division of Research and Statistics of the Federal Reserve Board (1922–1925); Vice President (1926–1927), Chairman (1930–1937), and President (1937–1938) at Case, Pomeroy & Co.; Economic Adviser at the Bank of England (1928–1930).

Strong, Benjamin, Governor of the Federal Reserve Bank of New York (1914–1928).

Subbarao, Duvvuri, Governor of the Reserve Bank of India (2008–2013).

Trichet, Jean-Claude, President of the European Central Bank (2003–2011).

Triffin, Robert, Belgian-American economist, notable for his critique of the Bretton Woods system (later known as the Triffin Dilemma).

Tucker, Paul, Deputy Governor for Financial Stability of the Bank of England (2009–2013).

Tüngeler, Johannes, Director of the Foreign Department of the Bank of German States (1948–1953); member of the Board of Directors (1953–1976), Board of Directors and the Central Bank Council (1957–1976), Deutsche Bundesbank; Reich Ministry of Economics previously (1917–1945).

Van Hengel, Adrianus Johannes (Arie), Delegated commissioner at the Rotterdamsche Bankvereenining (1924–1927); International Committee (1931); and Director General of Credit Anstalt (1932–1936).

Vanderlip Sr., Frank Arthur, President of the National City Bank of New York (1909–1919).

Vissering, Gerard, Governor of De Nederlandsche Bank (1912–1930).

Wilson, James Harold, Prime Minister of the United Kingdom (1964–1970 and 1974–1976).

Wilson, Woodrow, President of the United States (1913–1921).

Yellen, Janet Louise, President and Chief Executive Officer of the Federal Reserve Bank of San Francisco (2004–2010); Member of the Federal Reserve Board of Governors (1994–1997); Vice Chair (2010–2014) and Chair (2014–2018) of the Federal Reserve.

Young, Owen D., Chairman of General Electric Co. (1922–1939); Chairman of Radio Corporation of America (1919–1929); American Member, First Committee of Experts on Reparations (1924); American Member and Chairman of the Committee of Experts on Reparations (1929); Interim Agent General for Reparation Payments (1924); and Director of the Federal Reserve Bank of New York (1923–1940).

INTRODUCTION

> **Because a man I do not trust could not get money from me on all the bonds of Christendom.**
>
> —J. P. Morgan Sr. (Money Trust Investigation, 1912)

"I wished you could have met M. Franck—so very different from Hautain. A gentleman, who speaks English beautifully + opens his heart as well as his head + states his case firmly without being dogmatic . . . and Flemish instead of Latin!"[1]

This is what Montagu Norman, governor of the Bank of England, wrote to his counterpart in New York, Benjamin Strong, in 1926. Louis Franck had just taken over the post of governor of the National Bank of Belgium (NBB) from Fernand Hautain, during Belgium's interwar currency stabilization efforts.

The previous year, Strong, Norman, and J. P. Morgan bankers had discussed the issue of currency stabilization of the Belgian and French francs following the temporary cessation of the gold standard system after the First World War. For this, Hautain and Strong had arranged a line of credit from New York, supported by similar credits from Norman and other European neighbors. A series of loans to Belgium had been agreed upon between a handful of central bankers led by Strong.

Soon, Strong learned that Hautain had failed to inform him that the Belgian central bank had not secured its autonomy. Strong was disheartened about his experience with the Belgian central bank. Strong's position was now "so materially altered" that Norman could no longer "count on [his] participation in the central bank credit." Strong believed that they must "hereafter be fully informed of the bank's condition."[2] The loan fell through.

Strong's concerns with Hautain were bigger than the issue of the NBB's autonomy. Strong's discouragement did not arise "as much out of the figures and the facts as out of the way the situation was being handled"—in other words, a breach of trust. An official at the Federal Reserve Bank of New York (FRBNY or New York Fed) noted that Hautain "couldn't speak much English" and did not strike him "as a man of much mental calibre." Strong confided, "Very confidentially, I haven't confidence in Hautain" because he "never carried out his promise" to keep the Fed informed. Strong did not trust that Hautain had given them "all the essential information, notwithstanding repeated requests for it."[3] Hautain had "antagonised everyone and they all have lost confidence in him."[4] As Hautain's term ended, it was important to policymakers in Belgium and abroad that they "must be satisfied as to his successor."[5] When Franck took up the post, they were.

Franck's assumption of the position turned Belgium's fortunes around, with regards to accessing credits from New York and London. After Franck assumed the governorship in October 1926, cooperation grew "closer and closer" with the Bank of England and, by extension, with Strong in New York, as well as his counterparts in Germany and the Netherlands. Quickly and collectively, they arranged a credit to stabilize the Belgian franc.[6]

Norman and Strong had developed "a certain proprietary feeling about Belgian stabilization" and subsequent currency stabilization efforts across Europe. Little was known outside this handful of banks about these large loans that had been "secretly made" to support Belgium.[7] Even the governor of the Bank of France, Émile Moreau, was kept in the dark until later.

Norman and Strong's control over the interwar European economy had implications for their continental counterparts. Invitations to participate in stabilization loans were extended by Norman, who limited any cooperative efforts to his friends. Moreau, who Norman disliked and distrusted, groused that "the order in which the invitations were extended was, at the very least, undiplomatic."[8] Any questions that required Moreau's cooperation were, in Arthur Turner's words, "bedeviled throughout by personal animosities, misunderstandings, and deeply ingrained suspicion" of one another's motives.[9] As Charles Kindleberger notes, this rivalry "over which should take the leadership in restoring independence to central banks and stabilization of currencies in Eastern Europe would be pathetic, had it not run risks of instability for the system as a whole."[10]

Personalities, personal relations, and trust matter. They matter even in contexts where social scientists have largely tended to accept that they don't: policymaking in international finance. This short, and admittedly arcane story puts a face to finance to illustrate who is behind these policy decisions and how they make them. It also highlights how personal relationships, trust, and confidence among policymakers—here, central bank leaders—can enhance a country's access to financial assistance in times of need. Personal rivalries and animosities, and a lack of personal trust and goodwill, on the other hand, can hurt a country's circumstances.

Why are some financial pressures met with extensive central bank cooperation, such as the ad hoc credit arrangements extended to Belgium, while other pressures are allowed to escalate? And why are such arrangements available to only some economies but not others? Scholars have tended to lean on a wide set of political and economic explanations, from the perspective of various levels of analysis, for varying patterns of cooperation: the balance of power in international politics,[11] formal and informal rules and norms that institutionalize and constrain behavior,[12] the financial and national interests of states and domestic publics,[13] existing interstate economic or financial ties,[14] the functional necessity of cooperative solutions to shared problems or aims,[15] or because shared policy preferences and intersubjective understandings among officials from different countries naturally lead to such outcomes.[16] The role of particular individuals and leaders, and their personal relations, have rarely featured in these explanations.[17] Instead, political scientists and economists tend to view such policymaking as automatic and mechanical, with little attention paid to the agents who enact it.[18] We lack a theory that links leaders and their own social and personal relations to their job of policymaking.

Bankers' Trust is about how central banks have cooperated when faced with system-threatening financial pressures and crises over the last century (roughly 1920–2020) and why they failed to do so during the Great Depression. I focus primarily on the role of central bankers, usually central bank leaders, in arranging some of the most extensive, but relatively underexplored strategies for crisis management: ad hoc, bilateral credits, loans, and central bank currency swaps in the last century. I argue that interpersonal ties of trust between central bank leaders facilitates ad hoc and bilateral cooperation around these arrangements in times of crisis and uncertainty.

The lack of attention to interpersonal relationships is an unfortunate oversight, given that global governance does not happen automatically: people make it happen.[19] In normal times, systems of rules and conventions prevent leaders from engaging in arbitrary governance.[20] But even in rules-based systems, some agents retain meaningful discretion and can circumvent these constraints. In monetary affairs, central bank leaders' discretion is heightened in moments of market disequilibrium, or shocks, such as financial crises.[21] Normal rules no longer suffice, and conventional metrics lose meaning as assets and balance sheets become impossible to value plausibly.[22] In situations of crisis and radical uncertainty, market actors, and for the specific purpose of crisis management, monetary authorities, must intervene by making rapid, subjective decisions that rely on personal knowledge, familiarity, and trust.[23]

The interwar years were not normal times. They were marked by hyperinflation, banking crises, and dramatic political change, atop the ravages of the First World War. While Strong and Norman's ability to lend was constrained by the rules of the gold standard, it was not these constraints that made the initial loan to Belgium fall through. It was a breach of trust, misleadingly incomplete information, and disheartening interactions that changed Strong's mind. Only when Norman, satisfied with Hautain's successor, vouched for him to Strong, was this loan floated. But Norman's assessment had nothing to do with material concerns. He was not swayed by Belgium's economic position and resources; Franck's character, communication, and even Flemish identity instilled trustworthiness in him. Norman's judgment was personal and subjective.

How can we have an international financial system without trust? Money, after all, is trust instantiated. Rules and institutions, policy regimes, and market signals all serve to instill trust in global finance. In normal times, this trust is "just there," it is habitual, and people do not really need to think about it. In conditions of uncertainty and upheaval, this trust needs to be reclaimed or created, and quickly.[24] I argue that in these conditions, interpersonal relations of trust between leaders, independent of economic resources and broader political and economic considerations, can grease the wheels of financial governance and crisis management.

The central claim of my book is that when central bankers share personal ties of trust with their counterparts, especially with the key issuer of liquidity support, this enables them to engage in extensive, ad hoc, and bilateral cooperation, in conditions of crisis and uncertainty. The strength of these personal ties will influence the terms of these arrangements: strong interpersonal trust among leaders will have the most favorable terms. Looser ties will entail limits and safeguards. Absent these ties, leaders must turn to costlier alternatives.

The Politics of the Global Financial Governance

Today, crisis management relies increasingly on an extensive network of bilateral swap lines between central banks that, at least initially, emerged in a rapid, ad hoc manner, during the global financial crisis (GFC). The ad hoc nature of these arrangements raises worrisome questions about the robustness and durability of the global financial safety net. Yet we know little of how these arrangements come about in the first place.

I develop a relational argument to explain three interrelated outcomes: why central bankers have been able to employ these strategies in some crises but not others; why some central banks can access these tools but not others; and, where the terms of these credits and swaps are explicit and known, why they vary among recipients. Before turning to the argument, I briefly describe the types of liquidity assurance and crisis management strategies available to monetary authorities.

The core principles of financial crisis management have been informed by the insights of Walter Bagehot, a writer and banker in Victorian Britain, who proposed the principle of "lending freely against good collateral at a penalty rate" to guide the central banks, acting as lenders of last resort (LLR), to guarantee the liquidity of the whole economy.[25] Because financial crises starting in one country can quickly spread to others, there is also a need for an international financial governance system to manage systemic crises as a global public good. So, Bagehot's dictum, while domestically oriented, also guides international lender of last resort (ILLR) functions.[26]

In a financial crisis, monetary authorities have a host of unilateral, multilateral, and bilateral options to put out the fire. Each poses economic and political trade-offs, costs, and benefits.[27] First, unilateral strategies include drawing on reserves, domestic bailouts, and rescue packages. Drawing on reserves carries significant costs: it relies on substantial self-insurance policies of accumulating these reserves in the first place. Self-insurance comes at the cost of holding large sums of foreign exchange reserves, which must be invested in liquid assets. They may also not suffice when needed. Bailouts to specific banks or other corporate actors are contentious policy choices, often generating substantial domestic political pushback. But these options are speedy and require no international negotiations to arrange and deploy.

Policymakers may also turn to a second option to meet liquidity needs: multilateral strategies such as reserve pooling or international institutional arrangements such as International Monetary Fund (IMF) loans or other intergovernmental negotiated adjustments. These multilateral options usually carry stringent conditions and encroach on borrowers' monetary sovereignty. They may also not be adequate and can take a long time to negotiate between international financial institutions and debtor countries.[28] In a crisis, when days and even hours count, negotiation time is a crucial weakness of this approach. For these reasons, among others, even in multilateral arrangements, formal rules may be suspended and substituted by informal, modified governance arrangements or may be influenced by unwritten rules. While such informal governance in international organizations (IOs) is undoubtedly an important element of crisis management efforts, this book is focused on a third liquidity assurance strategy: bilateral assistance between central banks.[29]

Bilateral liquidity assurance strategies, such as swaps and credits between central banks, are much less costly than unilateral and multilateral strategies.

They offer a flexible, ad hoc, and rapid means to inject massive amounts of liquidity into the financial system without arduous negotiations with multiple entities. Recipient central banks are free to lend this foreign exchange to domestic banks in their jurisdictions on their own terms. However, bilateral liquidity depends on the availability of another country being willing to take the risk of providing liquidity.

In this book, I argue that the availability of these instruments can be influenced by central bankers' personal relations. Despite significant changes in currency and monetary systems in the last century—the move from the gold standard to today's fiat money and the shift away from sterling to dollar primacy—the nature of liquidity assurance and financial governance has stayed very much the same. And despite the extensive investment in creating institutions, norms, and conventions for crisis management, central bankers, time and again, circumvent these traditional mechanisms in favor of ad hoc, bilateral approaches to managing financial pressures. Each crisis decidedly shows central bankers' preferences for bilateral strategies (over unilateral or multilateral strategies) to meet liquidity needs. This happened all through the 1920s to address financial challenges after the First World War. It was repeated in the 1960s to patch up holes in the Bretton Woods safety net and, again, during the GFC that began in 2007. In the very worst of times, despite extensive ad hoc cooperation in the 1920s, no financing option seemed up to the task of stemming the Great Depression as it escalated.

I focus on the use of ad hoc, bilateral instruments during crises—central bank currency swaps and other flexible interbank loans and credit lines—that have emerged at the core of the global economy and the international reserve currency, be it the dollar, sterling, or gold. The technicalities of how these bilateral instruments operate has varied over time. But a common feature unifying these differences is a long but patchy history of central banks coming to one another's assistance in times of need. They are all ad hoc, short-term, liquidity instruments arranged bilaterally between partner banks. They are flexible loans from central banks to one another at very favorable terms: no costly conditionality.

Crisis and Uncertainty

My argument is specific to situations of crisis and uncertainty. Crises "signal the obsolesce of the status quo in markets and policy regimes and inject deep uncertainty into agents' decision calculus."[30] This world of uncertainty is different to the world of risk, as most lucidly and eloquently explained by John Maynard Keynes:

> By "uncertain" knowledge, let me explain, I do not mean merely to distinguish what is known for certain from what is only probable. The game of roulette is not subject, in this sense, to uncertainty. . . . The sense in which I am using the term is that in which the prospect of a European war is uncertain, or the price of copper and the rate of interest twenty years hence, or the obsolescence of a new invention. . . . About these matters there is no scientific basis on which to form any calculable probability whatever.[31]

Crises generate volatility beyond structural shifts in the economy or in the distribution of capabilities. Uncertainty poses a pervasive constraint. It limits agents' abilities to meaningfully assess future trends.[32] In such a context, agents can no longer think and make decisions in probabilistic terms.[33] As Keynes reminds us, "Human decisions affecting the future, whether personal or political or economic, cannot depend on strict mathematical expectation, since the basis for making such calculations does not exist."[34] When economic conditions are inauspicious and conventional signals of credibility no longer reliable, we fall back on subjective reasoning, personal knowledge, and familiarity, to inform decisions.

From this view, constructivist scholars show that intersubjective understandings and shared beliefs can facilitate cooperation and policy choices.[35] Central bankers' career trajectories can influence monetary policies and levels of central bank independence.[36] Shared career backgrounds and "the revolving doors" among policymakers across governance institutions also shape outcomes in financial governance.[37] They are embedded in social relations, which produce trust in economic exchange that influence individual actions and economic outcomes.[38] However, these works tend to overlook the complementary role that social relations and interactions play in economic processes. They ascribe policy outcomes not to the agents themselves but instead to agent attributes, thus treating embeddedness itself as the explanatory mechanism.[39]

Bankers' Trust similarly questions and challenges the assumptions of risk and rationality but departs from an attributional focus to give pride of place to the agents themselves. It joins a small but emerging literature on relational international politics as well as the study of financial diplomacy.[40] Crisis and uncertainty create room for greater agency, raising questions for how agents respond to events and contexts that necessitate change and how they act to "give meaning to such material changes."[41] Crises, therefore, pose distinct questions about global governance to those of routine governance supported by arm's-length ties in an "asocial market sphere."[42] Evaluating decision-making in crises necessitates a closer look at how agents operate within their professional, personal, and interpersonal relations, with attention to the agents themselves.

The Argument

Personal relations among financial diplomats can shape outcomes of crisis management. Interpersonal ties of trust between central bank leaders facilitates ad hoc and bilateral cooperation using currency swaps. Differentiated personal ties by degree—stronger, looser, or absent—of interpersonal trust can influence the likelihood of accessing ad hoc, bilateral liquidity assistance from partner central banks and the terms of the arrangement. Central bankers with the closest personal relations and trust to the core issuer of the reserve currency will be more likely to receive more favorable terms on credits or swaps. Where ties are looser, liquidity may still be extended but with some limits and conditions to hedge against risks. Leaders outside these circles, who do not enjoy personal ties of trust with the provider, may be forced to turn to more costly alternatives. Such cooperation, which is highly interpersonal and exclusive, is most easily conducted in secret.

Interpersonal Trust and Personal Relationships

In global financial governance, Paul Volcker and Toyoo Gyohten note that central bankers are "uniquely able to deal with each other on a basis of close understanding and frankness."[43] Their actions are not structurally determined solely by positions and roles but are comprised of histories and subjective preferences.[44] This is most crucial in the context of crisis and radical uncertainty, when normal functions and operations are set aside, calling for new interventions to manage crises.

Exploring the intersection between intimate relations and monetary transfers among individuals in various physical, familial, and other social relations—a context very different to central banking—Viviana Zelizer moves "beyond embedding." She notes that "producers are not just embedded in a market" but "actually constitute the market's interface in, and as a set of, their perceptions and choices";[45] economic transactions are thus shaped by meaningful interpersonal transactions. At the intersection of intimate relations and monetary transfers among individuals in social relations, in all economic activity, "people engage in the process of differentiating meaningful social relations."[46] It is not just the individual but, as Zelizer suggests, the "negotiated interpersonal transactions . . . that become the starting point for social processes."

The unique understanding and frankness of which Volcker and Gyohten speak is not available to all, and this has significant effects on outcomes of crisis management. Central banks negotiate the interface between national economies. In a crisis, how they do this is increasingly at the discretion of central bank leaders. The "differentiated ties" framework thus allows us to understand how people, here, central bankers, differentiate meaningful social relations by erecting boundaries, marking and distinguishing relationships with different practices, and designating specific economic transactions as appropriate to relationships.[47] Leaders distinguish interpersonal ties with varying and preferential economic transactions, which has important implications for central banks' options for meeting liquidity needs when faced with financial pressures. Through their relationships and cooperation, central bankers shape the landscape of global governance and reinforce hierarchies and inequalities in the global financial system.

In 1921, Strong wrote to Norman, "I suppose it is a fact that in none of our business relations has the personal relation played so large a part as in banking."[48] Their partnership transformed interwar central bank cooperation into a formal agenda. In the policy realm, Karl Otto Pöhl, a former Bundesbank president, also notes how interpersonal relations shape institutions: "It is the close friendships, not financial resources, that are the real strength of this institution. Different personalities could mean a different BIS."[49]

Central to the substance of these personal relations is interpersonal trust. By trusting we act under the belief that the other will not harm us or our welfare. We accept being vulnerable to risks, and do so in the absence of third-party supervision.[50] Actors who share *interpersonal* trust do not experience that vulnerability and indeed make themselves vulnerable as they do not expect to be exploited in their decision to trust.[51] Here, trust is thus a personal bond that enables risk-taking. It is especially important under conditions of uncertainty when conventional signals become unreliable, as it enables actors to undertake risky endeavors by relying on subjective cues and judgment.

Trust is also an emotional belief that indicates confidence in the goodwill and competence of another.[52] Feelings of goodwill, made up by the structure and the content of the actor's social relations, strengthen the interpersonal aspects of these trust ties. Such ties are rooted in friendship and a sense of obligation, and actors can rely on the support of those with whom they share such relations. Such ties have long been integral in international diplomacy, in questions of conflict, cooperation, and crisis. The influence of policymakers' personal relations in shaping outcomes in international politics is also certainly not limited to the monetary sphere.

For example, David Lloyd George and Woodrow Wilson's personal relationship differed from their ties with Clemenceau in France, and this mattered for diplomatic relations and cooperative efforts in the years following the First World War. Lloyd George and Wilson frequently dropped in on each other and met for lunches or dinners during the Peace Conference, while Clemenceau kept to himself. This social and personal distance was disadvantageous for the French during negotiations. The social element of Wilson and Lloyd George's working relationship was especially important, as Lloyd George noted: "If you meet for social purposes, you can raise a point. If you find that you are progressing satisfactorily, you can proceed, otherwise you can drop it."[53]

Such ties allow individuals to establish norms of frankness and reciprocity and then benefit from these relationships in times of stress.[54] Instilling a personal bond and a sense of obligation in trusting relations affords greater weight to the interpersonal element of these ties. Such bonds emerge from regular interaction and communication, both personal and professional, that allow central bankers to get to know their counterparts' personalities, beliefs, and temperaments and thus know how to engage with one another most effectively.

Trust can be built in several ways: incrementally, through collective identity-formation, by individuals with trusting dispositions, or a leap in the dark.[55] In diplomacy, trust as an *interpersonal* bond relies on positive identification of interests and humanization.[56] Interests must be internalized as collective interests, and through face-to-face interactions, leaders begin to view the other as not only a representative of cold state interests and relations but as human. Personalized diplomacy can break down formal barriers, allowing leaders to meet and engage with one another on a human level. Sharing meals that involve sharing personal-level conversations play a key role in breaking formal barriers; letter writing, email, and phone calls can reinforce interpersonal ties. These personal relations can enable cooperation between actors who share them, allowing them to cooperate over experimental, ad hoc efforts in times of uncertainty, bilaterally, and through personal and informal channels rather than more formal, institutional ones.

In finance, the company that states keep can signal their stability and risk profiles to investors.[57] The company that leaders keep has a similar effect. If leaders share trusting and sympathetic relations with counterparts where broader political and economic ties are looser, we may still see ad hoc cooperative efforts. In these instances, leaders will fall back on personal and subjective reasoning to justify decisions and, again, come to agreements through private, interpersonal discussions. However, risk concerns will call for safeguards such as through conditions, limits, or collateral requirements.

In conditions of crisis and uncertainty, interpersonal trust will enable actors to engage in experimental, bilateral cooperation through free and open personal exchange. The logic of my argument is best articulated by Strong in a letter to Norman in 1927:

> The point he makes about cooperation is, of course, of the greatest significance, but raises the question which you and I have discussed so frequently and fully. How can such a situation as the present one be met by any scheme or device, automatic or mechanical? Must it not be dealt with by this species of management and cooperation such as we have been attempting to give it, and if so, must not people generally trust someone, and therefore, does it not resolve itself to the simple question, "*Do they trust us?*"[58]

Individual, Political, and Economic Sources of Interpersonal Trust

While my analysis is focused on how interpersonal trust among central bankers matters for crisis management, by facilitating ad hoc and bilateral cooperation, it is still important to discuss the various sources of central bank leaders' interpersonal relations and illustrate how personal and interpersonal dynamics interact with political and economic factors.

Two broad categories of factors influence the patterns of leaders' personal relations and, consequently, their options for meeting liquidity needs in a crisis. The first set of factors are leader attributes: reputations, personalities, and perceptions of prestige.[59] Often, and especially in crises, central banks' final decisions need to be made quickly; this authority lies with the head of the central bank.[60] Milton Friedman even warned of the major impact that individual central bankers have on policy, especially in a crisis when leaders have the ultimate authority over policy decisions. Individual central bank leaders' economic philosophies have so significantly influenced the success or failure of economic policies in recent decades that a Fed chair can very likely fashion policy according to their views.[61] Leaders can also influence outcomes through their ability to create and maintain close-knit personal relations with their foreign colleagues. Their reputations, prestige, and personalities can affect their interlocutors' inclination to cooperate with them and even their willingness to engage in risky experimentation during uncertain times.[62]

Second, interpersonal trust is orthogonal to the broader political and economic explanations for cooperation discussed above. I do not refute these alternative facilitators of cooperation as they variously operate to bring leaders together to build interpersonal relationships and camaraderie and allow leaders to learn one another's personalities, temperaments, and dispositions toward trust, risk, and experimentation. But these factors neither systematically generate or explain interpersonal trust, nor do they systematically predict outcomes of cooperation. They do, however, offer important insights into questions of when and why cooperation emerges.

Traditional international relations theories suggest that the balance of power and state interests explain outcomes in world politics, which set critical baseline answers to the questions of when and why cooperation emerges and offer important insights into these questions.

The distribution and balance of power can shape economic activity, such as trade, cooperation, and lending.[63] Charles Kindleberger observed that "for the world economy to be stabilized, there [had] to be a stabilizer, one stabilizer." In international finance, this stabilizing role is played by the state that manages and issues the global reserve currency. Prior to the First World War, sterling had top billing, so to speak, and the Bank of England was the primary manager of coordination and cooperation to support the gold standard system. Since the end of the Second World War, the US dollar has been king.[64] The United States now plays this key function, either directly through the bilateral swaps and credits through the Fed or indirectly through the Bretton Woods institutions when that is more politically convenient for the United States.[65] The absence of this necessary stabilizing influence in the interwar period explains why the Great Depression was so long and so deep.

The power and willingness of leaders to play this role is undoubtedly a function of their national interests and preferences.[66] Currency power allows states to advance their foreign policy and security interests.[67] It also allows states to secure their national financial interests in an interdependent system. Obviously, then, central bankers and other monetary authorities have an incentive to assist foreign countries as a way of protecting their own financial interests from overseas pressures.[68] Given the international and systemic nature of these crises, not doing so would imply that leaders did not do their job.

But it raises the question of a leader's willingness to play its stabilizing role, especially when not playing this role has major ramifications for a state's national interests and material position, and why the United States was unwilling to play this stabilizing role in the 1930s. After all, the Fed willingly extended credits to its counterparts in Europe in the 1920s, as the opening anecdote in this book illustrates. Curiously, the slowdown of this cooperation led by New York and London predates the Great Depression, and the 1929 stock market crash, at a time when neither state's economic positions had changed.

And indeed, policymakers don't always do their job. Looking back, Benjamin S. Bernanke made this point in a speech honoring Friedman on his ninetieth birthday, saying, "Regarding the Great Depression. You're right, we did it. We're very sorry. But thanks to you, we won't do it again."[69] As chapter 4 shows, one area where Bernanke lived up to this promise was at the global level. With the support and cooperation of a handful of partner central banks, Bernanke's Fed engineered the currency swap program, the Fed's single largest program during the GFC, to provide liquidity to several large economies across the world.

The 1960s experience of a faltering Bretton Woods system points to another instance in which central bankers did not do their job, in the delayed extension of swaps and credits to the Bank of England due to the opposition of Bank of England associates to manage sterling pressures early on in the decade. This example also shows that preexisting economic and financial ties between states does not necessarily ensure cooperation in the face of shared problems. Despite the risks of sterling woes to dollar stability, and a long-standing partnership between the United States and Great Britain, interpersonal relations and mistrust delayed the US-UK swap line in the 1960s. In short, neither US monetary power nor financial ties between the two countries sufficed to speed up any cooperative efforts on their own.

Some might respond that domestic politics and interest-group preferences may explain these patterns.[70] In the late 1920s, the expansion of the franchise and the growth of labor movements undermined political and monetary leaders' abilities to pursue internationally oriented policies, thereby undermining central bank credibility and cooperation that were vital to gold standard stability. The period marked a shift away from domestic political and government stability and inactive labor movements that had previously supported international monetary cooperation to political and social instabilities that ultimately worked to undermine it.

Others would argue that the absence of formal and informal rules and norms, institutionalized in IOs to promote and facilitate cooperation, might explain the collapse of cooperation in the Great Depression.[71] Since the mid-twentieth century, the IMF and the Bank for International Settlements (BIS) have undeniably been important players in global financial governance.[72] But if that is the case, we should see that post-1945 crises met with a widespread multilateral, institutional response. Instead, these IOs could not overcome the unwillingness of the Bank of England to cooperate with the Fed in 1961, despite such assistance supporting domestic and interdependent financial interests. Recent crises also highlighted IMF inefficiencies and lack of resources to meet global needs.[73] IOs provided opportunities for face-to-face interactions and communication among monetary authorities. But in a crisis, engineering and deploying multilateral responses can be time-consuming and limited.[74]

In turn, scholars have suggested that in these situations, policymakers rely on their shared economic beliefs to guide decision-making in uncertainty. These shared beliefs are rooted in similar training and educational backgrounds, typically in economics departments in high-ranking US institutions.[75] Others suggest that similar career backgrounds generate common worldviews that guide policy decisions.[76] Certainly, it is also more likely that policymakers with similar training may already know one another before entering their central banking careers. However, leaders of some central banks that received bilateral assistance from the Fed during the GFC were not trained as economists at all. And in the early twentieth century, while some central bank leaders shared similar prior careers in private banking, they did not all hold the same views on how to manage the financial troubles at hand. More generally, shared careers or educational backgrounds do not necessarily prescribe the types of arrangements that central bankers have taken in the face of grave crises. Rather, the bilateral and ad hoc arrangements emerged out of cooperative experimentation among some bankers but not others.

The reality is that institutional rules and norms often cannot guide behavior in a crisis. State power, national interests, domestic preferences, economic ties, and shared beliefs among policymakers may inform agents' evaluations, and suggest important baseline answers to the question of when and why cooperation emerges, but they are incomplete. Functionalist explanations explain why cooperation emerges, that is, out of necessity in response to common problems, but not necessarily the form that cooperation takes. But these accounts cannot explain the chronic reliance on ad hoc, bilateral approaches to liquidity assurance. My argument supplements and strengthens our general understanding of cooperation that these accounts afford us; introducing interpersonal trust is *an* explanation for ad hoc central bank cooperation but not the *only* explanation for it.[77]

Differentiated Ties

In addition to the role of shared beliefs and intersubjective understandings discussed above, while these accounts can tell us why cooperation came about at all, they cannot explain particular patterns of ad hoc and bilateral cooperation over alternative approaches to crisis management. As such, my argument speaks to the existing discourse on the problem of international cooperation, broadly construed, and public goods provision of global financial governance.

No doubt, leaders in more interconnected economies, with strong financial ties, interact more frequently and so may be more likely to build trusting relations. Leader attributes and experiences interact with this larger set of variables that can shape patterns and outcomes of cooperation and crisis management.[78] While these variables neither determine chances of receiving a swap nor trust, they help explain the hierarchical and preferential nature of bilateral cooperation and reinforce differentiated personal ties that insulate the inner circle from outsiders.

There are important scope conditions to the argument. Per the Fed's criteria, banking and financial interconnectedness and economic size delineate the universe of possible swap partners.[79] In the contemporary context, larger emerging markets tend to be systemically important and have deeper financial and banking ties with the United States. While they meet the Fed's economic threshold for a swap, they are more fragile and riskier than advanced economies. In these instances, risk calculations will be moderated by subjective reasoning such as personal ties and trust. Smaller and lower income economies do not meet this threshold and are not borderline cases for swap lines. Even if interpersonal trust doubles the chances of receiving a swap, it would be doubling a near-zero probability to begin with. Personal trust cannot overcome risk nor can it alone bring smaller economies into the set of possible swap recipients.

Interpersonal trust also partially mediates the influence of institutional trust in establishing swaps. That is, the relationship between institutional trust and signing swaps remains operative when interpersonal trust is absent. Moreover, institutional trust does not guarantee interpersonal trust. Institutional ties are sustained through routine cooperation and may influence a bank's credibility to uphold arrangements. They influence which central bankers will more likely forge personal ties with counterparts as leaders in more interconnected economies will interact more frequently. Longer histories of interbank cooperation may instill trustworthiness in partners. However, in this book, I show that while institutional and other material considerations *can* shape the formation of personal ties, they do not do so necessarily or systematically. And even where institutional ties facilitated cooperation, central bankers still used informal channels and personal appeals to establish these arrangements, rather than formal institutional channels.

Different configurations of these factors help explain the hierarchical and differentiated nature of the swap network. Combined, they generate and reinforce differentiated ties among trusting actors, insulate the inner circle, and generate a set of testable implications of my argument. The strongest ties emerge where there is greatest convergence of the variables discussed above, to build personal ties or strengthen existing ones. In the contemporary context, these ties are most apparent among the G7 central bankers (and Switzerland), whose economies share strong financial ties and align with broader power and material configurations in the global economy. This largely reflects the historical balance of power, with Britain and the United States at the center of the financial system and Western Europe and Japan making up the core. Leaders in these economies likely interact with one another more frequently, formally, and informally and can build trust incrementally. While any type of cooperation among these economies is less surprising, I expect these ad hoc and bilateral arrangements to be made informally at the interpersonal level and without hedging beyond minimal collateral.

Outside the core, fewer factors will converge, and risk considerations may enter decision-making calculations. Here, interpersonal trust can moderate risk calculations and carry greater weight under conditions of uncertainty. Opportunities for interpersonal interactions allow trust to emerge among leaders, such as invites to BIS dinners and other social gatherings. If leaders, especially liquidity providers, share trusting and sympathetic relations with counterparts where political and economic ties are looser, we will still see ad hoc cooperative efforts to signal trust, obligations of reciprocity, and support. Leaders will use subjective personal and interpersonal reasoning to justify decisions and, again, come to agreements through private, interpersonal channels. However, risk concerns will call for safeguards in any resulting agreement.

The biggest gap in the hierarchy is between those inside and outside these trust communities.[80] Here, too, political and economic variables may loosely converge. These economies may also be emerging as systemically important economic actors. However, leaders who are less embedded in close-knit professional and social circles may be seen as outsiders, meet less frequently, and are thus less likely to build interpersonal trust relations with the core. Because the key liquidity provider has neither the trust necessary to engage in bilateral, ad hoc cooperation nor the personal bonds and goodwill that facilitate cooperation even with safeguards, they will not feel obligated to enter into agreements with these counterparts. These leaders may then be forced to turn to more costly liquidity assurance options. Where interpersonal bonds are absent, material conditions on their own are insufficient to offset risks.

Secrecy

Secrecy and privacy are essential for this type of cooperation, as in many other areas of global governance. It is an effective tool for eliciting information and encouraging cooperation in economic- and security-focused international organizations, where actors can provide sensitive information without fear of wider release of repercussions.[81] Security and military policymaking can be very controversial, so cooperation related to such issues is often secretive.[82]

Likewise, central banks' activities can have enormous market implications and distributional consequences for society, so their policies are likely to be economically and politically controversial. In dealing with such sensitive issues, working in exclusive settings and behind closed doors allows for more open and frank discussion to generate solutions. Secrecy can allow a handful of individuals to develop stronger bonds within the inner circle than with those outside it. Secrecy also allows policymakers to avoid the inefficiencies that may arise from these constraints imposed on negotiating parties that can affect their bargaining power.[83] Finally, it also helps prevent major market reactions from even hints of major monetary and financial policy decisions. To minimize further financial disruptions, it is necessary that major policy announcements be choreographed and orchestrated carefully.

Identifying Interpersonal Trust

At the heart of my argument are two key claims. Central banking is *highly personal*, and central bank leaders' influence is significantly heightened in a crisis, when leaders have the ultimate authority over policy decisions.[84] Changes in leadership in central banks should change the trajectory and policy stance of their banks.[85] Central banking is also *highly interpersonal*: leaders are also influenced by their foreign colleagues. Changes in leadership can change the form of liquidity assurance strategies available to a central bank based on their interpersonal relations with their counterparts overseas.

While most studies focus on trust between enemies and in conflict situations, I argue that interpersonal trust is necessary even among friends, in times of radical uncertainty. In such a context, actors will fall back on subjective reasoning, personal knowledge, and familiarity to inform their judgment. Global financial crises offer fertile ground to explore these dynamics of interpersonal trust and differentiated ties in international monetary affairs. I focus on the role that interpersonal trust plays in explaining varying outcomes of cooperation and crisis management.

International relations scholarship identifies three indicators of trust relations—"the incidence of cooperation; discourses expressing trust; or the calculated acceptance of vulnerability."[86] Keating and Ruzicka suggest that the act of adopting or removing existing hedging strategies may provide better strategies to identify trust relations; Wheeler identifies absence of risk calculations in decision-making as an indicator of *interpersonal* trust.[87]

I argue that interpersonal trust need not imply an absence of risk calculations. Rather, agents who share interpersonal trust will work to help trusted partners, despite risks, while also hedging against them. Interpersonal trust

TABLE 0.1. A framework for identifying interpersonal trust

	THEORETICAL EXPECTATION	EVIDENCE OF EXPECTATION
Why rely on interpersonal trust	Absence of system trust	Crisis and radical uncertainty
	Policy experimentation	Limited and selective cooperation
	Preference to avoid institutionalized governance system and costs	Bilateral and ad hoc liquidity provision
How it is executed	Use of personal and/or informal channels	Discursive interview account, personal and formal correspondence, official records of decision-making
	Private, closed-door discussions	Discursive evidence, absence and/or avoidance of official records of decision-making
	Ad hoc cooperation absent material and functional conditions	Discursive evidence of social, subjective, and personal-level justification for bilateral assistance
Evidence of absence	Absence of cooperation *despite* meeting material and functional conditions	Preference to send requesting counterparty to formal, institutional channels of liquidity provision

will carry greater weight in risk calculations in conditions of uncertainty. Trust cannot substitute for risk calculations, but it can moderate how central bankers evaluate their counterpart's credibility as borrowers who will honor the arrangement. In the absence of interpersonal trust, concerns of country and economic risks cannot be overcome.

I add to these observable indicators (see table 0.1): first, by showing that it is not system trust—defined as "trust in the continuity of the overarching, shared sociopolitical order"—that is doing the work.[88] Crisis and radical uncertainty may suggest the absence of system trust to start. The choice of ad hoc responses over institutionalized strategies already in place in the system suggests an absence of trust in the system. And if we attribute cooperation to the environment of either system trust, or crisis and uncertainty, we should see more widespread cooperation within the system than selective, bilateral assistance that has emerged repeatedly, in the gravest crises.

Moreover, if interpersonal trust is an operating variable, *how* it is acted upon is key. We should see that in establishing bilateral arrangements during a crisis, trusting leaders do not conduct negotiations through formal channels but make direct, personal appeals to their trusted counterparts. Mutual trust is important for a central banker to request a swap. But given the power asymmetry between the borrower and liquidity provider in any lending agreement, it is important that providers trust borrowers, especially where country risks are prominent. Discussions will occur privately, among trusting counterparts, and precede domestic deliberations—leaders will come to agreements before involving their institutions.

We should also see actors allude to their personal relationships and conversations, and the importance of trust, reciprocity, and goodwill (such as helping risky but trusted counterparts to avoid less attractive policy options), in justifying decisions: personal and interpersonal reasoning will complement material considerations. Contra Wheeler, I suggest that interpersonal trust need not imply an absence of risk calculations. Trust is looser where risk concerns are higher. However, actors who share interpersonal trust will go the extra mile to help trusted partners, *despite* significant risks, but will take steps to hedge against them—interpersonal trust will factor into risk calculations and carry greater weight in conditions of uncertainty; where interpersonal ties are absent, such efforts will not be made. Interpersonal trust can open the possibility of ad hoc and bilateral cooperation in undertaking risky actions, even if political and economic factors do not support it. Where interpersonal trust is absent, these factors alone will not suffice.

Research Design: Evidence and Case Selection

Interpersonal trust is an affective bond that relies on personal perceptions, judgment, and inclinations to trust. While interpersonal trust can be observed through the indicators discussed above, it can neither be predicted ex ante nor can it be quantified or measured. Instead, I rely on personal, subjective assessments of leaders and their perceptions of their counterpart's trustworthiness, friendship, and goodwill. I therefore chose to support my claims with qualitative evidence from the archives and twenty-nine elite interviews that I conducted with current and former central bank leaders and officials.

Archival sources provide the bulk of my evidence, triangulated with secondary texts, for my analyses of the interwar period (chapters 1 and 2) and the Bretton Woods era (chapter 3). These materials were collected from the Federal Reserve Archival System for Economic Research (FRASER, online), the Columbia University Rare Book and Manuscript Library in New York City, the archives of the Bank of England in London, and the Bank for International Settlements in Basel. I consult the personal papers of central bank leaders at the Bank of England, the New York Fed, and the Bank for International Settlements, including their correspondences with their colleagues in Germany, France, Japan, and other concerned central banks. These files offer firsthand details and insights into how central bankers approached the crises that they faced, their relations with their foreign and domestic colleagues, and how they arrived at solutions to these issues through open and friendly deliberations. I also consult historical texts, biographies, autobiographies, and memoirs written about or by the key individuals around whom each narrative is focused.

My analysis of central bank cooperation during the GFC (chapter 4) is substantiated primarily with evidence collected from elite interviews that I conducted with current and former central bank leaders, most of whom were in office in leadership positions during the crisis. My interview pool includes Benjamin S. Bernanke, chairman of the Fed; Mervyn King, governor of the Bank of England; Masaaki Shirakawa, governor of the Bank of Japan; Jean-Claude-Trichet, president of the European Central Bank (ECB); Duvvuri Subbarao, of the Reserve Bank of India (RBI); and their deputies, including Charlie Bean and Paul Tucker (Bank of England), Donald Kohn (Federal Reserve), and twenty-one bank officials in foreign departments or at the Bank for International Settlements, who asked to remain anonymous. These accounts offer important details and insights into how central bankers approached the crises they faced, their relations with their foreign and domestic colleagues, and how they arrived at solutions to these crises.

Given the opacity around the initial swap arrangements during the GFC, to understand these dynamics better, I chose to interview individuals at the center of these policy decisions. I interviewed officials from the Fed, the key provider of dollar liquidity, from recipient countries, and from India and Iceland, whose requests were denied, to achieve variation in my interview pool. Many asked to remain anonymous. I was unable to secure interviews with central bank leaders from some Fed swap counterparties—namely, Mexico—and some whose swap requests were denied, such as the Central Bank of Iceland. However, this does not challenge the integrity of my analysis as, given concerns of currency or financial risk in these countries, the burden and need to trust falls on the provider, who did share insights on some of these cases in interviews. I triangulate these materials with official meeting reports and transcripts from the Federal Open Market Committee (FOMC), and the Federal Reserve's Oral History Project interviews, as well as journalistic and scholarly accounts of the crisis written both during and after the crisis. My analysis is novel in that I identify the personal and interpersonal underpinnings of ad hoc and bilateral cooperation for crisis management with insights from the perspective of central bank leaders themselves.

Case Selection

The particular evidence necessary to illustrate and support my argument influences my case selection, as well as the treatment of the point on the "terms" of bilateral arrangements. I discuss the latter point first. Specifically, that the issue of differentiated terms on bilateral arrangements is addressed in depth in chapters 1 and 4. The variability of the terms of bilateral arrangements does not feature in chapter 2, on the Great Depression, as it is focused primarily on the collapse of ad hoc, bilateral cooperation on the eve of and during the crisis. With regards to chapter 3 on central bank assistance under the Bretton Woods system in the 1960s, the issue of the terms of these arrangements did not really even feature in the discussions of these loans during this period, as per the archival and secondary record. However, this does not negate the element of how stronger or weaker trust influences the differentiated arrangements altogether. I show how weak ties between key American and British central bankers influenced the watering down of the amount of the Anglo-American swap line, as well as the speed of arranging this line in the first place.

I present four chapters on the 1920s, the Great Depression, the 1960s, and the GFC. I develop and deploy narrative analyses of why and how moments of financial shocks and crises are met with ad hoc, bilateral cooperation among central bankers. My selection of the first, third, and fourth cases follows the most different systems design, following the logic of causal inference through case studies.[89] I show why such cooperation emerged more frequently within these periods and explain the variation in access to liquidity assurance strategies for different central banks. In the second case, I evaluate the early years of the Great Depression and show how leadership changes across key central banks weakened personal relations between central bank leaders at the cost of crisis management. The comparison of the 1920s and the 1930s follows the "most similar" case logic.

Each case advances the argument and empirical analysis in a distinct way. The cross-case variation between these periods allows for controlled comparisons to establish the correlation between my independent variable—interpersonal trust—and outcome of interest—ad hoc, bilateral cooperation—to answer the question of *why* such cooperation is possible sometimes but not always. Close examinations of each period allow me to demonstrate *how* it emerges through interpersonal channels. My goal is to look deeply into these distinct periods to identify and distill what is common about crisis-time cooperation within disparate institutional and economic settings. These cases allow me to assess whether interpersonal relations in facilitating cooperation are independently influential in shaping outcomes or not. The universe of potential cases is limited to systemic, or system-threatening, financial pressures that warranted liquidity assistance that did or possibly could occur.

The 1920s present a "most likely" case for my argument. At this time, central bankers, which were then private institutions, were less constrained than their successors. The institutional apparatus for financial governance was also nonexistent at this time. We should therefore expect ad hoc and bilateral cooperation to emerge more easily in this less constraining context. My analysis of the Great Depression demonstrates the converse—weak interpersonal ties among a changing cast of characters, and low levels of trust among central bank leaders, hindered interbank lending to arrest the Depression and closed all possible avenues for any type of cooperation at the 1933 World Economic Conference in London.[90]

The crises of the 1930s were not exogenous shocks but endogenous to the economic and political climate of the decade before. The political and economic environments right before the 1929 Wall Street crash had not changed markedly from that of 1927–1928. What changed before the Wall Street crisis and the Great Depression was not the structural context but the leadership that operated within it, when Strong died in 1928.

The 1920s case is vital for theory-building and illustrating the mechanisms and dynamics central to the argument, to link personal relationships to outcomes of liquidity assistance. Although the mini cases in this chapter are not directly akin to all-out crises like the Great Depression, each presents a problem of financial instability and shocks from wartime hangover that are related to the departure from the gold standard parity and stumbling efforts to return to it, which emerged alongside banking crises, hyperinflation, and political upheaval. The Great Depression is a critical counterfactual case that shows how in the absence of personal relations (central to which is Strong's sudden demise), this mode of crisis management is severely hindered.

The case studies on propping up the Bretton Woods system in the 1960s, and the creation of the Fed swap program during the 2007–2010 GFC, allow me to evaluate the generalizability of the argument. These periods present "hard cases" for my argument. The postwar institutional environment is marked with established rules and institutions to manage financial pressures and the problems of liquidity, adjustment, and confidence. Central banks today are also more constrained by domestic institutional and legal structures, limiting individual bankers' influence in these institutions. Finally, the academization of central banking may generate ideational homogeneity that lends itself more easily to cooperation. These contexts do not translate easily to an interpersonal argument of trust facilitating ad hoc and bilateral cooperation. Still, central bankers engaged with one another on a person-to-person level with their trusted counterparts overseas to get bilateral, cooperative arrangements off the ground.

The Bretton Woods case is important to show that even when central banks faced growing political, institutional, and legal constraints and evolved into highly technocratic and bureaucratic institutions, interpersonal dynamics played a core function of supporting governance efforts and generating bilateral solutions to systemic problems. The GFC case is important for extending the insights of this paper to the contemporary period. In addition to growing constraints on central banks, they are now increasingly also guided by groupthink through the academization of the profession—or so the existing research suggests. My analysis here shows that in fact this was not the case; interpersonal cooperation facilitated the crisis management effort where central bankers across countries initially disagreed on the causes and resolution of the crisis.

There are also notable absences in this book, namely the emerging and developing economy crises of the 1980s and the 1990s. Indeed, these cases are not completely distinct from the periods of uncertainty considered in the book, and so I explain why they are not included in the text. These absences speak to a broader methodological comment about research limitations in doing archival and interview work and how the data-generating process and evidence necessary to substantiated arguments also determine case selection.

By the 1980s, policymakers were past the point of letter-writing, with increased use of telephone correspondence and, many years later, email and cell phones. This changed the nature of recordkeeping and truncated the availability of the types of data and historical materials that the archives may keep or make public. This points to a key aspect of historical research and archival silences—not only what archives choose not to keep but also what they cannot keep and how these records shape the inferences we can make.[91] While transcripts from FOMC meetings during these crises are now available, they are limited in what they can tell us on their own.

Interviews for this period are also difficult as many policymakers involved in this period are no longer around, unavailable to speak, or poorly recall these distant memories. While transcripts from FOMC meetings in the 1980s are available, they are limited in what they can tell us on their own. There is also a lack of additional primary and secondary material to generate the type of evidence to support the arguments I make in this book—firsthand accounts triangulated with real-time discussions and secondary reports on the same period.

My analysis of the GFC is focused on just the Fed swap program, not swap lines provided by the ECB. The kind of evidence necessary to illustrate and support my argument in the context of the ECB swap network—interview accounts from recipients of ECB swaps or real-time transcripts of the ECB's negotiations and decisions to extend these lines—as I provide in the Fed case, are unavailable. There is therefore a substantial gap between what is in the written record and what is being asked in the book, which makes similarly detailed inference for this period difficult.

A Safety Net with Gaping Holes?

As Jeffry Frieden observes, a striking feature "of the political economy of the crisis is just how similar it looks to previous" crises.[92] What I show is that its resolution was also similar, in that it reminds us that the global financial governance system frequently does not work. Contrary to arguments that the system worked during the GFC, and successfully prevented a second Great Depression, financial governance, time and again, has relied on improvised stopgap fixes for a system that is ill-equipped to deal with the troubles it generates.[93] When rescue efforts have prevented the worst from happening, the underlying problems inherent in the financial system have remained largely unaddressed.

This pattern is reminiscent of the past and is thus a recurring theme in this book: the global governance system's record has always been patchy, and this reliance on ad hockery is suboptimal economically. In the last century the system has sometimes worked; at others, crises have spiraled out of control. When trouble struck at the end of the 1920s in the years before the Great Depression, those in charge of the system were unwilling or unable to provide the fixes necessary. So, since 1945, states have invested tremendous amounts of time and resources toward building a more robust framework of rules and best practices for global financial governance. And still, when crises hit, the system suffers from political infighting, tedious negotiations, and inadequate resources.

What holds the international financial system together is often an ad hoc patchwork of arrangements grounded in leaders' interpersonal relations. While a second Great Depression was prevented between 2007 and 2010, it was not to the credit of a robust and reliable "system" but to the credit of central bankers who were willing and able to engage in experimentative and ad hoc governance to provide the necessary measures. This constant feature of global financial governance has three broader theoretical and empirical implications that I highlight in this book: the need for more work on interpersonal ties in international relations, hierarchy in global governance, and the tensions between crisis management and the norms of democratic governance.

First, I challenge the political science "assumption of motivational homogeneity" that individuals merely carry the interests or characteristics of states, institutions, or attributes.[94] The extension of liquidity has historically relied not only on the coffers of great powers but their willingness to provide them. This willingness depends greatly on the leaders of these banks and their personal ties with their counterparts across the globe. *How* power and resources determine patterns of crisis management often depends on the leaders who animate them. Technocratic global governance is not immune to policymakers' personal preferences and relationships. So, to better understand the robustness and durability of global governance arrangements it is essential to understand the individual and interpersonal dynamics underpinning them.[95]

Second, I identify another channel through which agents shape and reinforce hierarchies in the playing field. My case studies demonstrate that diplomatic agency influences both exceptional and improbable outcomes and more routine and predictable ones. The reliance on temporary governance is not only suboptimal economically, but it is also suboptimal politically.

The actions of the most powerful central banks do not affect their domestic economies and markets alone; they also have a dramatic influence on their foreign counterparts.[96] This is an almost unavoidable by-product of central banks' positions at the intersection of national economies and international markets. For some countries, the hierarchies of this interconnectedness are contractual relationships.[97] For those disadvantaged in their international competitiveness, facing high barriers in accessing the support in a crisis, these hierarchies are imposed upon them.[98]

In financial governance, central bankers, through their personal relationships, agents can construct and reinforce hierarchies in the global economy through the transnational reach of their power and discretion. These concerns are even more troubling than we think. The inordinate power of central banks during crises is so concentrated in the hands of a few leaders within them. In a crisis, one, maybe two, unelected, domestic institutions decide who sinks and who swims.

While valuable in a crisis, interpersonal ties pose significant political tensions. They can serve as mechanisms for gatekeeping; notions of prestige also play a role in how individuals perceive their counterparts, in terms of their intelligence or intellect, or in the idea that "people like us" should be in certain places and are worthy of certain things. These close-knit networks are deliberately exclusionary and extremely hard to enter. Only those few who have access to the connections, position, pedigree, and resources to enter them are allowed in.[99] In doing their job, central bankers can replicate hierarchies and inequalities in global financial governance.

Finally, this book speaks to debates on the rationale of central bank independence based on concerns of its legitimacy and its undemocratic nature.[100] After the GFC, several financial experts, critics, and political actors called out the Fed for overstepping its mandate and acting with little transparency and political accountability. The outsized role of central banks has generated considerable political and public pushback since the crisis.[101] Central banks world over have been called out for independently expanding, or overstepping their domestic mandates, and acting in a manner that is at odds with key democratic principles.[102]

Crises highlight the inordinate power of central banks and have brought public attention to their contentious positions in democratic societies.[103] In viewing monetary policymaking as a technical activity and removing it from the hands of politicians, the roles and activities of central banks have been justified as depoliticized.[104] Delegated authorities rely on their autonomy from political interference. But by acting as international lenders of last resort, powerful central banks' unique ability to govern interdependent economic relations and influence policymaking abroad raises new questions about the international acceptability of this role.[105]

Plan of the Book

To show that individuals matter, Michael Horowitz notes, "There have to be reasons to think that having a particular leader in power at a particular period of time mattered."[106] A change in leadership should lead to different outcomes. At the relational level, having particular leaders, *plural*, in power at the same time also matters. A change in leaders should change the nature of interpersonal relations between counterparts and therefore lead to different forms of crisis management.

In the rest of the book, I take this argument on a historical tour to reexamine key periods of economic uncertainty in the twentieth and early twenty-first century to substantiate my argument. I start with the first half of the interwar years, focusing on the 1920s in chapter 1. I explain patterns of central bank cooperation and discord over postwar reparations, reconstruction, and the return to prewar parity in the early interwar years. I highlight the decisive roles that Strong and Norman played managing the 1920s postwar economy. I show how their varied relationships with Hjalmar Schacht at the Reichsbank, Inoue Junnosuke at the Bank of Japan, Emile Moreau at the Bank of France, and several private bankers in New York helped or hindered the arrangement of the bilateral and multilateral loans and credits to manage four interconnected economic problems of the decade: financing German reparations; banking crises in Japan; the return to prewar parity in Britain; and currency stabilization in Poland, which followed that of Belgium, discussed in the opening of the book.[107]

In chapter 2, I show that this breakdown of the ad hoc cooperation coincides with the sudden death of Strong in October 1928, and a new cast joins Norman: George L. Harrison takes over the governorship at the New York Fed, Schacht is replaced by Hans Luther, and Clément Moret takes over from Moreau. Weakened relations between Norman and his new counterparts in New York and Berlin after Strong's death, and Schacht's departure from the Reichsbank, hindered key attempts to rescue the global economy in the early 1930s. I evaluate the failure of central bank liquidity assistance to rescue the Austrian and German banking systems, Britain's abandonment of the gold standard, and the tripartite meetings alongside the 1933 World Economic Conference in London.

Chapter 3 considers the creation of the "Basel Arrangements," the Reciprocal Currency Arrangements (also known as the Fed swap network), and the sterling arrangements of 1964 and 1967. I show that differentiated personal ties among key players—Charles Coombs in New York, Max Iklé at the Swiss National Bank, Julien-Pierre Koszul in the Bank of France, Guido Carli of the Bank of Italy, Johannes Tüngeler at the Bundesbank, and Lord Cobbold and his successor, Lord Cromer, at the Bank of England—shaped central bankers' responses to the troubles brought on by the Bretton Woods monetary system in the 1960s. I illustrate how interpersonal trust facilitated the creation of the swap networks by the Fed and by central bankers in Basel in the 1960s. Moreover, despite favorable economic and political conditions for bilateral cooperation, weak trust between Bank of England associates and Charles Coombs at the New York Fed in 1961 hindered cooperation between their banks.

Chapter 4 leaps forward to the twenty-first century, with an evaluation of the emergence of the Federal Reserve's swap network in the wake of the GFC. I show that the creation of the Fed's swap network by Ben Bernanke would not have been possible without the support of Mervyn King, Jean-Claude Trichet in Europe, and Masaki Shirakawa in Japan. I also offer two brief analyses of why two important and highly interlinked economies, India and Iceland, did not benefit from privileged access to the Fed's swap network. I demonstrate how differentiated ties among leaders influenced access to liquidity arrangements during the GFC: unconditional swaps to the G7 economies and Switzerland, limited swaps (including additional authorization requirements and limits on drawings) to four emerging markets with a focus on Mexico, and the Fed's rejection of swap requests from India and Iceland.

Moving chronologically through these canned histories, my case studies emphasize that with the dramatic changes in the structure of the international monetary system, the distribution of monetary power, and the institutional governance apparatus over the last century, one constant remains. When crises hit, central bankers, time again, shed these systems of rules, norms, and conventions and turn instead to one another, relying on their interpersonal ties to get cooperative arrangements off the ground with trusted counterparts.

To conclude, I return to the theoretical and political implications of my argument and findings. First, the outsized influence of individuals and interpersonal interactions in creating what may evolve into central features of the global financial governance framework. Second, that technocratic global governance is not immune to personal preferences and affinities influencing policy. I consequently draw attention to the fickleness and sensitivity of financial management and policymaking to the "who" of global governance. Finally, I return to the tensions at the core of my argument: the need for a nimble and flexible central banking system as part of a larger robust and reliable international governance system and the norms of democratic governance that guarantee and enforce the public and political accountability of the actors guiding our economies and our politics through future financial turbulence.

1

STRONG MEN AND STRONG'S MEN

Central Bank Cooperation in the Interwar 1920s

The First World War threw the global economy into disarray. The gold standard system had been suspended, global trade had collapsed, and European states, reeling from the war, were consumed by disputes over enormous debts and reparations. The politics and economics of the interwar period have been exhaustively documented and explained. The aim of this chapter is retelling some of this history and focusing on one significant section of these problems: the management of monetary and financial affairs. Specifically, with this well-known history in the background, I shine a light not only on how international monetary affairs were conducted but also by whom, foregrounding the interpersonal dynamics among central bank leaders—their interpersonal ties of trust—that facilitated the arrangement of the bilateral loans and credits to manage four interconnected interwar economic problems: financing German reparations, banking crises, the return to prewar parity, and currency stabilization.

Each of these problems is linked to the broader issue of liquidity shortages of sterling, dollars, and gold, necessary to achieve these domestic goals or alleviate financial pressures, placing central banks at the center of postwar monetary and financial affairs. But these economic problems emerged in a world of shifting alliances and strained interstate relations. Domestic political systems also began to be radically transformed with the expansion of suffrage and shifting power to labor. In addition to these constraints, the management of international financial affairs was also undoubtedly shaped by the global balance of power, as well as the need for the Bank of England or New York Fed to provide liquidity and credit to partner banks.

Political and economic constraints alone cannot fully explain the kinds of cooperation witnessed in the interwar 1920s but speak to the questions raised in the introduction. Namely, why some central banks benefited from extensive cooperation but not others, despite the risk of contagion, even when the resources necessary were available and cooperation could have been a straightforward undertaking. Or why, at other times, vast amounts of resources were mobilized even when financial conditions created heightened risks attached to extensive lending.

To answer these questions, I draw attention to key themes regarding the politics of this unusual, interpersonal manner of cooperation that reappear throughout the book. Cooperation, spurred by crises and liquidity shortages, emerged at the discretion of central bank leaders and was influenced by their personal relations. Central bank leaders in this period were viewed as more credible and reliable when they could and would act independently from political pressures at home. Cooperation was guided by central bank leaders who regularly circumvented domestic political constraints, as well as international considerations, such as alliances or disputes.

In the absence of a coherent and robust financial governance system in the 1920s, personal relations among leaders of key central banks had great bearing on global financial governance, which facilitated the creation of temporary solutions to stem financial pressures. While central bank independence was not an institutionalized practice, the interwar period was an important moment for the emergence of this idea, and central bank autonomy enabled central bankers to approach contemporary problems through interpersonal channels and in an ad hoc manner.

Next, I describe the economic and political questions facing policymakers after 1919 and the events that created a favorable environment for central banks to chart their own course. I then turn to the four key economic problems that called for central bank intervention: reparations, banking crises, the return to parity, and currency stabilization. To explain how they were managed, I show that leaders' differentiated personal relationships influenced outcomes of cooperation, conditional assistance, and noncooperation to manage the economic problems of the decade. I trace how these close personal ties among some central bankers emerged or faltered. Given the centrality of sterling and dollars in the international monetary system, Montagu Norman of the Bank of England and Benjamin Strong of the New York Fed are protagonists in this period. Their supporting cast includes Hjalmar Schacht of the Reichsbank and his predecessor, Rudolf Havenstein; Émile Moreau from the Bank of France; Junnosuke Inoue from the Bank of Japan; their deputies and associates; and several private bankers in New York and London.

The International Monetary System after the First World War

International politics after the First World War soured as states became consumed with settling war debts and reparations. Europe was teetering on the brink of bankruptcy; only the United States and, to a lesser extent, Japan, came out of the war relatively stronger. The arrival of the New York Fed on the international stage in 1914 was consequential in cementing its position during and after the war, changing the landscape of international monetary affairs and central banking.

The war shifted a great amount of political power to the central banking community. Alfred Hayes, later president of the New York Fed, observed that "western democracies were experiencing a reaction against government management of their economies—of which they had had their fill during the war. . . . As governments withdrew from economic management, central banks were left to carry virtually the whole responsibility of maintaining economic stability."[1] It was now central bankers, who dread war and seek financial stability, who faced the Herculean task of reconstructing the international financial system following the devastation of the war. Their primary goal was to stabilize currencies and return to prewar parity of the classical gold standard, which had collapsed with the war.[2] This goal, however, was motivated, in Kenneth Mouré's words, not by careful analyses "of the operation of the prewar gold standard and war time changes, but on retrospective longing for the stability of the prewar system, and a desire to reverse the most obvious changes that had taken place since 1914." Still, among those in charge, there was "no consensus on how to get back to gold, nor on how the restored gold standard should operate."[3]

Certainly, international and domestic factors had implications for interwar monetary management and, in particular, the collapse of credibility and cooperation necessary to maintain the gold standard. At the system level, Charles Kindleberger has highlighted the need for a singular leader to provide global public goods of liquidity, adjustment, and confidence to maintain system stability.[4] Before 1914, the gold standard system rested on British hegemony, where the Bank of England provided leadership and played "lender of last resort" to stabilize the system.[5] But the war brought on the beginning of the end of Britain's hegemonic reign and the Bank of England's monetary leadership. The New York Fed was still relatively young.

In a crisis, international cooperation was key, and stability rested on governments' commitments to maintain gold convertibility.[6] But after the war, states' interests had turned inward, and they faced growing political tensions with one another; at home, the expansion of voting rights across Europe, and an emergent labor movement, created new demands on governments and central banks. Now, Britain was no longer able to lead, and the United States was unwilling: the international system benefited from neither hegemonic leadership nor international cooperation during the interwar years.[7]

This new leaderless environment, marred with disputes and economic turmoil, impeded prewar cooperation, questioned the credibility of governments to honor the terms of the gold standard, and hindered quick adjustments to payments and currency imbalances. Before 1914, central banks supported one another through loans and credits, or by buying foreign currency bills, and accommodated gold and currency inflows and outflows to support parities. As Beth Simmons notes, the gold standard system was upheld by "instantaneous international cooperation" that ensured system stability but relied on widespread belief that governments would do so.[8]

After 1919, currency crises and devaluations were rarely met in the same way. Barry Eichengreen argues that national policies and domestic preferences shaped states' economic adjustment strategies in the interwar period, consequently compromising the credibility of central banks' commitments to uphold the gold standard system.[9]

These impediments were aggravated through the decade to thwart a timely resolution of the Great Depression, as I discuss in chapter 2. But they began to manifest early in the 1920s. The stabilization of the mark was hindered by political disputes over inter-Allied debts and German reparations between Britain, France, and Germany in 1924. Not long after, the Bank of England, the New York Fed, and J. P. Morgan & Co. allowed the French franc to sink, as governments could not credibly commit to implement policies to prevent outflows. Domestic political shifts and a tense international environment dampened a once cooperative approach to monetary management.

Although mechanistic cooperation and hegemonic leadership did not work as well in the 1920s and 1930s as they did in the prewar system, central bank cooperation certainly did not stop but took a new form. While the automatic prewar cooperation was interrupted, a different form of cooperative management emerged in the 1920s, and it was not just between central banks but among central bank leaders. Some of this history has been laid out in Clarke's monograph focused on the 1924–1931 period, Mouré's study of French interwar monetary affairs, or Bytheway and Metzler's study on interwar central bankers in New York, London, and Tokyo.[10]

Drawing on insights from these studies, combined with additional archival materials, my analysis of interwar monetary affairs in this chapter and the next offers a theoretically grounded narrative analysis of how interpersonal relationships of trust and mistrust can influence cooperation in times of crisis and uncertainty. I do not refute explanations of the collapse of cooperation attributed to changing domestic politics and the emergence of social democracy, shifts in the international balance of power, or policymakers' shared preferences to return to the prewar gold standard system. It is in this complex landscape, which has been thoroughly documented and explained, that the interwar financial troubles emerged; from there, central bankers' preferences—to secure autonomy, avoid political constraints, and operate in secret—were solidified and remain central to the practice of central banking today.[11] In turn, I provide an explanation for why a new form of cooperation, one that was more ad hoc and informal, emerged to fill in the void left by more routine and mechanistic arrangements, which foregrounds the role of individuals' personal ties among central bank leaders.

Acting together in secret and seeking to preserve their autonomy, central bank leaders regularly circumvented the domestic and international constraints on their activities. Where they chose to, they ignored intergovernmental disputes and governmental pressures to assist their counterparts through sizable ad hoc loans and credits. Who benefited from these efforts was often much less dependent on purely economic and financial ties, national interests, and shared preferences than on personal relationships and trust among central bank leaders.

Political Roots of Relational Central Banking

The Treaty of Versailles, signed in 1919, failed to establish an effective system to govern international affairs.[12] Under David Lloyd George, Britain's main concern was to maintain the strength of its empire, along with the security of France, and the establishment of the League of Nations. In France, Georges Clemenceau was determined to see Germany weakened militarily and economically. Despite Woodrow Wilson's support for the League, the United States neither joined nor ratified the Treaty.[13] Germany negotiated a separate peace agreement with the Bolsheviks, who took power in Russia in 1917, but both countries were excluded from talks and from the first League meeting in 1920. John Maynard Keynes warned that stiff reparations against Germany would lead to the collapse of the German economy with spillover effects on the rest of Europe. But the Treaty succumbed to France's vengeful spirit, setting impossible terms for restoration in Germany, beyond what the country could fulfill.[14]

Keynes's foresight was realized much sooner than the start of the Second World War; "revisionist sentiment against the Paris Peace Treaties erupted even before the ink was dry," and the victorious allies' coalition quickly unraveled.[15] As Keynes predicted, the economic costs of the war and the reparations payments dampened any hopes for European recovery. By 1921, Weimar Germany was swept by runaway inflation, induced by the government's issuing more money to meet its reparations obligation and revive trade. The peace settlements needed revision.

In 1922, the Genoa Conference was tasked with restoring the international gold standard and rehabilitating European trade and production, as well as coming up with a strategy for German reconstruction and negotiating an arrangement between Russia's new Bolshevik regime and Western Europe to rebuild ties to create peace and stability in Europe. This time, all sides were represented, including Weimar Germany and Russia. As a non-League member, the United States did not participate, although James A. Logan, from the New York Fed, attended in an informal capacity.[16]

Unfortunately, before the conference, Germany and Russia signed the Treaty of Rapallo, which Logan noted to many "came as a shock. It indicated an underlying atmosphere of suspicion and distrust at Genoa, which did not indicate much hope of substantial results as to either Russia or Germany, and possibly this incident served to prepare our winds for the rather barren outcome."[17] New sources of friction emerged across Eastern Europe prior to the conference, so Allied powers attempted to forge their own agreements to no avail. The lack of unity and leadership, failed to "give substance to Genoa's conciliatory façade."[18]

But while governments fought their political battles on the continent, cooperation between central banks developed in private, outside the public eye, to sustain the flailing global economy and national economies within it. Eichengreen suggests that the arrival of the Fed on the international stage "disrupted the clubby atmosphere" where ad hoc arrangements among European central banks "proved increasingly difficult to reach."[19] I show that influential central bankers, namely Norman and Strong, recreated this exclusive atmosphere, which facilitated interpersonal cooperation to extend bilateral central bank assistance.

The Genoa Conference, although an intergovernmental affair, catalyzed the recreation of clubby, bilateral, and ad hoc central bank cooperation, led by Montagu Norman. The proposals presented by the British delegation at Genoa was, in Stephen V. O. Clarke's words, "by far the most ambitious official attempt of the 1920s to organize central bank cooperation."[20] Among other recommendations, the proposals called for central bank independence and suggested that central banks should cooperate with each other continuously.[21] It was decided that the Bank of England would hold an international conference of bankers.[22] Norman embraced the task and, with Strong's support, "sought to crystallize the doctrine" of international central bank cooperation.

Norman corresponded with just a few bankers to create a practice of bilateral cooperation. Strong was disinclined to bind himself to European norms and rules of central banking. Instead, he and Norman developed ad hoc and informal lines of cooperation as the Genoa resolutions dissolved: "effective personalities were emerging and becoming a team lead by Norman, with Strong at first partnership."[23] By 1924, twenty central banks had opened accounts with the Bank of England, in contrast to the four that had existed before the war, laying the essential groundwork for ad hoc and bilateral cooperation that continued through the decade.

The Norman-Strong Partnership

Interwar cooperation was markedly hierarchical. Economic power and centrality in international finance were paramount in determining the core of the hierarchy: Britain and the United States. Given the centrality of Britain and the United States, and their currencies, sterling and the dollar, Montagu Norman, governor of the Bank of England, and Benjamin Strong, governor of the New York Fed, were the linchpins of the central banking community during the decade. Although the First World War and the interwar period marked sterling's twilight years, the United States and the dollar were only commencing their rise;[24] together, they decided the central bank hierarchy.

Lord Montagu Collet Norman, "the Alchemist," was deputy governor of the Bank of England in 1917 and governor of the Bank of England from 1920 until 1944.[25] For Norman, the return to the gold standard was tied to "London's leadership of the world's financial and monetary affairs." He was troubled by the shift of economic power toward New York. The growth of the working class's political power through the vote also put new pressures on central banks' activities. In charge of Britain's financial position in the interwar years and during the Second World War, he was a man of extraordinary power, the most influential central banker in the world: his speeches could sway markets. Norman came from an old and respected banking dynasty. He was also an infamously difficult, peculiar, and troubled man, whose mercurial ways led to regular nervous breakdowns that often brought about decisive consequences for the British and global economy.[26]

The New York Fed, led by its governor, Benjamin Strong, was the only entity that Norman saw as an equal. Liaquat Ahamed describes Strong as a "man of action" who "represented a new generation in America" that wanted to bring its power to bear in world monetary affairs.[27] He was known for his take-charge attitude and was admired within private financial circles for his dominant personality and aptitude for addressing practical problems. He was well connected in New York, having spent his career at the Bankers Trust, a "bankers' bank" that worked alongside J. P. Morgan during the rescue of the Panic of 1907.

Strong briefly served as the Bankers Trust president in 1914 before taking up the position of governor of the New York Fed.

As an architect of the Federal Reserve system alongside key US bankers, Strong was not one to wait around for orders.[28] Although isolated from the goings-on on the continent, his personal charm and shrewdness in financial matters won him many friends among central bankers internationally. But he was also physically weak, frequently very ill, and regularly could not travel. This did not stop him from seeking out and developing personal connections, which he believed were deeply important for cooperation to maintain financial stability.

Norman and Strong shared an internationalist outlook. They also insisted, as Émile Moreau, governor of the Bank of France after 1926, recounts, on the absolute independence of central banks vis-à-vis the state and believed that central banks "should be master of the money markets."[29] For Norman, Britain's interests aligned with those of the international financial system. Central bank cooperation was "a doctrine and a program, a prescription of how things *should* be."[30] He was more interested in international than domestic affairs, often, as his associates suggest, to the point of neglecting the Bank's role in London.[31] Strong was particularly interested in European reconstruction and committed to "internationalism." He was an Anglophile who believed that Anglo-American cooperation was fundamental to postwar reconstruction, but he did not weigh the American national interest less than the interests of the international system.

Strong first traveled to Europe as the new governor of the New York Fed in 1916, where he met with Walter Cunliffe, then governor of the Bank of England, and Norman, then deputy governor. During this trip, the Bank of England and the New York Fed opened reciprocal accounts, which were crucial for cooperation between the two banks.[32] From then, Norman and Strong stayed in touch frequently, formally and informally. They regularly sought one another's counsel and kept each other up on their correspondence with other foreign central bank leaders, their policy positions, and their plans. Their personal relationship was uniquely intimate: they often went on vacation together, kept each other informed of their home lives, spent some Christmases together, and even arranged for their mothers to meet.

Together, Norman and Strong transformed interwar cooperation and central bank autonomy into a formal agenda, and their close ties within private banking and financial circles allowed them to mobilize private funding that often made up large parts of international central bank credits and loans. They developed and routinized practices of operating in secret, to insulate central banks from political pressures and governmental interference. Central bank autonomy also became a preferred practice, as Norman and Strong avoided engaging with governments or even central bankers who were under political and governmental influence. This vision was put down by Norman in a 1921 manifesto detailing central banking principles:

1. Autonomy and freedom from political control are desirable for all Central and Reserve Banks.
2. Subject to conformity with the above clause a policy of continuous cooperation is desirable among Central and Reserve Banks.[33]

Central bank cooperation was often exclusive to independent central bankers; important discussions and meetings often excluded bankers Norman or Strong saw as tied to their governments or that they did not like or trust. As the main hubs of the central banking world, they dealt with several central bank counterparts all over the world, but primarily in Europe and Japan.

As important wartime allies and economic partners, French central bankers should have been much closer to Norman and Strong. Britain was France's "principal ally," and France relied greatly on Britain for its military security; but relations between the Bank of England and the Bank of France were less friendly, and this chilly relationship was exacerbated by difficulties at the purely personal level in the 1920s between Norman and Moreau, who assumed the French governorship in 1926.[34]

Despite deep political ties with Britain and the United States, cooperation with the Bank of France was influenced by who governed it and not only material economic and political considerations. During Strong's first European visit, he met Governor Georges Pallain, but his efforts to establish reciprocal services between their banks failed, and again with Georges Robineau. Strong believed that Norman "will be an earnest advocate of the Bank of England arrangement," "while in Paris [Strong] had not felt, for various reasons, willing to develop the matter with Monsieur Pallain." His new friends in England regarded "Pallain here as being a little difficult to deal with." He was advised by Cunliffe that the Bank of France is "distrustful, do not cooperate."[35] Regular cooperative relations between the Bank of France and the New York Fed were not secured until Moreau assumed the governorship in 1926, but at the same time, Norman's close ties with Schacht in Germany generated increasing mistrust in Norman among the French.[36] These interpersonal squabbles had important governance ramifications. Norman kept France far outside of the core as he viewed the Bank of France as "hopeless."[37]

Norman and Strong sought to keep central bank discussions informal where possible and limited participation to only a few trusted and friendly counterparts. Soon after Genoa, Norman found that any official meeting would succumb to "too many political stumbling-blocks and too little goodwill in many quarters" and should come down to a "half-way house in the shape of a small, private and informal meeting."[38] Strong similarly believed that central banks' objectives were best achieved "without subjecting them to a formal agreement."[39] Many central bank meetings in the 1920s were informal and "without publicity and without commitments," narrowing attendance to a handful of individuals, finding "some reason for the dividing line between the sheep who were invited and the goats who were not."[40] Strong and Norman's personal relationships with their various counterparts determined the hierarchy. The largest beneficiaries were Germany and Japan, who Norman and Strong respectively actively brought into their circles.

Following correspondence from Strong, who suggested that such a meeting could be "simply a fortuitous 'happenchance,'" they could invite only their friends and include Schacht at the Reichsbank, even though Germany was not "of a free gold market" then. And indeed, if they did not "have a meeting but just [happened] to meet, then there would be no difficulty in drawing the line," as any official central bank meeting would need to include more leaders and would have to be publicized and on the record.[41]

By the mid-1920s, while Hjalmar Schacht's rehabilitated Reichsbank had gained increased international weight, the Bank of France adopted a more combative approach with its foreign counterparts, as Norman's "crusade for cooperation among central banks did not include" it.[42] Norman limited close cooperation to his friends, Strong and Schacht, occasionally Moll in Sweden, Vissering in the Netherlands, and Inoue Junnosuke and Eigo Fukai in Japan. There was no mention of including Georges Robineau or any French representative in these private gatherings.

These plans took a while to develop because, as Norman explained, in "some European countries a growing sentiment of nationality [had] increased the difficulties of financial or any other cooperation," and the "question of the German reparations [was] now a worse muddle."[43] This meeting eventually took place in July 1927 in Long Island. It was a secret gathering of only Strong, Norman, Schact, and Charles Rist, standing in for Moreau to represent the Bank of France; the French were only brought in later, as Strong developed closer ties with Moreau. The meeting was not publicized, and the bankers traveled under aliases. No official record was kept, and it is reported that talks were shaped by the "accidents of personalities and personal relationships"; Norman spent most of his time with Strong and did not engage with Rist.[44]

German Reparations

Germany came out of the First World War massively in debt from financing the war through external borrowing. After Versailles, approximately a third of

Germany's deficits were comprised of its reparations obligations. Under Rudolf Havenstein, the Reichsbank's response to financing these repayments, with gold stores now depleted, was to print more bank notes to buy foreign currency. Distributional conflicts within Germany were also worsened by the international disputes around the reparations that fueled inflation in Germany. Keynes and others on the committee of experts suggested that a moratorium on reparations could restore confidence in the mark and in Germany's financial position. By 1921, shortly after Germany made its first reparations payment, the value of the mark began to depreciate rapidly. In 1923, for a short period, inflation exceeded 1,000 percent a month.[45]

Economic collapse had led Germany to default on its reparations and to the French and Germany military occupation of the Ruhr. Germany was so overcome by hyperinflation that even German officials, including Havenstein, believed that Germany's financial position was hopeless, and inflation worsened due to the reparations imposed on them. Havenstein's policy of buying foreign currency with depreciating marks only made matters worse, wiping out the domestic financial assets of many families in Germany and reducing the Reichsbank's gold reserves to the small sum of $111 million, almost half of which were pledged against foreign credits.[46] It was not until November 1923, when Hans Luther, Germany's finance minister, established the Rentenbank and the Rentenmark, tied to gold bonds, that inflation was halted.

But even once the problem of inflation was resolved, the financial pressures on Germany imposed by the agreement of Versailles remained. What Germany needed was liquidity to honor its debt and reparations payments. These efforts only truly got off the ground after Schacht took over the Reichsbank at the end of 1923, following Havenstein's death. New leadership at the bank allowed new and strong personal ties to emerge and shape cooperative efforts. Schacht's unusually close ties with Norman, and by extension, Strong, changed the Reichsbank's fortunes, through Norman's help in financing the Golddiskontbank (the Gold Discount Bank, or Gold Bank) in the Rhineland, and in arranging the Dawes Loan. Havenstein, who did not have similarly close ties in London and New York, had been unsuccessful in reaping the benefits of central bank cooperation to finance the reparations.

Norman, Schacht, and the Golddiskontbank

Schacht's ascendence to the Reichsbank presidency was surprising, as he was relatively unknown in central banking circles at the time. He was better known in Berlin's banking communities but was distrusted by many "for his questionable financial dealings."[47] He later came to be known as "The Old Wizard,"[48] "Hitler's Banker,"[49] or the economic dictator of interwar Germany, although this is not the version of Schacht we meet in this book.[50] He was an arrogant figure, perceived as out of tune with the Germany for which he spoke—weak and defeated—a circumstance that his predecessor, Havenstein, better embodied.

Norman and Schacht developed a very close and trusting relationship. They shared many personal and social similarities. Schacht looked the part of a Prussian banker; his understanding of the world outside Germany, along with his fluency in English, proved invaluable. Schacht shared Norman's elitist sense of superiority and was contemptuous of "the masses—of 'vulgar' democracy—and of the classes—to them, equally vulgar plutocracy."[51] Like Norman, he was a peculiar person, and few understood him. Norman was difficult to work with and picky in his likes and dislikes. One central banker said that Norman "picked people who were congenial to him, & blind to talents of those not congenial."[52] Schacht was skilled in finding people abroad who would help him strengthen his position at home. He had a knack for moving with the times. Both men were extremely private. Norman was regarded as a man of mystery.[53] As for Schacht, as his secretary described, "What did he do? He sat in his dark room, which smelled of old cleaning rags, and he smoked. Did he read letters? No. And he dictated no letters. But he phoned a lot all over the world, about domestic and foreign currency. Then he smoked some more. We didn't eat much. He usually left late and took public transport to go home. That was all."[54]

Even before they met, they admired one another. Norman was eager to befriend Schacht and was eager for him to step into his new role. Schacht recalls that Norman met him at the train station on his very first, and infamous, visit to London on December 31, 1923. When Norman made plans for them to meet at the Bank the follow morning, Schacht said, "But Mr. Governor, tomorrow is New Year's Day. Surely you won't be going to the Bank tomorrow?"

"That doesn't matter, I want to have a talk with you as soon as possible and I shall expect you at eleven. I do hope we shall become friends," was Norman's reply.[55] While many at the Bank of England were put off by Schacht's vanity, Norman "went out of his way to cultivate him for the good points he might possess and blind himself to the rest" and "saw largely what he wanted to see" in him.[56] Their personal trust that had emerged before they had even met, and rapidly grew, played a central role in determining the fortunes of the Germany economy. They talked frankly to one another about their positions and financial needs, which facilitated extensive cooperation between them.

In fact, Schacht broached his idea of establishing a new Credit Bank in addition to the Reichsbank during their first encounter, which he proposed would be funded with capital "of two hundred million marks in foreign currency, half of which should be raised in Germany. The remaining half [Schacht] should like to borrow from the Bank of England." This bold proposition left Norman perplexed but struck by the clarity and logic of Schacht's proposals.

While discussing the French banking syndicate, Schacht solicited Norman's opinion for his plans to create a separate central bank—the Golddiskontbank—in the Rhineland. The success of this scheme depended on the support of other central banks. Norman opposed the French scheme as it "reeked of politics" and was pleased to learn that Schacht was also opposed to any project which sought to "restrict [the Reichsbank's] supreme power in matters of currency."[57]

Everything about Norman and Schacht's very first interaction spoke to Norman's vision for central bank autonomy, a shared opposition to French political projects, and a mutual admiration and desire to be friends. Norman's personal ties with Schacht allowed Schacht access to monetary assistance that Havenstein could not. When Schacht left London, he had secured a three-year loan from Norman of $25 million for his new bank. Schacht's new bank would "push francs out of Germania." Even more, this bank, funded by British capital, could issue banknotes in sterling, a right that had been rolled back in Scotland and Northern Ireland.[58]

Norman and Schacht's immediate connection and personal cooperation in 1924 set the precedent for extensive personal cooperation between the two central bank leaders all through their tenures. Norman praised Schacht for his Gold Bank plan publicly and to Strong.[59] He went on to say that foreign support, from central banks and not public officials, was essential, and if such a scheme came into effect "it would be a grand thing from every point of view for [Strong] to co-operate" and to keep this idea entirely to himself until then.[60]

Such openness to cooperation had not been extended to Schacht's predecessor. Norman's belief "that a gradual revision of the more punitive provisions of Versailles was essential if the European peace was to be maintained" strengthened his relationship with Schacht.[61] This same shared view had not made him more sympathetic to Havenstein. Norman vouched for Schacht, writing to Strong that Schacht "seems to know the whole situation from A to Z and to have, temporarily, more control of it than I believe possible: he is acting more resolutely than his predecessor Havenstein." Strong's perceptions of Havenstein had also discouraged extensive credit assistance from the Fed to the Reichsbank to navigate hyperinflation and reparations.

Strong and Norman's contact with the Reichsbank and Havenstein had begun late in 1921. Under Havenstein, the Reichsbank had demonstrated a tendency toward being entangled in domestic politics, which brought into question his affinity for politics and politicians. Norman was adamant to limit his interactions with German authorities regarding German stabilization to himself and

Havenstein but was concerned that the Reichsbank's lack of independence would affect its position and capacity domestically and its foreign interactions. Norman wished to see Havenstein strengthen the Reichsbank's position vis-à-vis the government as "a Central Bank which is so much dominated by its own Government as to have no independence or initiation and even no right of protest is not in a fair position and therefore cannot play its part either within its own country or, still more, alongside other Central Banks. That is for instance the present position of the Bank of France, and we all lose by it."[62]

Strong wrote that Havenstein "presents a sad picture of an old man heartbroken and disappointed and apparently helpless in the face of events. I have been told that he is a most reliable and conscientious banker, but that he has lost his prestige in Germany because of the failure of the Reichsbank to withstand the pressure of political domination."[63]

Concerns around Havenstein's inability to withstand political pressure on the Reichsbank were shared within the Fed that the "Reichsbank is said to be somewhat discredited in Germany because it has yielded to political influence" and it was therefore unwise "to enter into close reciprocal relations with the Reichsbank such as we have with some of the other foreign banks." Dealings with the Reichsbank would be best done through formal agreement, not extending Fed credit in furthering and continuing "the present reparations muddle."[64]

Strong and Norman believed that friendly relations with Havenstein were important to creating cooperative working relationships. Strong had attempted to reach out to Havenstein, with little success. As he wrote to Norman, his efforts were "simply a friend pursuit . . . with the idea of cheering him up and indicating that we are really friendly, that we want to do something, and indicating something of the technique involved in developing these relationships."[65] These relationships did not always emerge automatically, especially where personal similarities and backgrounds did not align; as Strong noted, there was a technique to developing these ties.

Norman similarly found value in "bringing about a more intimate and sympathetic relationship between the various banks of issue than has heretofore existed, or been possible." He regarded such relationships "as depending upon personal acquaintance, understanding, mutual respect and confidence, than upon the here formal understandings that can be arrived at my correspondence."[66] But he did not hold the same admiration for Havenstein as he did Schacht, and Havenstein did not share Norman's elitism, nor his prestige and autonomy.

For Schacht, any assistance from an individual or institution with the authority and prestige of the Bank of England would foster increased support for Germany and himself. In the years that followed, Schacht wrote that his "relations with Norman developed into a genuine friendship. . . . For all [Norman's] characteristic mellowness and outward calm he was a man of great personal determination and tenacity of purpose."[67] Norman was even named godfather to Schacht's third grandchild, who was given the names Norman Hjalmar.

The Dawes Loan

With time, extensive correspondence, and frequent personal visits by Norman, Strong, and Schacht, strengthened their relationships and enabled more and more extensive interpersonal cooperation. Their early communication illustrates the delicate nature of developing these relations and the need to not antagonize preexisting relations. Strong held that "inaugurating" these correspondences was best done when opportunities arise naturally; these objectives are best achieved without making them the "subject of formal agreement."[68]

The power that these men enjoyed, their relative immunity from any sort of accountability, and the turbulent nature of the times made these rare friendships potentially extremely valuable. Their personal ties, with each other and with private bankers, central banks' primary stakeholders at the time, were vital for Strong and Norman to mobilize private finance for central banks' lending. These ties proved crucial to bringing about more cooperation between Schacht and the US bankers J. P. Morgan Jr. and Thomas Lamont, which was facilitated by close relationships with Norman.

The reparations disagreements with Germany at the Paris Conference in 1919 had got thrown off again in Genoa in 1922. It was then proposed in 1923 that an Experts' Committee of international experts and Allied politicians be appointed to reexamine Germany's reparations. While Norman was consulted on their decisions, he declined to serve on the committee because "Central Bankers should be left outside international quarrels," and politics would make things very difficult. This "guaranteed him a free hand."[69] The Dawes Loan was a political arrangement designed to resolve the reparations "muddle," including the stabilization of the German mark.

Although key central bankers were not committee members, they along with commercial bankers in the United States influenced "the frantic negotiations that preceded the flotation of the Dawes Loan."[70] Throughout 1924, they cooperated closely over temporary solutions through short-term credits to manage gold flows and stabilize currencies. J. P. Morgan, who was "on almost as close terms with Norman as Strong himself" had already discussed with Norman the idea of an international loan to address the reparations issue.

Schacht was frustrated with the committee for its "policy of delay" over arranging "credit for the final stabilization of German currency."[71] With long-drawn-out negotiations and political obstacles predominantly from the French government, the Golddiskontbank helped manage the mark and the expansion of German exports. Norman saw it as a "last chance" to prevent an outright collapse of the German economy that could not wait for the Experts' deliberations.[72] When Norman reported his plan with Schacht to establish the Golddiskontbank, the Committee approved "an advance of £5 million to the Reichsbank" to assist with its establishment, which was critical for maintaining currency stability in Germany before the final Dawes Loan.[73]

Andrew Boyle suggests that Norman "depended to a greater extent than any modern central banker on the cooperation of individuals" to navigate political obstacles.[74] Initially, he and Strong disagreed and debated for a long time over their currency's role in the Dawes Plan with Norman reminding Strong that sterling was "very much the exchange of Europe, so far as the dollar is concerned," and so the mark should be based in sterling.[75] Strong pointed out that if Germany was to return to a gold-valued currency, it ought to hold all credits in New York "because it is the gold market" and the credit burden on London could impede its return to par.[76] Schacht found himself somewhere in the middle.[77] But their regular correspondence and shared trust enabled Norman, Morgan (on Strong's behalf), and Schacht to engineer this arrangement in Germany in a way that would later facilitate England's return to gold and put pressure on Norman "to commit himself to an early 'return,' and it is not inconceivable that he had indicated as much to Schacht."[78]

The final negotiations between Norman, Morgan, and Schacht were "neither prolonged nor difficult." However, political, and public opposition to lend money to Germany put pressure on governments to stop this arrangement; "in Paris the bankers were especially balky."[79] So, Morgan and Lamont negotiated with the wavering French government, threatening not to float loans to France if they did not cooperate. Norman rounded up British banks to underwrite the London tranche, despite political pressures from the prime minister against the loan.[80] Privately, Norman, Strong, and Schacht, supported by commercial banks, overcame political disputes against the Dawes Plan to float a loan to Germany in October 1924.

Richard Sayers highlights that under Schacht, the reconstituted Reichsbank became "a major star in the central banking firmament."[81] Schacht frequently appealed to Norman, and his determination and virtuosity in financial matters impressed Norman. While Strong was less infatuated by Schacht, he admired Schacht's handling of the Reichsbank. His friendship with Norman made him a third member of the central banking triumvirate, with Strong. Between 1924 and 1926, Schacht sought to minimize pressures on the gold market in London and transfer that pressure to New York, "which was willing and able to take it."[82] Along with strengthening the Reichsbank with the help of the Dawes

Loan and credits from American bankers, Schacht was able to gradually ease the credit rationing policy and lower interest rates through the year.[83]

Schacht benefited greatly from his growing trust and friendliness with Norman, Morgan, and Strong, which facilitated the arrangement of sizable loans and credits to Schacht and the Reichsbank. In many cases, central banks did not need to draw on foreign credits; the availability of a large supply of foreign exchange created "so much confidence in the nation's currency that withdrawals were obviated."[84] When these credits were used, it was to "retire some of its short-term debt," achieving the double purpose of reducing floating debt and increasing the central bank's foreign exchange reserves.[85] In 1926, following a personal visit to New York, Schacht wrote to Strong, thanking him for his goodwill and friendly conversations: "May people more and more realize how largely personal contact, knowledge and friendship are bound to foster such a development of the good of all[.] I hope we shall continue along these lines on many other occasions to come."[86]

Manias, Panics, Crashes, and Earthquakes

Alongside Germany's hyperinflation and reparations woes, a crisis had ensued in Japan. Japanese industry and financial markets had expanded substantially during the war, and the economy experienced a short-lived economic boom. In 1919, the governor of the Bank of Japan, Yatarō Mishima, died, and Junnosuke Inoue took over the bank after an eight-year hiatus from the institution. Inoue was the star of a new generation of central bankers and financiers. Toward the end of the war, Inoue observed the shift in global financial power: "America is becoming England's successor, which is to say, New York is becoming the central market of world finance."[87] Upon his return, Inoue was warned about a possible reaction to the postwar boom, and indeed, wartime trade surpluses had already turned into a deficit.

Although Inoue first recognized the speculative nature of the postwar boom, he was far more optimistic about Japan's prospects than those who warned him about this U-turn. Inoue set out to do in Tokyo what "Strong had been doing for several years at the Federal Reserve Bank of New York, as part of his own drive to make the US dollar a major international currency and New York City a world financial center to rival London"—and introduced new instruments to ease trade financing.[88] He was deeply committed to deflationary policies and returning to prewar parity and had a vision that Tokyo would one day have a free market in gold, a key requirement to be an international center.[89] However, he also took an activist stance in dispensing Bank of Japan credit.

In March 1920, the predicted reaction arrived, when Japan's commercial and financial markets crashed. The panic "was one of the greatest in Japanese history."[90] The decade that followed was a "new age of limitation" for Japan, marked by domestic political tension, economic stagnation, and depression. Many of Japan's economic woes were seen as a result of the imbalances created by the wartime boom. And before the wounds of the panic had healed, the Kanto earthquake and fire hit the country in 1923. Japan was now left to rebuild its economy from the devastation of the earthquake, which also exacerbated its existing debt crisis. All this at a time that scholars suggest represented the height of influence for political parties and financial circles in Japan, and political power swung back and forth between Japan's major parties.[91]

Liquidity and financing were essential to rebuild Japan's economy from its crisis and the earthquake in the midst of constant political change and growing nationalism through the 1920s. Inoue's personal relationship with Strong and private bankers in the United States was consequential in securing Japan's international position and access to dollar liquidity for reconstruction and the banking rescue. Inoue and Eigo Fukai, the Bank of Japan's director and later vice governor, benefited from extensive cooperation with the New York Fed, Norman, and Strong, as well as private bankers in the United States, especially Thomas Lamont at J. P. Morgan & Co. Inoue "knew modern fiscal and monetary theory, spoke and read English fluently, had numerous friends abroad, and operated in the international world of finance as equals to their European and North American counterparts in the pre-war twentieth century. Thomas Lamont of the Morgan Bank grieved when his friend Inoue was assassinated in 1932."[92]

Through Inoue, Fukai, Strong, and Lamont, Japanese finance developed an intimate relationship with the New York banking circuit, which had been weaker prior to Inoue assuming the governorship. During the war, American suspicions of Japan's intentions in China had intensified. But central bankers' personal relations did not fall prey to intergovernmental disputes; rather, they helped overcome obstacles imposed by them: "Those of us who have the opportunity to promote better relations and better understandings must not fail to take advantage of it and what little I could do towards that accomplishment has been one of the most agreeable occurrences of the past two years."[93] Strong wrote to Inoue of his wish to foster and expand cooperation, "to be based upon the known and intimate relationship and interdependence . . . and in the sympathy which we both wish to cultivate between the people of our two countries."[94]

Strong made huge efforts to befriend Inoue and Fukai. Close relations with American financiers also developed quickly after Paris. Lamont traveled to Japan "to negotiate Japan's entry into a revived, American-led international banking consortium" and interacted primarily with Inoue. Vanderlip of the

National City Bank of New York visited Japan soon after.[95] They shared Strong's view of the importance of personal relations that were "built on personalities rather than stockownership," as Morgan once said to Vanderlip.[96] Their visits were followed by Strong's long visit to Japan to include Inoue "personally, into the international central bankers' club that he and Montagu Norman were organizing."[97] When Strong died, Fukai talked of the close relations he and Inoue had developed with him in the early 1920s, and the evenings they passed together in New York at Strong's home when their "conversation became intimate enough that [they] ventured to talk about personal matters."[98] With the help of his American friends, Inoue secured "several large loans" during the decade.[99]

Closer personal relations with Strong also brought Inoue and Fukai closer to Norman, despite the termination of the Anglo-Japanese Alliance and dwindling financial ties between London and Tokyo. Inoue "gained a very influential connection placed even more highly in the firmament of international finance" than his predecessor, who had been left out of the Anglo-Saxon protestant inner circles.[100] Strong noted, "Nothing could be so pleasing as to find upon our arrival that the friends I had looked forward to making are already made."[101] Strong wrote to Inoue in confidence about his plan with Norman about central bank cooperation with other European bankers, with no mention of inviting the French. They all lacked faith in politicians, as Strong wrote to Inoue in 1921: "The time has arrived, or is approaching, when some constructive and helpful program is going to be needed to mitigate the distressing consequences of the war. I must say quite frankly that I dread the point of view of politicians in these matters, and if I must say so without discourtesy to people of such importance, I dread their blunders in economic matters."[102]

After the Kanto earthquake in 1923, Inoue was called to the post of minister of finance in the government. But by 1924, American loans to Japan to finance the Japanese cause during the Russo-Japanese War that were due to mature in 1925 risked default, as were Japanese loans to China; yet Japan found itself taking out loans of its own. In the years prior, Strong and his fellow American bankers had stayed in close contact with Inoue. By this time, the Fed's primary shareholder, Lamont, had unseated Kuhn, Loeb, & Co. as Japan's chief foreign banker.[103] Right before his departure, in February 1924, Inoue negotiated a massive loan of $150 million from Strong and Lamont to Japan for earthquake relief, which was followed by the $190-million Morgan-backed loan to Germany in the Dawes Loan.

During this time, central bankers across the world longed to return to the prewar gold standard. This was also Strong's interest, as well as Inoue's and their foreign counterparts', to return Japan to the prewar gold standard. This shared aim often drove interwar financial and monetary policy.[104] However, Strong did not attach this condition to the Japanese loan, and even cautioned Inoue not to hurry this move; Inoue also did not pursue parity until later. Much of these loans were used not for reconstruction after the earthquake but to roll over the Russo-Japanese War loans and replenish the Bank of Japan's gold reserves in London.[105] They were also not widely welcomed within the Japanese government itself, and Inoue pursued these bilateral central bank credits against Japan's political preference.

In 1924, Inoue was called to the position of minister of finance. This move interrupted his ties with Strong until he returned to the bank. Strong expressed his disappointment, writing, "Of course, I think you will readily understand that the news of the honor which you have received in being made Minister of Finance was not received entirely with great pleasure. . . . In some ways I felt that it might interrupt our contact, although I am sure it can in no way affect the deep friendship which I feel we have had ever since my visit to Japan."[106]

But Strong offered advice on financing Japan's rehabilitation "to be based upon the known and intimate relationship and interdependence which we have upon each other . . . and in the sympathy which we both wish to cultivate among the people of our two countries," which would be a bankers' transaction that would be undertaken with the participation of his entire banking organization. Strong's suggestion was "inspired entirely by [his] friendship and a desire to see the utmost success in any financing done in [Japan]." His "even more personal" note was his assurance to Inoue that "any advice or information which you need from me or from our organization will be furnished promptly and effectively by cable and you must not hesitate at any time to call upon us. It will be disinterested and frank and I should hope that it might prove useful."[107] Inoue acknowledged this support, responding to Strong that "when the time comes, as it should, [he] would not fail to avail [himself] of [Strong's] good offices" as was suggested.[108]

Despite Strong's disappointment at Inoue's departure, he and Lamont negotiated the loan to Japan to help Inoue, in his last month at the Bank in January 1924. Their personal affection for Inoue was crucial for this loan. Inoue was Lamont's main contact in Japan, assuring his partners of Inoue's ability and prestige that "Inoue speaks the same financial language as . . . all of us. I have never found him to deviate from a straight line."[109] The private bankers in the United States, most of whom constituted the shareholders of the Fed, particularly Lamont, were very close to Strong and to Inoue. The Morgan-backed loan was broached by Strong and orchestrated by Lamont to the tune of $150 million. This was, at the time, the largest long-term foreign loan that had been arranged by New York. This bank-led bond issue from New York was carried out jointly with assistance from Norman in London, issuing an additional £25 million, in

February 1924. Norman's assistance to Inoue and to Schacht were contrived to help Inoue, Schacht, and himself, through terms that had the reciprocal effect of allowing them to help finance Britain's return to parity in 1925.

This loan set a precedent for several more, albeit smaller, municipal loans from Strong, Lamont, and Norman to Fukai, until Inoue returned in 1927, tasked to pull Japan out of a grave banking crisis. As he left the Bank of Japan, Inoue cabled Strong sending him his "heartfelt thanks" for Strong's "kind assistance re formation of longwishedfor [*sic*] powerful and influential group."[110]

Inoue then embarked on a year-long trip to Europe and America, where, before his official departure from the bank in 1924, he joined a secret meeting with Strong and Norman. To Inoue, this was not strange, nor was it surprising they traveled under false names and in disguise. In addition to the personal correspondence and informal discussions behind the Morgan loan to Japan, this private meeting was held to discuss Britain's return to parity in 1925. On his return, he wrote to Strong that their time together was the "most enjoyable and interesting one in my present visit to America and Europe" and that he was exceedingly grateful for the best opportunity afforded to renew his friendship with Strong and enjoy such a nice time together.[111] Norman shared these sentiments, writing to Inoue after their visit that he "greatly appreciated having the opportunity of discussing affairs with a Central Banker of such experience as [Inoue]" and hoping for the opportunity to renew their friendship at some later date.[112]

When Inoue moved to the finance ministry, Strong "wondered whether [Inoue's] short political career might subject us to the misfortune of our not having any further association or contact . . . which would be a source of grief to us all."[113] And indeed, their correspondence was interrupted when Inoue joined the finance ministry. At least, per records of Strong's papers held in the Fed's FRASER Archive, there was no correspondence after December 1924 until 1927.

Early in 1927, Japan experienced a grave banking crisis. Japanese banks were carrying over large sums of bad debt from the 1920 crisis and the 1923 earthquake. The urgency of the situation brought Inoue back to the governorship to orchestrate the bailouts and restructuring.[114] On his return, Strong cabled Inoue: "Hearty congratulations and welcome back into the family."[115]

Britain's Return to Gold

The German and Japanese loans brought about a new optimism in Europe. Next was Norman's "conquest of $4.86," to return to prewar parity, pushed by a belief in the gold standard orthodoxy that was shared by central bankers across the world, and by British authorities in the Cunliffe Committee tasked by the government to oversee Britain's currency restoration.[116] Norman was instrumental in sidestepping the governmental authorities at home charged with this task, and together with Strong, arranged large credits from the New York Fed to the Bank of England.

A multitude of factors influenced sterling's return to parity in 1925. First, ideas and a seemingly blind faith in the gold standard dogma that motivated treasuries and central banks to return to the prewar system. Second, this decision was preordained through the Cunliffe and later the Chamberlain-Bradbury Committees created to pursue this goal as the First World War came to an end. Third, Norman's influence in shaping Britain's trajectory. Notably, he alone was not alone in this radical transformation—John Maynard Keynes influenced how policymakers, including Norman, thought about the prewar orthodoxy.

The role of domestic policymakers' contradictory preferences and influence on what Britain's goals were are reflected in some of the concerns that motivated Norman to bring sterling back to its prewar levels, as shared by the Chamberlain-Bradbury Committee, as well as Keynes's interpretation of the shift away from the orthodoxy toward a dollar parity of $4.86.[117] With that background, I highlight the role of agents, with attention to the interpersonal dynamics that enabled Norman to steer the transition as he wished, with the cooperation of Strong, Schacht, Inoue, and Fukai.

Cooperation between Britain and the United States was indeed more straightforward and not entirely unsurprising. Still, given domestic obstacles to resorting to international assistance, credits to Britain were marshaled through informal and interpersonal channels between Norman and Strong, against British governmental preferences not to rely on foreign lending. The Cunliffe Committee on Currency and Foreign Exchanges, and the Chamberlain-Bradbury Committee on Currency and the Bank of England Note Issues were tasked by the government to oversee Britain's return to parity after the war. However, Norman strong-armed these committees to adopt his preferred interest-rate policies at home, with regards to timing and to credit, rather than appreciate the value of sterling, and speed up the restoration of $4.86.

In the urgency of sterling's return to parity, Norman and Strong were on the same page as Lord Bradbury, who chaired the Chamberlain-Bradbury Committee. They held that "the return to gold would save Britain from living in a fool's paradise of false prosperity and would force the export industries to become competitive." Britain's return to parity could not be done at a rate lower than the prewar level, or it would jeopardize London's future as an international center. Norman and Strong both feared that Britain's failure to do so would be "too serious to contemplate."[118]

While the Cunliffe Committee believed in the "automatic machinery" of the gold standard orthodoxy and the need to use Britain's own resources, Norman chose to steer gold markets "through relationships among leading central bankers" to finance his conquest of $4.86 with help from Strong, Schacht, and Inoue.[119] The pace and means of pursuing this agenda were a significant source of contention in Britain. Norman initially favored capital controls and delaying sterling's return to gold. While Norman preferred initially to "hurry slowly" on conclusion of the Dawes Plan, he was also encouraged by Victor Moll of the Sveriges Riksbank in Sweden "to lead the way back to gold."[120] He was pressed by Strong, who urged Norman in 1924 that "sterling cannot return to par and gold payment be resumed without an act of 'force majeure.'"[121]

Eventually, Norman picked up the pace. Britain's return to gold was facilitated by his use of "the very methods explicitly denigrated by the Cunliffe Committee," and also within the Bank of England, of cooperation and foreign borrowing. In January 1925, Norman received cables from his associates that if Britain were to return to gold, "it should do so solely on the basis of its own resources" as foreign assistance would cast doubts on its ability to maintain sterling at prewar parity at all costs. At the heart of this borrowing was the interpersonal support and cooperation that Norman received from Strong, who assured Norman, "You know with what earnestness and sympathy we would consider any suggestion or endeavor to enter into any agreement which would make your plan a success whenever you have one."[122]

Norman and Strong always preferred to discuss matters "face to face, in the spirit of friendship, and avoid public discussion in this way."[123] Given how controversial the subject was at home, Norman wrote to Strong of "how secretly [the issue of future gold policy] must be treated; so much so that not a word can be breathed until some decision much be reached," which would be "to declare a free market" at the end of 1925. To do this, they would "get together and devise a plan which will probably need to include some sort of credit operation."[124] While they privately deliberated arrangements between their banks, Norman emphasized his "preference for secrecy."

In 1923, Norman wrote to Strong that in England they could not "get along without you. . . . I want your help from your international mind: it's not common in the FRB in Washington or elsewhere!"[125] Around this time, an announcement was due as to who would take over the governorship in England. The prospect of a change of guard was also a source of angst for Strong. When it was announced that Norman would continue in his post, Strong wrote to him: "You will now have another year within which to complete a splendid work [the return to parity], which I know is very near your heart. Probably you are the one person in the world who knows me better than anyone else how anxious I am that you shall succeed in everything that you set out to accomplish, not the least important being to leave the Bank of England with the pound sterling and the gold dollar firmly established as before the war. What a great achievement, indeed, will this be!"[126]

Strong believed that their "success in accomplishing anything depends so much on these personal relations that I look forward with dread to the day when you will be succeeded by some unknown person with whom I may not have the same intimate and affectionate relations that I have enjoyed so greatly with you."[127] During this time, Norman wrote to Strong, "And you know, Ben, I am grateful for your all your welcome and hospitality: & for all you do for me & are to me."[128]

Credit lines of support from the Fed and J. P. Morgan & Co. to support the stabilization of sterling came about with ease. Norman negotiated, with very little difficulty, a loan from Strong and Morgan up from $300 million to $500 million, which Strong saw "as not excessive." The Fed would be consulted as to which credit and how much would be used. Through their credit line, central bankers could coordinate monetary policy with their counterparts overseas, manipulate exchange rates, and through central bank cooperation, "fend off a speculative attack."[129] Previous studies on this matter overlook, however, that due to some delays, the bank-led US loan engineered by Strong and Morgan was finalized at $300 million. One notable request from Strong to Norman was for Norman's assurance that he would stay on as governor for at least another year, if not two.[130]

Strong "urged that [their] proposed gold transaction should be entirely separate and distinct from any credit or borrowing conducted by the British Government"; he had "always felt that the successful conduct of this matter depends upon the spirit of cooperation which can be and has been developed, and that that spirit, which is obviously present in this matter, is all that is needed."[131] Despite the reduced loan size, Strong and Norman engineered this in a manner which had the advantage of reducing the Treasury's share of the credits by $200 million but maintaining the line between the New York Fed and the Bank of England as planned. All through the decade, and as Britain returned to parity in the spring of 1925, Norman and Strong kept one another abreast of discount rate changes and other policy developments at home.

In Britain, there was "reluctance in some quarters" to be too dependent on the Fed or the US gold market; financing the return to $4.86 through Fed assistance went against the means prescribed by the Cunliffe Committee. On learning of this political interference in Norman's endeavors, Strong reiterated, "The most important consideration to preserve is the right spirit of cooperation and helpfulness, which cannot be made the subject of written agreements and obligations." Norman was extremely grateful to Strong for "all the trouble which [Strong had] so kindly and willingly taken in connection with these arrangements."[132]

Norman also orchestrated help from Schacht and Fukai. Following Britain's loan to Japan in 1924, Norman solicited the help of the Bank of Japan to join a handful of central banks to provide credit to the Reichsbank to capitalize the Golddiskontbank, which would conduct its business in sterling, which was important for Norman's goal of restoring the currency's international position. Although the Bank of Japan was not technically or legally authorized to participate in a foreign loan, Fukai and Norman worked out a plan through which Japan would assist the Reichsbank through the Bank of England's account for the Reichsbank. Norman orchestrated a convoluted scheme in which the Bank of Japan would effectively lend the Reichsbank $500,000 through its Bank of England account, which could be presented as an unofficial fee for the 1924 loan to Japan.

The following April, in 1925, this balance was withdrawn from the Reichsbank account and the $500,000 was credited to the Bank of Japan account at the Bank of England, to support sterling's return to parity in 1925. Because these accounts paid no interest, deposits could conveniently be viewed as de facto loans to support Britain's return to gold by withdrawing these funds from the Reichsbank's account and credited to the Bank of Japan later. This same mechanism was used in 1926 and 1928, in which Japan credited the Bank of England the funds to provide the Belgian and Italian central banks the necessary credit to finance currency stabilization.[133]

Steered by Norman's strong hand, and the help of Strong, Schacht, and Fukai, Churchill announced Britain's return to gold in April 1925. This decision had been made outside Cabinet and executed predominantly by Norman.[134] In the years that followed, sterilization policies continued secretly through Strong's bank. Because these operations were carried out in the New York money market, and by the Fed, Norman's manipulation of gold reserves in the Bank of England was not traceable. As Simon Bytheway describes it, "Norman operated a bank within the bank, known only to himself and a few key confidants."[135] Norman's own associates described him as "secretive and devious and would not ever tell you what was being done, or who did them, and surmised that Norman would probably finalise it himself."[136]

European Stabilization Efforts

The need for liquidity, in sterling, dollars, and gold, remained a concern for all of Europe that sought to stabilize their currencies, and return and maintain gold standard parity in the 1920s. Postwar goals over currency stabilization and returning to parity were shared across Europe. Indeed, following Britain and Germany's return to gold, many more countries sought to follow suit. Not everyone, however, had the privilege of these clubby networks to facilitate this goal. In this section, I turn to the influence of interpersonal relationships and hierarchies in shaping central banks' access to liquidity and financing for currency stabilization across Europe between 1925 and 1928.

Norman and Strong orchestrated these efforts, but negotiations were often slower and disrupted. Interpersonal relations shaped stabilization efforts and loans again, but these loans were different. They were granted to "outsiders" from Norman and Strong's usual circles, arranged *multilaterally* by central banks and the League of Nations, and carried limits and conditions.[137] When Émile Moreau and his Bank joined these efforts, this brought new complications.[138] While I do not go into the minute details of every stabilization effort here, I illustrate general patterns of how personal friendships and, more so, frictions, especially between Norman and Moreau, impacted loan negotiations and currency stabilization in Belgium and Poland.

Belgium and Poland were less embedded in financial and central bank networks than those in the larger and richer economies, so Norman and Strong knew their counterparts less well in these countries. Consequently, Belgian and Polish central bankers had much less influence in negotiating their stabilization packages. Autonomy from politics was therefore an important signal of trustworthiness for these banks. Distrust and mistrust influenced who was included in negotiations, and who was not, and how negotiations progressed. These dynamics manifested in currency stabilization efforts, through the Norman-Moreau vendetta.

Norman and Moreau

In 1925, Norman, along with Strong and private bankers in England and New York, discussed the issue of stabilization of the French and Belgian francs. The Bank of France was excluded from these discussions, as French central bankers early in the decade had not established close interpersonal ties with Norman and Strong and because the French franc had not yet been stabilized. Even after the French franc was stabilized in 1926, Bank of France leaders were still excluded from secret meetings and negotiations over currency stabilization elsewhere in Europe. When its new leaders, Émile Moreau and Pierre Quesnay, entered office in 1926, they were only occasionally invited to participate in credit agreements.

Moreau, in Liaquat Ahamed's words, was "a taciturn man" from the French provincial countryside. Although he rose rapidly in the civil service ranks to enter the elite administrative class in France, "he proudly went out of his way to remain" provincial.[139] When he was appointed as governor in 1926, French public finances were in complete disarray and the franc was on the brink of collapse. Moreau played a crucial role in rescuing the currency and restoring France's public finances. But he had no formal independence from the central government, frequently bowed to the Treasury's demands, and "proved to be unusually adept at bureaucratic infighting."[140] He clashed with several figures in the Bank of France, in the private banking sector, and across national boundaries. He distrusted Anglo-Saxon banking practices and was suspicious that the Bank of England did not possess all the gold it claimed it did; indeed, he was proved correct in 1931.

Norman and Moreau's mutual distrust was rooted in suspicions in their political goals, preventing them from finding common ground to cooperate. Ivar Rooth, former governor of the Swedish National Bank, observed that Moreau "was [very] unwilling to do anything with foreigners; just a Frenchman—de Gaulle's kind"; "Moreau made a great mistake in imagining an anti-French plot—didn't understand that [Norman] wanted central [bank] cooperation [and to] keep clear of politics."[141] British monetary and financial authorities found Moreau to be "the greatest obstacle to intelligent international cooperation in monetary policy" and "quite ignorant of modern ideas, full of prejudice and personally difficult."[142]

Jacques Leon Reuff, a French economist and adviser to the government, noted that there was great distrust of Norman in Paris. "Moreau disliked and distrusted" Norman.[143] Norman's lack of trust and warmth for the Bank of France emerged from what he saw as "a lack of closeness between" the Bank of France and the New York Fed; Norman was keen to keep New York in with Schacht.[144] Robert Lacour-Gayet recalled that Norman's closeness with Schacht created suspicion among the French in "anything peculiarly English" and exacerbated suspicion between Norman and Moreau.[145] Moreau believed Norman and Schacht saw each other often to "hatch secret plans."[146]

Moreau understood the need "to gain the confidence and, if possible, the friendship" of Strong. "Norman spares nothing in his efforts to flatter him or gain influence over him."[147] Strong found that the French were "gradually . . . beginning to think of the Bank of France in terms of independence from Treasury domination."[148] As the Bank of France grew more powerful, the "development of central bank relations with Norman serving as a hub for European contacts closely linked to Strong in New York was no longer viable" as Moreau's Bank established its own relationship with Strong.[149]

Meanwhile, Strong was concerned that his meetings with Moreau would be misinterpreted by Norman and kept them secret. But with time, Strong's friendly relationship with Moreau posed problems for Norman and ultimately to the interests of cooperation.[150] It helped Moreau that Strong knew that in France, Italy, and Belgium, "there is much suspicion as to whether the attitude and arrangements are at all times free of political motives or purposes. . . . They seem to be afraid of [Norman] and somewhat distrust him."[151]

Likewise, Norman did not like the French and distrusted Moreau for his lack of autonomy and independence from the Treasury and from government, expressing that "he would appreciate it if the independence of the bank could be demonstrated not only through its policies but perhaps also by a change in its own statutes and constitution. In any case, he believes that his 'friends,' that is Strong and Schacht, if not himself, would like to see such an external demonstration."[152] Norman and Moreau competed over currency stabilization efforts, seeking to achieve their own strategic aims. Neither was unfettered from politics as they claimed.[153]

As discussed in the opening of this book, the Belgian stabilization was handled privately by Norman, Strong, some colleagues in the Netherlands and Switzerland, and Morgan. Moreau was kept in the dark until later. Norman and Strong's control over the trajectory of the interwar European economy had implications for their counterparts on the continent. Invitations to participate in stabilization loans were extended by Norman, who, in an undiplomatic manner, limited any cooperative efforts to only those who he liked. Attempts to include Moreau on questions that required cooperation were thwarted by mutual mistrust and suspicion.

In Belgium, Fernand Hautain's breach of Strong's trust led to an initial loan agreement between New York and Brussels to collapse. Belgium's fortunes changed only when Louis Franck replaced Hautain. Norman, Strong, Schacht, and Vissering in the Netherlands floated a credit to the National Bank of Belgium.[154] Moreau felt slighted when he later learned of this arrangement and grew even more suspicious of Norman's imperialist agenda, intensifying their rivalry.[155] As Kindleberger highlights the stakes of their squabbles, this rivalry "would be pathetic" were it not to jeopardize the stability of the system as a whole.[156]

Polish Stabilization

In Poland, initial de facto stabilization was achieved in 1924, following a period of hyperinflation, akin to that in Germany, Austria, and Hungary. Austria, Hungary, Greece, Bulgaria, Estonia, and Danzig all undertook adjustment and stabilization programs through the League of Nations; Germany had support from Norman and the Dawes Loan. Poland received little external assistance at first. Stabilization this time was short-lived and fell victim to Norman and Moreau's continual feud and an emerging fallout between Norman and Strong.

Bank Polski had received a $10 million credit from Strong at the request of Felix Młynarski, then vice president of the Polish central bank in 1925. The government had received a loan from the private financiers Dillon, Read and Company, who were then the financial agents of the Polish government in the United States. After a period of stability following this loan, ensuring the stabilization of the złoty faced many complications. When this initial attempt was not successful in helping Poland return to parity, Edwin Kemmerer, famously known as a "money doctor," was commissioned to study the Polish economy. However, before the study began in 1926, and through that year, the złoty continued to fall and any attempt to secure private loans to the government and avoid going the League of Nations had broken down, and such agreement was never reached.[157]

Currency stabilization in Poland could be approached in three different ways. Each, however, was unsatisfactory to at least one involved party. First, Poland could go to the League, which the Poles refused to accept. The government tried to avoid Norman (who preferred this route) and the League to acquire a stabilization loan "perhaps because they did not want to be identified with the losing parties of World War 1 that had programs with the League."[158] By the time of Polish złoty stabilization, policymakers had a better idea of what League loans looked like, in particular, the austerity measures and surveillance, from the Austrian experience.[159] In fact, later in 1925, Jan Ciechanowski, the Polish minister to the United States, approached Strong for support, as well as assistance to "win Governor Norman away from the League of Nations program, which he said was utterly impossible for Poland."[160] A second option was to expand the Kemmerer mission to include other European banks, although this would have had to be led by the Americans, which Strong was eager to avoid. Indeed, the United States did send financial expert advisers, including Charles Dewey, to follow Kemmerer, which some portray as engineered by the United States to exert financial power over the financial system, which had an air of new dollar imperialism.[161] The third option was an entirely American program, which Norman refused to accept.

A version of the second option was adopted, and it reflected the impasse among monetary authorities: a joint loan issue from a handful of European banks, led by the Americans, but with notable influence from Moreau. The effort was disrupted by a series of personal disagreements—an emerging disagreement between Norman and Strong, an illness that forced Strong's absence from the final negotiations, and misunderstandings between Norman and George L. Harrison, then deputy governor of the New York Fed who later succeeded Strong as governor. Indeed, Polish officials capitalized on these disagreements, as Martin argues, and "played foreign banks off one another until a loan with the weakest control provisions was found."[162] Moreau and private bankers in France were able to sway the outcome and the terms of the final agreement.

By August 1926, the Kemmerer Commission provided hope for a new stabilization attempt. Soon, Poland sought external credits and the Polish central bank governor Młynarski asked Strong to approach Norman to find an alternative. But the stabilization of the Polish złoty was disrupted by a combination of personal preferences, disagreements, and distrust among all the central bankers involved. Młynarski found Norman to be "more sympathetic and friendly than he had been a year ago" but had not moved in his preference that they go through the League. He also found that "Strong was not quite as interested as he had previously been in aiding Polish monetary reform and that he felt that Mr. Strong apparently wished to 'back off.'" Apparently, Strong had previously agreed to coordinate his and Norman's views, while the Poles would deal directly with Strong. In the end, they dealt directly with both parties whose views "could scarcely be considered coordinated. . . . Nor were the Poles apparently telling quite the same story to both banks."[163]

Norman and Strong found that too many central bankers in Poland acted without coordination, sought political influence, and were too suspicious of other people's motives. Initially, Strong was eager to go to the League, while Moreau wanted to take charge in the credit. Norman wanted Młynarski and his bank to go through the League and believed that any credit arrangement should be made with the support of a preliminary expert committee. After all, Germany had now joined the League and sought stronger controls on the loan. Poland was wary of Germany's involvement in any loan, as it was then seeking to reconnect the Polish corridor. Poland could not afford to give Germany any additional leverage in its affairs.[164]

During negotiations, a lack of communication and Strong and Norman's misgivings hindered progress. Norman wished to limit cooperation only to central banks and keep politics out. For him, any stabilization credit "would be necessary to go into all the conditions of the program and require all sorts of protections required in a wholly independent credit such as he and Schacht had suggested." Strong and Harrison preferred to grant development loans "as part of an effective program of stabilization than unconditionally," which were granted a few months later.[165]

Młynarski went to see Strong in 1927, with the goal of securing US cooperation in Poland's stabilization. A rough loan-issue plan was drawn up between Polish and American central banks, and a few private bankers in New York, of $50 million, which would be exercised by a committee of international experts, including an adviser each from the United States, Britain, France, and Switzerland. Strong, who was often ailing, was not present at many meetings with Młynarski and his associates, nor at subsequent central bank gatherings on the continent. Strong's absence had a significant effect on Norman's influence and willingness to cooperate, as Norman did not share the same intimate friendship with Harrison as with Strong. Everyone, even Norman and Schacht, agreed on the need for a loan. Norman, losing interest in the issue, now proposed that Moreau and the Bank of France take on responsibility for the loan "as a way out" of the impasse, and follow Strong's lead. Schacht disagreed "because that would give rather a political aspect to the whole matter."[166]

Eventually, Strong agreed on the proposal with the Fed's limited participation, entrusting Moreau to enlist European partners. Most subsequent discussions were held between Młynarski, Moreau, and Harrison, and only occasionally, Strong. Moreau, still salty about the Belgian credits, opposed Norman's preference to go through the League. He thought the League was disproportionality staffed with Britons and saw it "as little more than a vehicle for extending the Bank of England's interests."[167] He was advised by the League's secretary general, Joseph Avenol (who was French): "At the moment, efforts are underway to put a stop to the veritable tyranny which the Bank of England exercises over European Banks of Issue." Avenol and French central bankers saw the League's Financial Committee as "synonymous with the Bank of England."[168]

Strong found himself mediating the strained relations between Moreau and Norman over the stabilization plans in Eastern Europe. In lieu of Strong, who was ill, Harrison went to Europe to discuss Polish assistance with his counterparts. Strong had urged Harrison that "above all . . . Moreau should not be left with the feeling that things had been arranged with Norman and Schacht before Moreau had had the opportunity to express his views, and that Norman must not get the idea that the conclusion of a stabilization plan for Poland depended on Norman's attitude."

But now, the stabilized French franc allowed France to enjoy a strong economic recovery from the crises it faced between 1923 and 1926 and was one of the strongest currencies in the world. Norman and his associates were disgruntled by the success of French policy, as it had managed to stabilize the franc with little recourse to international assistance and secured a significant write-down of its debts to Britain. While Moreau and his bank were neither "quite big enough to have responsibility forced on" them nor "small enough to afford the luxury of irresponsibility," they were powerful enough to destabilize and, only with help, act as a stabilizer.[169]

Already sensitive about Strong's relationship with Moreau, this intensified a growing dispute between Norman and Strong, which was exacerbated by Norman's irritability and Strong's illness. Strong and Harrison gradually moved to support Moreau's multilateral program, with protections for central banks that gave credit. In fact, they privately met Jean Monnet, on behalf of the Bank of France, who had returned to banking in New York after spending some time in the family cognac business, and Młynarski, in New York to discuss the credit in 1927.[170]

On his trip to Europe, Harrison first saw Norman, and from his meeting, believed that Norman was satisfied with the terms of the agreement. Norman largely saw the advantage of stabilization in Poland, with some reservations as to whether reforms would ensure political and financial stability.[171] Harrison recalled Norman had previously indicated that he would participate in a credit approved by an expert committee "as long as it had been developed this way."[172]

Norman, who did not share the same ability to have frank discussions with Harrison as with Strong, did not fully convey that he did not feel as Harrison believed he did. Harrison believed that a deal had been reached. Norman, however, was still eager to have Młynarski and his bank go through the League and was upset at Harrison's move away from this route. He soon realized that an American scheme was going to go on and "chances of League [were] almost nil."[173]

After speaking with Harrison, Norman wrote about his misgivings of the failure of going to the League to his own Bank of England associates, indicating they might split with New York over this difference in principle.[174] Norman and Schacht renewed their demands to go to the League, which were rejected by Harrison and Moreau.[175] Norman, now upset at the handling of the situation, was no longer willing to appoint an Englishman to such a committee. While he admitted that "it was to the advantage of [all participating banks] for him to be helpful," Norman "would not say he would be helpful."[176] If no agreement was going to include the League, Norman wanted the Fed to assume responsibility for the loan; Norman "was not willing to give enough ground to enable an agreement to be reached on the Fed's terms.[177]

Norman told Rist, of the Bank of France, that he "would be willing to join in a central bank credit organised by the Federal Reserve, or, if he were to be asked, by another central bank." But at this time, any such loan could be interpreted as France being Poland's ally.[178] Harrison found Norman to be reneging on his word and pushed him on it and wanted to see a more "favorable and cooperative point of view on [Norman's] part."[179] Norman believed that all participating bankers, especially himself and Schacht, should limit their participation to an invitation from the Fed. The Fed could then scarcely be unwilling to assume responsibility for the loan, as without Norman and Schacht's support, the program would likely fail. Harrison had felt that Norman's "refusal to aid or [give] advice or even be tacitly in favor of a committee would indicate a lack of desire to cooperate in a constructive way."[180] Norman made no definitive commitment on the credit or appointing anyone to an expert committee. On the other hand, Harrison found that so far as Moreau was concerned, Harrison "could tell him quite frankly how we all feel."[181]

An emerging rift between Norman and his associates at the Fed, heightened by Strong's illness and inability to actively participate in loan negotiations, turned the tables for Norman's influence in Eastern Europe. Harrison turned to Moreau instead, to lead the way, requesting Moreau to approach other banks of issue, except Norman, to participate in the loan. This was the first time that Moreau was given any sense of coresponsibility with the Fed, which aggrieved Norman even more. In June 1927, Moreau, Harrison, Norman, Schacht, and a handful of their European counterparts agreed to float a $20 million annual credit to Poland. Following delays, renewed negotiations with American bankers and the Polish government reached an impasse over the terms of the loan, which was only overcome that October.

At this time, no Fed representatives participated in the final negotiations. Moreau had close contact with private bankers, including Jean Monnet, who were in direct negotiations with the Polish central bank. Like Norman and Strong had done in the past, Moreau used these connections to influence the terms of the agreement, especially as Fed representatives were not involved in these negotiations, to further French political interests in Poland. But he anticipated looser control over the Bank of Poland than the League had had over Germany, Austria, or Hungary.[182]

In the end, Moreau used his position to pursue French political aims, binding borrowers "with military and political ties." He also successfully secured French control over monitoring these credits and the Bank of France's leading position in mobilizing these international credits.[183] Moreau ultimately arranged a very short-term credit from several banks of issue with Strong, where Strong requested Moreau that "all interested parties will keep existence of credit strictly secret." Strong followed up this comment with his "grateful thanks for your splendid cooperation and our congratulations for the way you have handled a most difficult problem."

In 1928, Moreau similarly disrupted Norman's stabilization plans through the League and organized an international credit to Romania, on his own terms, without involving the League. Norman's bitterness at this blow to his pride and prestige was exacerbated by Moreau's success in achieving France's political ends in the region.[184]

Strong's Men

In the interwar period, there was no one stabilizer that was willing or able to lead. But Norman and Strong provided this public good and played that part at their discretion, in a selective and exclusive way. Their personal ties with their counterparts influenced central banks' access to liquidity and the stringency of any conditions on these loans and credits.

The strongest and most unique relationship was between Norman and Strong, which allowed the two men to control and steer Britain's return to gold against the preferences and manner dictated by the British government. Schacht and Inoue were also privileged in their personal relations with Norman and Strong, which allowed them to circumvent international political disputes and the domestic dictates of their governments and institutions in securing the necessary liquidity to finance currency stabilization and bank rescues. For long, the French were excluded from this inner club. Those outside the center, such as Belgium, and at the periphery, such as Poland, had very differential treatment, through enforced and monitored multilateral loans that were arranged by the core. Not only did trust and goodwill facilitate extensive liquidity assistance, but distrust and personal disputes could also serve to frustrate efforts.

The interwar years laid important foundations for central bank independence as a more institutionalized practice. Central bankers viewed governments as responsible for inflation. Central bankers' political insulation allowed them to enact anti-inflationary policies and instilled trustworthiness and confidence among their peers. Interbank loans and credits were also used to secure central bank independence among borrowers. These institutional preferences were solidified among the most powerful and insulated central banks under Norman and Strong. This autonomy was critical for avoiding the constraints of democratic practices and preferences.

The swings from boom to bust and back and recurrent crises of the 1920s also illustrate the contradictions of central bank independence. Specifically, central bank autonomy is believed to allow policymakers to avoid short-termism and political whims from encroaching into monetary management and limit inflationary pressures from politicians. However, central bankers' responses to addressing financial pressures has also tended to be ad hoc and short-term, tackling the most immediate problems. But often these strategies simply kicked the can down the road, failing to address the sources of financial pressures in the first place. The interwar years are an important moment in central bank history in regularizing contemporary practices that sit at odds with democratic governance and failed to provide more than temporary solutions to resolve the more deeply seated problems in the international financial system.

Strong's leadership was critical for the Fed's involvement in international cooperative efforts. And without Strong, Norman would also have been more isolated in his endeavors to pursue his central banking agenda. In the latter half of the 1920s, Strong was a key mediator in managing disputes arising from Norman's "petulant treatment of Moreau" in his personal capacity as a close and trusted friend to both men. As his physical condition deteriorated in 1928, Strong felt ill-used and aggrieved by Norman's increasingly uncooperative attitude toward Moreau.

While they ultimately "patched up their differences by post . . . their personal reconciliation had not reconciled their views" of the Bank of France and of Moreau. Strong noted the personal disagreements between Norman and Moreau; Moreau had found Norman so "torturous" (which is exactly the word he used) that, plainly stated, it was almost impossible to do business with him.[185] Strong also noted the intimacy and affection he shared with Norman "despite certain personal qualities of which [he] heartily disapprove[d]," and despite a definite dispute between them, "it would prove most unfortunate if at this stage and with the circumstances as they were [they] had a third party introduced into the situation, where a like dispute would arise, and [Strong] begged Governor Moreau and his colleagues to do their utmost to forget all the questions of personality and deal with the Bank of England matters on an institutional basis with regard to the main purposes to be accomplished, rather than those of passing personalities."[186]

Despite their disagreement, Strong convinced Moreau "not to create any unnecessary trouble for Britain" and Moreau agreed to try and protect the Bank of England so long as they "made it possible for him to do so."[187] Strong made a similar appeal to Norman, but for Norman, developing friendlier relations with Moreau "involved more questions of personal equation than of institutional relationships, and Governor Norman was so sensitive that anything of that sort might prove fatal."[188] Moreau also notes Strong's influence in overcoming personal differences in this and the need to turn to institutional support when personal relations soured: "Speaking of relations between the Bank of France and the Bank of England, M. Strong confides that if Norman fails to reach a reasonable and pacific frame of mind, he will use his own methods if necessary to get certain members of the Court of the Bank to stand up for a policy of conciliation."[189]

Unfortunately, Strong's peace mission came too late. Strong died in October 1928 and "Moreau was now too determined to make Norman dance to his own tune."[190] Now, both Norman and Moreau found themselves at the center of the central banking profession in a world soon engulfed by a stock market crash with the Great Depression just around the corner.

2

THINGS FALL APART

The Collapse of Cooperation and the Great Depression

Through the 1920s, central bankers developed an understanding that the international financial system could not be left to run itself.[1] In the absence of a robust system and an automatic and institutionalized means to maintain stability, the management of international monetary affairs relied on extensive, ad hoc cooperation among central banks. Montagu Norman at the Bank of England, and Benjamin Strong at the New York Fed, cultivated tight personal relationships among themselves and a few of their counterparts, namely Inoue Junnosuke at the Bank of Japan, and Hjalmar Schacht of the Reichsbank. The Norman-Strong partnership lay at the heart of central bank cooperation after the First World War. Together, they could circumvent international and domestic obstacles to cooperate informally to support one another's currencies through ad hoc bilateral assistance.

Strong died suddenly in October 1928. In this chapter, I show that his death played a central role in the breakdown of interwar cooperation in three ways. First, under Strong's successor, George L. Harrison, the New York Fed faced increasing interference from the US government and the Federal Reserve Board in Washington. Second, under Harrison and Norman, Anglo-American cooperation slowed down as they did not share the trust and familiarity akin to Norman and Strong. Third, Strong's death dealt a blow to Norman's power and position in the central banking world, for which Norman had relied greatly on Strong's support.

This period was also marked by significant personnel changes in central banks across Europe. Just as the Great Depression began, Schacht was briefly replaced by

Hans Luther, to the detriment of cooperation between the Bank of England and the Reichsbank. Émile Moreau was replaced as governor of the Bank of France by Clément Moret in 1930. Norman himself frequently took ill or was indisposed, often turning over monetary leadership in London to his deputy, Ernest Harvey. These leadership changes had important implications for bilateral and ad hoc central bank cooperation in the 1930s. Norman, the hub of the international central banking community, now dealt with different spokes, without the close personal friendships and trust that he had enjoyed with their predecessors.

These new leaders were also more constrained by political pressures or interference and often could not overrule or circumvent governmental interests. They were therefore less free to participate in international central bank activities than their predecessors. These changes were consequential impediments to extensive central bank collective action at the outbreak of the 1929 stock market crash and the Great Depression.

The collapse of bilateral cooperation that persisted through the 1920s tells an important story of how individuals navigate the structural and domestic constraints within which they operate, and the role of individual agency in shaping outcomes in international monetary affairs. Individual agency was inhibited by structural, institutional, and political preferences. There were now institutions that could challenge the leadership of the Bank of England and especially the New York Bank. They were the Federal Reserve Board, the US government, and even governments in Europe. These leadership changes created new space for extensive political involvement at the New York Fed. Moreover, as the package of players changed in the decade after 1928, the absence of interpersonal trust, goodwill, and friendship left central bankers incapable of meeting their counterparts more than halfway to cooperate over financial rescue measures. Central bank cooperation gave way to governments' priorities and political pressures, thus obstructing informal and ad hoc cooperation during the Great Depression.

In this chapter, I provide a brief overview and timeline of the emergence of the 1929 stock market crash and the Great Depression. I then review accounts of why the Depression was so long and so deep and introduce a new cast of characters. The rest of the chapter focuses on how the weakness or absence of interpersonal relations contributed to central bankers' failure to undertake bilateral cooperation to provide liquidity assistance to partner banks. As such, the Great Depression was prolonged in part because of the absence of interpersonal trust among central bankers in office that prevented a consorted rescue effort. I focus my analysis on the failure of cooperation to rescue the Austrian and German banking systems, Britain's abandonment of the gold standard, and the tripartite meetings alongside the 1933 World Economic Conference (WEC).

The Crisis and Depression after 1928

In the United States, the 1920s were a period of unprecedented economic prosperity. From late 1928 to 1929, the New York stock market "seemed spectacular." The market was described as "an orgy of speculation, a mania, a bubble," but, as Kindleberger also points out, it denoted "a loss of contact with reality."[2] The New York Stock Exchange was at the center. The Dow Jones Industrial Average increased almost sixfold from 1921 to 1929. Irving Fischer, one of the most well-known economists of the time, was quoted in the *New York Times* on October 16, 1929, saying that "stock prices have reached 'what looks like a permanently high plateau.'"

Not ten days later, on October 24, the roaring twenties came to a crashing halt. On October 28, dubbed Black Monday, the Dow Jones Industrial Average declined nearly 13 percent; and then another 12 percent the next day. By mid-November, the Dow had lost nearly half its precrash value and continued to slide in the years that followed.

The crash itself did not halt economic growth—economic output was already in decline. In light of this emerging recession in the summer of 1929, the Federal Reserve was already assessing how to respond in the months leading up to the crash. When the recession began, and as it turned into a depression, it was neither immediately obvious nor inevitable that the crisis would be so severe or last as long as it did.

Because of the exceptional nature of the crisis, finding an explanation for it has been described as the "search for the Holy Grail."[3] In the context of the United States, there is consensus within the scholarly community searching for this explanation *that* the Fed failed to act appropriately during the crisis. There is less of a consensus as to *why* it did. Milton Friedman and Anna Schwartz blame the Fed's failure to stem the banking panics that began in 1929 on the structure of the institution—disagreement over what policy action to take and the power struggle between the New York Fed and the Board. The Fed's actions at the start of the recession-depression were distinct from those of the 1920s, and Strong's death also played an important role in determining Fed policies. As they argue, Harrison did not have "the confidence and backing of other financial leaders inside and outside the [Federal Reserve] System, the personal force to make his own views prevail, and also the courage to act upon them."[4]

David Wheelock suggests that Strong's death in 1928 led "to a redistribution of authority within the [Federal Reserve] System that caused a distinct deterioration in Fed performance." Authority was transferred to other Reserve Banks that were less knowledgeable and failed to recognize the need for aggressive policies.[5] But Wheelock disagrees on Strong's influence over Fed policies, suggesting that they represent a continuation of the Fed's 1920s policies, focused on defending the gold standard and maintaining dollar parity; they did not focus on domestic economic activity.

Allan Meltzer highlights the Fed's flawed policies, focusing on its actions and inactions. Fed leaders had no coherent policy strategy in place, and the lack of agreement among the governors of regional Feds exacerbated the recession then turned it into a Depression. Several Board leaders believed that speculation misdirected resources away from more productive activities such as commercial, agricultural, or industrial activity. Many authors of the 1913 Federal Reserve Act, and leaders within the Federal Reserve System, prescribed to the theory of real bills, which essentially called for procyclical policy: "The central bank should issue money when production and commerce expanded, and contract the supply of currency and credit when economic activity contracted." The Fed's adherence to the real bills doctrine contradicted the prescriptions of the gold standard mechanism, and so policy was deflationary. Per Meltzer, because Strong also adhered to the real bills doctrine, had he been alive, he would similarly have failed to take the necessary aggressive action.[6]

The Federal Reserve Board in Washington opted for a policy of more direct action to reduce the surge in call loans by asking reserve banks to deny credit to any bank that used these funds for loans to stock market speculators. As early as February 1929, the Board was worried about Federal Reserve credit seeping into security markets and warned against speculation.

Harrison sought a different approach to raise the discount lending rate to 6 percent when he made his first appeal to the Board for this change.[7] His applications for this move were repeatedly shot down. While Harrison believed that higher discount rates would bring about lower call loan rates, the Board believed the opposite effect to be more likely.

Between February and May 1929, the Board shot down ten appeals by Harrison to increase discount rates. In this time, conditions in New York changed drastically. The Board was being asked to raise rates amid falling Federal Reserve credit and increasing reserve ratios, which "according to the canons of banking practice called for lower rather than higher rates!" Even more, Harrison's plea was for an increase to 6 percent *to start*, with the possibility of further increases should it not "correct the situation." The Board, however, believed that the "present fever of speculation could not be curbed through the discount rate by any increase short of such extremes as would produce a cataclysm in the market, which, as stated above, would injure business as much as or even more than it would injure the stock market."[8]

Perhaps they were right. But the Board finally acquiesced to Harrison's appeals in August 1929, raising the discount rate in New York to 6 percent. This step pushed foreign central banks to increase their own interest rates, and tightening monetary policy tipped European economies into a recession. While international commercial and economic activity contracted, the financial stock market boom continued, and commercial banks continued lending money to speculators. By that September, stock prices began to fluctuate increasingly in the United States and collapsed in October.

While commercial banks were protected by the New York Fed's intervention, the stock market dashed investor and consumer confidence, hurt commerce and industrial activity, and reduced consumer demand, especially for higher-priced goods usually purchased using credit. Large manufacturers saw their demand decline, leading to lower production and furloughs. As unemployment increased, the economic contraction that had begun in the summer of 1929 was accelerated by the stock market collapse, turning a recession into the Depression.

The Depression in the United States was marked by regional banking panics that spread nationwide by 1931, with the collapse of the commercial banking system in the United States that March. The United States saw a series of regional banking crises and failures, starting in the south, in Tennessee, and moving north to the Midwest that December.

These crises reached the heart of American finance. On December 11, the Bank of the United States in New York City failed, then the largest commercial bank to have ever failed in US history. The New York Fed's intervention failed, depositors panicked, and the bank was closed. This panic created fears of a repeat of the 1907 crisis, the first worldwide financial crisis of the twentieth century that led to the creation of the Federal Reserve System in 1914.

Between 1929 and 1933, the US economy experienced the most severe business cycle contraction of the century. The money stock fell by over 30 percent. Firms faced higher prices to access working capital, and others found it hard to get credit at any rate.[9] This created further deflationary pressures, reducing the overall monetary base deposited in banks, and pushed many banks and firms into bankruptcy, reducing consumption, and generating high unemployment. The long bout of bank runs was capped by President Franklin D. Roosevelt's bank holiday across the United States from March 6 to March 13, 1933. The deflationary spiral only ended with the bank holiday, the suspension of the gold standard, the reflation of prices, and a slew of domestic financial reforms, including the creation of deposit insurance and recapitalizing commercial banks.

But this was by no means the end of the crisis. Even more, these efforts came too late to prevent the Depression from being exported to other industrial economies. Beginning in 1929, Britain began to bleed gold, losing a significant portion of its reserves. Banks in Germany and Central Europe were also especially vulnerable to stock market pressures from New York. In response, central banks across Europe lowered discount rates in 1929 to provide some relief from the crash.

Soon, Europe met with its own slate of banking crises, starting with the collapse of Credit-Anstalt in Austria and Danatbank in Germany. In the summer of 1931 the German mark collapsed, followed by similar currency crises of the pound and the dollar. The Bank of England alone did not have adequate reserves to help the failing Austrian bank. Politics closed another solution to the problem, making international rescues seemingly impossible: the French refused to do so without the promise of specific political concessions by Austria. Central banks were constrained by the fetters of the gold standard system in their abilities to address their own troubles, let alone those overseas, ultimately causing several states to abandon it. In September 1931, Britain left the gold standard, triggering fears in international markets that other nations would follow suit. Some did.

To explain why the Depression went on so long, Charles Kindleberger points to the absence of a hegemonic leader to stabilize the global economy: "No longer London. Not yet New York."[10] Britain's inability and American unwillingness to lead meant that there was no stabilizer to manage the international gold standard system—to provide liquidity and stability through international cooperation.

Eichengreen identifies the breakdown of credibility and cooperation, both inextricably linked and sourced in the rise of mass politics and labor unions, as impeding central bank policy during the crisis. Emerging domestic political pressures and an unstable international economic climate—generated by the fetters of the gold standard mechanism—constrained governments in their ability to commit credibly to adhering to the international monetary practices that kept the system going. This resulted in a collapse of monetary cooperation in the interwar period, leading to a series of banking and currency crises, the Great Depression, and ultimately a world war. Central bank internationalism that kept the gold standard system going was on the ebb.

Central banks' inability to credibly commit to upholding the gold standard system was in part rooted in the rise of labor unions, in the latter half of the interwar 1920s, in Britain, and Germany, and elsewhere in Europe that put upward pressure on wages. In the United States, wages rose to fend off the threat of unionization. High wages and downward inflexibility were a problem within the gold standard system. Attempts to end the Depression by cutting wages ended in disaster. Domestic priorities led policymakers to lose sight of international monetary stability as a collective good, rendering the gold standard system incapable of working.

A unifying aspect of these accounts of the depression is, as Eichengreen and Peter Temin highlight, "the ideology, mentalité and rhetoric of the gold standard led policymakers to take actions that only accentuated economic distress in the 1930s. Central bankers continued to kick the world economy while it was down until it lost consciousness."[11] The doctrine of the gold standard and the "masochistic strand of the gold standard mentalité" hamstrung policymakers throughout the Depression in a manner that allowed the crisis to worsen, even in their efforts at rescuing domestic and international economic activity from collapsing.[12]

These seminal studies together provide key insights into what caused the Great Depression, and why it went on as long as it did, pointing to a failure of central bank policies and an inability to collectively manage crises during this period as they unfolded. However, they underplay the impact of key leadership changes within central banks that altered and inhibited their room to maneuver their way through their troubles. In this chapter, I tell the story of how central bankers tried and failed to mobilize resources to rescue the global economy from its worst collapse. I bring the role of central bankers to the forefront of the discussion and debate around why attempts to arrest the Depression failed. I show how relationships of trust, or their absence, fed into the policymaking process of arresting the Depression and illustrate the interpersonal nature of the mission.

I pick up the line of inquiry set up by Friedman and Schwartz, of the impact of Strong's death on Fed policy on the eve of, and during the Great Depression. While their analysis focuses on Fed policy specifically, I point to another set of changes in the Fed's ability to act in Strong's absence: the weakening of cross-border relationships between New York and Europe, when Strong was replaced by Harrison following his untimely death. The greatest effect of this change in leadership in the central bank community was in the detrimental impact it had on the Anglo-American partnership, which hindered attempts at bilateral central bank assistance and crisis management.

I also provide a more general story of how interpersonal relations among central bankers during this time were too weak to overcome political and economic obstacles to rescue attempts, unlike in the 1920s. Not only was Norman dealing with a new counterpart in New York, he was also dealing with Hans Luther in Germany, who had taken over the Reichsbank presidency from Schacht. While Norman's relations with Clement Moret at the Bank of France were an improvement to those with Moreau before him, they were not strong enough to manage or overcome disagreements between Luther and Moret and his associates in France. In a sense, this chapter illustrates the microfoundations of why system leadership, as had been provided primarily by Norman and Strong in the 1920s, was nowhere to be found because leaders changed. The package of players tasked with dealing with the Great Depression did not possess the right types of personal ties necessary to collectively provide this public good.

The 1929–1933 years mark a period of key turning points, opportunity, and crucially, missed opportunity, that allowed the crisis to escalate and explain, to use Charles Kindleberger's words, "why the Depression went so deep, and lasted so long."[13] In this chapter, I evaluate some of the many efforts made domestically and internationally to arrest the Depression. I start with the attempted rescues of Credit-Anstalt and Danatbank in Germany and Austria. I then consider the crisis in Britain that prompted sterling's departure from gold. Finally, I look at the failed tripartite meetings during the WEC held in 1933 to revitalize international trade, stabilize currencies, and fight the Great Depression, which were "torpedoed" by Roosevelt.

While the chapter ends with WEC tripartite meetings in 1933, this was not the end of the Depression. The Tripartite Agreement was signed in September 1936 by Britain, France, and the United States to facilitate currency stabilization following the collapse of the gold standard during the crisis. But the recovery of output and employment only occurred during the Second World War; the Dow Jones only returned to its precrash levels in 1954.

I do not address the post-1933 efforts as they present a distinct context to the pre-1933 years and are outside the scope of this book. Germany left the League of Nations in 1933; Italy was denounced by it. The remilitarization of the Rhineland in March 1936 broke the Versailles and Locarno Treaties, and Europe was now more decidedly on the road to war. The long recovery was then interrupted in 1937 by a double dip recession. By then, military tensions were the main focus: Hitler's expansionist aims had turned violent, and the United States had abandoned neutrality against aggressor states. The Anschluss, the annexation of Austria by the German Reich, took place in March 1938. Diplomatic appeasement efforts such as the Munich Agreement, or Roosevelt's letter to Hitler seeking peace, were underway. The Second World War was around the corner, and the Depression was no longer the focal crisis, as states began to build up military and war efforts.

A Changing of the Guard

The turn of the 1920s to the 1930s was marked by more continuity than change. The most significant changes related to international monetary affairs were not structural but personnel changes in major central banks, yielding consequent changes in the internal institutional apparatuses of these banks, and the creation of the Bank for International Settlements (BIS).

Strong's international influence, especially in Europe, started with Norman. The two relied on one another to exercise their influence and undertake their operations as they wished; both were keenly aware of the prospects for their joint efforts if one of them were to leave their post. Early in their tenures, Norman wrote to Strong, "You are an international asset + almost unique in your own country: with you we hope to gain the whole world: without you we should not know where to turn for instructed support: do not jeopardize that support, especially at this stage, by endangering the powers or the health of yourself as its channel."[14] Indeed, both expressed their discomfort at the prospect of a change of guards at one another's banks, as Strong wrote to Norman:

> It has long been the cause of some uneasiness to me that when the time comes for you to retire as Governor of the Bank, your successor may not feel the same interest and be inspired by the same purposes that have characterized your attitude from the start in building up an understanding between your institution and ours. There is so much to be done from now on that is important to both of us, and our success in accomplishing anything depends so much on these personal relations that I look forward with dread to the day when you will be succeeded by some unknown person with whom I may not have the same intimate and affectionate relations that I have enjoyed so greatly with you.[15]

Although seven years later it was Norman who faced this change of guards, the implications of these concerns were apparent. With Strong's departure, "the intimacy of the transatlantic relationship evaporated."[16] Norman was "desolate and lonesome at Ben's sudden death." While it was unclear whether he realized "how mountainous were the odds stacked against him," his circle of friends in the financial world was dwindling.[17]

Harrison, a lawyer by training, replaced Strong as governor of the New York Fed, having served as deputy governor from 1920. His appointment was welcomed by the private banking industry in the United States; J. P. Morgan saw it as "most natural" and "had the advantage of continuing unchanged the friendly and important relations the Federal Reserve has had so many years with the central banks of issue abroad."[18]

But Harrison was markedly distinct from his predecessor. Under his "less forceful" governance, the Fed's power shifted from New York to the Federal Reserve Board and the US Treasury headquartered in Washington, DC.[19] DC's influence and opposition to the BIS was so strong that Harrison actively avoided Basel when visiting Europe.[20] He enjoyed friendly relations with his European opposites and maintained Strong's tradition of consulting with Norman. But the nature and the intimacy of his relationships were not as deep and personal as were Strong's, and he did not share Strong's "readiness to go more than half-way to meet the wishes of Norman."[21]

In Germany, in 1930, Schacht was replaced by Luther as Reichsbank president. He was trained as a civil servant and was a nationalist who "had faith in the government and the army," a "politician without a party."[22] He had previously served as chancellor, and before that as the Reich finance minister, was involved in fighting inflation in the early 1920s, negotiated the Dawes Loan, and was known to be a skilled diplomat. Luther shared credit with Schacht for Deutschmark stabilization following hyperinflation in the early 1920s. But when he took over the Reichsbank in 1930, he was viewed by his counterparts in Britain as a politician.[23]

Moret took over from Moreau at the Bank of France in 1930. For most of his tenure, Moreau had "leaned to passivity in relation to international gold movements." Moret's governorship improved relations with Norman and his Bank, even if old political loyalties and governmental influence remained. Moret, along with his assistants, had learned how to interact and cooperate over gold movements. Under Moret, Norman's cooperation with the French now "had a highly practical slant."[24] Moret "did not inherit the aggressive distrust Moreau had shown toward the British"; he was more cooperative from the outset, indicating his inclination toward reciprocity by saying that the Bank of England "will find here all the support it might require."[25] Unlike the poor relations between Norman and Moreau, Norman, Moret, and Harrison enjoyed mutual respect; their assistants were closer than any of their predecessors.

Strong's death brought on significant system-level changes: the first was a change in the relationship between the New York Fed, the Board, and the US government, restricting the New York Fed's freedom. Moreover, with Strong gone, Norman could no longer rely on the trust and good faith of his overseas counterparts. Leadership changes on the continent similarly reduced central bank autonomy and their willingness to prioritize international issues. Two institutions most keenly affected by these personnel changes were the New York Fed and the BIS.

In many ways, Harrison's policy preferences represented continuity from Strong's tenure, especially on domestic policy, or his position on the League of Nations.[26] Still, Strong's death made way for increased intervention by the Board and US Treasury in Washington. This changed the New York Fed's capacity as an international leader in the absence of what Lester Chandler prescribes as "some powerful man, with sufficient understanding, imagination, and personal force to weld the Board members into an efficient unit capable of vigorous and timely action."[27] Harrison did not share Strong's international influence or his internationalism to the same extent.[28] According to the economist Lester Chandler,

Strong's death left the Federal Reserve System "with no [center] of enterprising and acceptable leadership" to consolidate the position of the FRBNY vis-à-vis Board and other Reserve Banks.[29] No clear policies could be agreed to within the institution in 1929. Harrison's replacement of Strong changed the position and interactions of the New York Fed in the United States and overseas.

Norman had a good relationship with Harrison, and they maintained regular contact.[30] However, Harrison did not share Strong's interest in Europe and was more tied to Washington's position in international monetary affairs, leaving Norman "baffled to know how to proceed in the situation."[31] The influence of the New York Bank with the Board shifted and constrained Harrison's ability to sidestep institutional and domestic political influence to cooperate with Norman and his other foreign counterparts. Harrison was wary of overstepping his position or engaging in conversations that were governmental concerns.

A second change was the establishment of the BIS. In the early 1920s, Norman and Schacht had drawn up a framework for the functions and policy of what became the Bank for International Settlements.[32] In 1929, Owen Young, an American diplomat, chaired a committee revisiting the issue of German reparations. The BIS was established under the Young Plan, in 1930, as a central bank for central banks, to formalize Norman's agenda of central bank cooperation and autonomy. This realized Norman's dream of creating an international central bankers' club, to "provide the machinery for bringing together and offsetting the demands on the gold reserves of Central Banks, which as things were, tended all to be converted into claims upon London."[33]

The first role of the BIS was to arrange the Young Loan, which reduced the German reparations payments agreed to in the Dawes Plan and abolished the control over German economic life that Dawes had imposed. But its combined functions, of managing German reparations and coordinating central bank cooperation, "proved fatal." The Fed's absence in the BIS, due to constraints on Harrison's participation, meant that cooperative arrangements had to continue on an ad hoc basis.[34] Moreover, as Henry Clay observes, the Young Plan "came at a time when the financial sky was overcast, economic depression was deepening, and the flow of international loans drying up."[35] The BIS was unequal to the task of preserving the gold standard and stemming the Great Depression. In its early years, the Bank has been described by Eichengreen as proving "singularly ineffectual" in managing the Great Depression.[36]

Banking Crises in Austria and Germany

The new cohort of central bank leaders did not have the tools or experience to manage it. Given the unprecedented gravity of the Great Depression, their experimentation was neither quick nor adequate to stem the crisis as it emerged. The BIS had hardly begun its operations when the world was in the throes of the Great Depression. An unfavorable economic environment, combined with weak personal ties and political pressures upon BIS members further inhibited international cooperative solutions to arrest the Depression.

The crisis in the United States triggered a collapse of banking systems all over the world. President Hoover passed the Smoot-Hawley Tariff in June 1930, and trading partners soon retaliated by imposing protectionist measures at home, leading to a collapse in international trade. Heavily indebted economies were most affected by the global economic collapse at first. For them, default and devaluation seemed to be the only ways to get their domestic finances under control.

These troubles were not limited to debtor states. The banking crises in the United States quickly engulfed creditor countries, including Britain, leading to losses in interest earnings and mounting balance-of-payments pressures. The most significant consequence of this development was the collapse in international lending, which consumed central European banking systems, leading to a financial collapse that began in Austria and spread to Germany.[37] I look at two failed efforts at resolving the banking crises in Austria and Germany: first, Norman's International Committee in London and Basel, and second, Germany's fraught attempts to secure French credits. I show that central bank leaders were now free to float interbank assistance but did not make extensive efforts to circumvent intergovernmental constraints to coordinate central bank credits to Austria and Germany, as they had done following the Genoa Conference and in the Dawes arrangement in the 1920s.

Crisis and Contagion

In the 1920s, under Schacht, German banks had become extremely dependent on foreign capital through the flotation of foreign bonds. American investors were attracted to the higher rates compared to New York, and Germany borrowed in the ballpark of $600 million a year to finance both its reparations and to boost consumption. Austrian and Hungarian banks had similarly grown reliant on foreign deposits. By 1929, long-term investment from the United States was attracted to Wall Street's high returns, catalyzing the financial crisis in central Europe and in Britain.

As banks could no longer meet depositors' demands, they turned to their central banks. National balance-of-payments pressures mounted in Central and Eastern Europe, resulting in a growing loss of confidence in policymakers' abilities to defend the gold standard parity.[38] In Austria and Germany in 1931, the withdrawal of foreign deposits following central bank and government liquidity injections triggered a series of severe banking crises, first in Rothschild-owned Credit-Anstalt, Austria's largest deposit institution. Support from the Austrian government, central bank, the Oesterreichische Nationalbank (or the Austrian National Bank), and the Rothschilds raised alarm bells about its stability. And a proposed Austro-German customs union provoked the French to withdraw credits from the bank, prompting a bank run.[39] This proposed union further complicated rescue efforts in Austria and Germany in the summer of 1931.

In response, central banks raised interest rates and restricted credit after depleting their reserves through efforts to maintain parity. They also injected liquidity into the banking system by purchasing securities and discounting bills that commercial banks held. But rather than restoring confidence, these actions provoked fears of capital flight and further devaluation. The loss of confidence triggered a run on Credit-Anstalt in May 1931, the first of several significant banking failures in the next two months.

Late in May 1931, risks that the crisis would spread to Germany and that Germany would cease repayments on the Dawes and Young Loan continued to grow. The German chancellor Heinrich Brüning called for reparations concessions and talked of plans to stop meeting its reparations obligations. At this time, Schacht, now out of the Reichsbank, continued his campaign against the Young Plan (over which he had resigned) in his US lecture tour. While this proposition became increasingly attractive to Brüning, invoking it would cause further panic and result in the devaluation of the mark as short-term US credits to Germany remained unsettled. Germany's financial position was tenuous, and its trade surplus was only adequate to meet its current reparations obligations. Contagion from Austria and the fear of capital from Germany was a real possibility.[40]

Brüning's calls hurt confidence in Germany's finances and stirred international diplomatic tensions over reparations. Combined, the large exposure of foreign deposits in Germany, the Austrian crisis, and Brüning's vocal calls to cease reparations payments caused a panic among investors in Germany. The Reichsbank followed Austria in credit rationing and liquidity injections into the banking system, to little avail. Nordwolle, a large textile company, collapsed, provoking a run on DanatBank, a German credit institution, which was heavily exposed to foreign depositors. By July, Germany had a full-fledged banking crisis on its hands.

Central bankers, private banks, and governments all pursued several policy strategies to rescue these failing financial institutions in Austria and Germany. Before the crisis spread from Austria, the Austrian National Bank sought a foreign loan, but these efforts were met with disagreements and diplomatic squabbles over each creditor's share in the loan—France, Belgium, and Italy were reluctant to lend sufficiently. Only after much delay did the Austrian National Bank secure a meager, given the scale of the crisis, $14 million. The loan came with limits and overt reluctance from Austria's creditors and failed to revive confidence among investors. As the Austrian crisis continued to escalate, both domestic and international efforts failed to arrest the crisis and prevent further contagion.

This failure to rescue the Austrian and German banking sectors was a break from the extensive crisis management and rescue efforts from the previous decade. Even in the 1920s, the Genoa conference, and the Dawes agreement were primarily negotiated and orchestrated by squabbling governments, not central banks. Yet Norman, Strong, and Schacht circumvented these traditional channels to shape international agreements and financial assistance outside formal avenues through their private correspondence and meetings. A key change in 1931 was a shift in central bankers' abilities and willingness to make similar efforts to arrest the Great Depression. In the face of weak economic conditions and interstate tensions, this exacerbated cooperative efforts in an already difficult situation: Norman's International Committee to rescue Austria and Luther's attempt to secure a billion-dollar rescue package.

The International Committee

Credit-Anstalt's position only became known to the government and central bank in May 1931, but it had been weakening steadily since early 1930. So, when the crisis first broke out, not only were Austrian authorities caught by surprise, but so were US bankers, including partners at J. P. Morgan & Co., international investors, and bankers in London and Paris. The Austrian economy was in a stronger position to handle the crisis than its fellow Europeans. But the combined effort by the Austrian National Bank, government, and the Rothschilds to inject liquidity into the banking system proved insufficient and reduced market confidence in Austria's finances.[41]

As the crisis worsened, it was clear that the $14 million credit that central bankers had balked at could not save the banking system. In London, Norman was eager to do something about the increasingly intensifying crisis in Austria and Germany. Norman had a soft spot for Austria and feared contagion of these crises elsewhere in Europe. But he saw the Austrian intervention as insufficient. Norman had known more about vulnerabilities in Credit-Anstalt and held that Austria faced the gravest problem, but he incorrectly believed that Germany would make it through.

To deal with the bank runs in Europe, Norman assembled a special International Committee in London to arrange support for failing banks. He believed that the BIS was the right venue to float any assistance.[42] This Committee would support a cooperative loan through the BIS. But Norman's efforts proved inadequate and slow, and failed to prevent the banking crises from becoming a systemic problem in Europe.

Credit-Anstalt's dire position soon became clear in London, Paris, and New York. A combination of incompatible state interests, inadequate communication among central bankers, especially through informal and personal channels, and a reliance on private finance complicated the problem. This time, central bank leaders did not make the same efforts to work around these disagreements as they had done in the past. There was also a lot of confusion about who was vulnerable to the crisis, among foreign creditors. As Harrison wrote to Gates McGarrah, an American banker and the first president of the BIS, regarding Norman's International Committee, "No one seems to know who are the American creditors outside certain larger concerns in New York."[43] McGarrah also wrote of the concern among foreign central banks and the BIS that none of them would be willing to "support the [Austrian] National Bank's exchange responsibilities if it has to take upon its shoulders the credit liabilities of the Credit Anstalt." The mismatched legal and financial concerns in Austria and overseas complicated the matter, even though McGarrah noted that the BIS was ready to defend Austria if the central bank took up this course of action.[44]

The French government urged the Bank of France to extend a credit to Austria, hoping that such a line would be coordinated internationally, and with the help of J. P. Morgan Jr. in the United States. However, this was not possible for Morgan partners in the United States.[45] Norman was now doubly concerned and confused that previous rescue efforts for Credit-Anstalt had collapsed.

Norman then called on a J. P. Morgan partner bank, Morgan Grenfell, in London, which was able to get J. P. Morgan in New York on board. Through Strong, Norman had developed very close relations with Morgan bankers in the United States. They had played an important role in floating credits to Japan in 1924, to Britain to return to the gold standard in 1925, and during Dawes negotiations, which Norman influenced behind the scenes, with Strong. At the same time, New York bankers, including Harrison at the Fed, were able to secure the support of Paribas in Paris.

Despite finally getting together a handful of private creditors, the International Committee and the BIS were unable to finalize any agreement. Very soon, these efforts at coordinating a rescue for Credit-Anstalt were hindered by central bank leaders' inabilities to avoid political interference in their banks and cooperate with their counterparts over international loans and credits. Norman's Committee "worked daily to disentangle the situation, which [continued] to obscure."[46] Because Austria's economic position was stronger than Germany's when it faced its worst crisis, the crisis also took much longer to unfold, as more information about Credit-Anstalt became known.

In June 1931, following discussions among private bankers, BIS officials and central bankers across the continent, a Dutch banker, Adrianus Johannes (Arie) van Hengel, was approached by the Austrian National Bank. Van Hengel had previously overseen the reorganization of Rotterdamsche Bankvereeniging in the Netherlands in the 1920s and was seen as a strong man from the outside who could right the problem and the right person to act for the International Committee of creditors in Austria.[47]

But as information about Credit-Anstalt's position became clearer, the private bankers that Norman had brought together failed to agree on how large their credit lines would be. Indeed, many non-Morgan New York banks *reduced* lines already in place or canceled them outright, which Morgan bankers were not consulted about.[48] As a result, concerns among Morgan bankers grew. Eventually, the BIS was unable to pull these banks together to coordinate any assistance without Morgan support.

The slow speed at which central banks and private banks moved through their negotiations and decision-making for an Austrian credit proved calamitous. Political disputes and an incapacitated BIS hindered any forceful rescue effort among creditors. Van Hengel communicated these concerns to Norman and McGarrah separately, writing, "'*Faites moi de bonne politique et je ferai bonnes finances* [Give me good politics and I'll give you good finances].' None of us are politicians, but circumstances may force us to meddle with politics, especially when finances can only be asinined by political measure." In van Hengel's view, Western finances were "absolutely unsound because of the stupid financing by short time investments [of] long term capitalization." Given the crises of confidence these practices had caused, the only options were to either pay everyone who wants to get paid or stop payments.

To him, in Vienna "the wrong solution has been chosen out of fear for revolution," but concerned parties were not only domestic but also in Eastern Europe and Britain, as well as creditors in France and the United States. It was therefore necessary that any paying had to be "effected through the bank of issue" and so, through the BIS. And considering the troubles involved in organizing creditors to Credit-Anstalt, van Hengel wrote to McGarrah and to Norman that it gave him "little confidence that the creditors of Germany can be organized when an energetic effort is made. Measures ought to be taken by you, by the B.I.S., the Federal Reserve Board, perhaps the Banque de France on one side, and the Reichsbank and German state on the other." He hoped to discuss this possibility with McGarrah and "the other gentlemen before it is too late."

The problem was the BIS, although an "Institution to warrant confidence in International Finance, its foundation is a calamity."[49]

Van Hengel's concerns about politics and the BIS remained obstacles as the Austrian crises progressed and spread. Political developments in Germany had become evident that contagion from the Austrian crisis was now underway. Before Norman's committee or the BIS could arrange any sort of Austrian credit, the crisis had now engulfed Hungarian banks, who were heavily exposed to the Austrian crisis, and to Germany, by June 1931.

One might expect the involvement of the BIS, an international institution that guarded central bankers' secrecy and allowed for regular exchanges, would facilitate cooperative efforts. But this was not so. The institution proved to be yet another avenue to channel central bankers' restricted reins and their diminished autonomy to act outside of governmental preferences.[50]

The Federal Reserve Board and the US government's attitude toward the BIS curbed Harrison's ability to intervene and "deprived him of the opportunity to exchange views." Harrison was embarrassed by the losses suffered due to the lack of direct contact between himself in New York and with McGarrah, a US banker and the first president of the BIS.[51] As Norman sought the BIS to assemble some small assistance for struggling Austrian banks, the Federal Reserve, who wanted to stay out of BIS and other international efforts, was unwilling to take any credits to prevent bank failure in the United States, and chose to make unilateral discount rate adjustments instead, which added to concerns about the stability of Austrian banks.[52]

Harrison could neither act autonomously from the Board nor could he participate in the BIS in an official capacity. Strong had also been constrained and had avoided official multilateral meetings and venues. But Strong instead continued to participate in and indeed spearhead cooperative international central bank activities throughout the 1920s, to provide funds to partner banks, with the help of his closest associates on Wall Street, and more crucially, with Norman, through ad hoc, informal channels. The Norman-Harrison pairing shifted central bank policy to one that bent more in favor of the Board and the government than Norman and Strong.

The Luther Conquest of $1 Billion

During the efforts to float the Austrian credit through the BIS and Norman's International Committee, the crisis spread to quickly consume the German banking system. Germany initially pursued many of the same liquidity and credit rationing policies that Austria had done in the months before, to the same effect. Pressures on Reichsbank reserves made further central bank interventions difficult. As foreign withdrawals from German banks began, Hans Luther, now president of the Reichsbank, turned to the option of securing foreign assistance.

When Luther assumed the Reichsbank presidency, Bank of England associates noted that Luther "comes to an office of which it is most desirable that the holder should be non-political, with a record which, while showing marked successes, both in the political and the financial sphere depends mainly on his personal characteristics of his activity, energy, strength of will and capacity for undertaking unusually difficult tasks." Although he had been seen "to be a politician in spite of himself," his success would depend on his ability to keep free of any political intervention. At the time, regarding external affairs, there was "little ground on which to base an estimate of his power to cooperate successfully with the leaders of other central banks."[53]

The crises in Austria and Germany quickly put this to the test. As he had done in the 1920s, Norman sought the cooperation of his colleagues in New York and Berlin. While working to arrange support for Austria, Norman, who had just "spent two enthralling days in Schacht's company" had stated that what Austria needed was "a foreign butcher."[54] He similarly shared with Harrison and Walter Stewart in Basel that "more financial brutality was needing in Austria, that to this end *Schacht* was the right type" to address the collapse of Credit-Anstalt in Austria.[55] While he trusted Schacht, Norman was uncomfortable working with Luther without Harrison's involvement, who in turn insisted on the involvement of the French. But the Bank of France opposed any such plan and could not advise both the Austrian National Bank and the government, whose views would be conflicting, without political concessions.

Policymakers were picky about whom they dealt with abroad. Harrison noted that Charles Rist of the Bank of France was "not acceptable to Austrian government"; Norman also suggested that Rist "could not advise the Austrian National Bank and the Government whose positions would doubtlessly be conflicting."[56] Personal preferences against dealing with Rist in Austria and New York impeded cooperation between Austria and France as the crisis worsened in June. And while Harrison sought the involvement of the French, Norman's views on credit to Austria generated pushback in Paris, which "would not occur if Basle contained more discretion and less gossip."[57]

When the European banking crises began in May 1931, Norman believed that Austria needed more help than Germany if they faced similar crises. But when Germany began hemorrhaging its gold reserves, Luther needed the help of his counterparts. At first, it seemed as though central bank assistance was more forthcoming than it had been in Austria. Cooperation among central banks to provide Luther with the necessary credits seemed promising, given the risk of contagion from Austria. Luther approached Norman for a credit of $100 million, which he received a week later, with support from the Fed, the Bank of France, and the BIS.

But this was not enough to resolve the German crisis. Norman's belief that Germany would be more resilient than Austria was mistaken. The success of this package was short-lived: just weeks later, Nordwolle's collapse triggered a run on DanatBank that began on June 17, 1931. Capital continued to leave Germany all through June, further triggered by Brüning's threat to suspend reparations payments. Luther could not garner the support of the German business community to loan the Gold Discount Bank the liquidity necessary to rescue its financial system. In trying to rescue the DanatBank, Reichsbank reserves fell below the legal minimum. The DanatBank collapse quickly exhausted any monetary flexibility that Luther had at home.

On June 20, 1931, President Hoover announced a one-year moratorium on all reparations and debt repayments from the war, recognizing Germany's assessment of the crisis, which France opposed. But the moratorium did not relieve the Reichsbank of reserve pressures, and the Hoover government had made it clear that that was all the US government would do for Germany.

Harrison and Norman both found that "much of the good that could have been accomplished by Mr. Hoover's proposal [was] being lost to the delay [in getting the initial loan to Luther] and the withdrawals from various countries in Europe, especially Germany."[58] As the German position worsened, Luther drew upon a credit arranged in the 1920s with a consortium of New York banks to the amount of $50 million, available through the Gold Discount Bank. Luther drew on the entire amount, hoping assistance from the German industrial and business communities would follow. It did not. By July 9, Luther had completely exhausted the Reichsbank's policy room and withdrew support for DanatBank.

Having exhausted all domestic options, Luther sought central bank assistance of no less than $1 billion. He boarded a private plane—"the first such resort by a desperate central banker"—to Amsterdam to begin his hunt for it. He then journeyed to see Norman in London and accompanied him to Basel, where Norman realized that "the German position was now irretrievable."[59] Uncertainty about Germany's position and reparations payments made Norman apprehensive. Norman emphasized that "he was only talking about what was possible or impossible in the circumstances of that moment"; if Luther were to raise the issue again in the future, it would be approached differently, given the constantly changing, uncertain environment.[60]

Luther met a similar sentiment in the United States. Considering that the Hoover moratorium had provided Germany some relief on the reparations front, up to an amount of $400 million, US bankers were irked that Germany had also suspended its obligations on the Young Loan. This further impeded the Reichsbank's ability to secure any foreign assistance, considering it was these US banks on whom Luther would have relied.[61]

Harrison faced pressure from the Board in Washington and could not support Luther through the crisis. Hoover's decision had exacerbated international tensions with France, who blamed the United States for the situation in Europe. Harrison later learned from McGarrah that reservations about Hoover's bill that had been attached by Congress to the moratorium indicated to European policymakers that, outside of the year-long moratorium, "America was not cooperatively interested in solving that situation."[62] Harrison expected Luther to request a credit enlargement, but he was surprised at just how large the amount was. He emphasized to Norman that he saw the need to do something, and only found it valuable to "be adequate rather than inadequate." But Harrison expressed that he did not trust that Luther had "done everything within its power effectively to protect its own position" first.[63]

The politics of these issues had become too big for central banks and required government interest. Harrison could do little more than have informal and personal discussion with central bankers about the possibility of credits, without any commitment from the New York Bank. He could not speak for the Board or the government, nor could he visit Basel in an official capacity to coordinate efforts with other central bank leaders.[64] He had hoped that some arrangement could be worked out with central bankers in Europe, who would have been in Basel that weekend. He would only consider joining any credit arrangement were this initially supported by Britain and France. Meanwhile, Luther, who hoped for US assistance, had not even requested a credit from Harrison when he approached his European counterparts.

Once again, the BIS proved ineffectual in facilitating any type of central bank cooperation. During this time, Norman appeared "to be in a very bad frame of mind." He did not favor any input from the BIS; to him, the situation was more "political and governmental."[65] McGarrah later shared with Harrison that regarding Luther in Basel, "the governors there felt that the matter is for the governments and not the central banks; Luther had no program whatever."[66] They noted how Luther and Schacht differed from one another in their position and ability to manage the current situation were Schacht to return to the Reichsbank: "If Schacht is appointed there will inevitably be a conflict between Luther and Schacht sooner or later; that Schacht will come out on top and will eventually become financial dictator. [Leon Fraser, director of the BIS] said Luther had not ever yet got a program, that he had stayed over this morning in Basle and that they could not find anything constructive for him; that he left Basle at noon and had been quite helpless during the meeting."

Even as the banking crisis unraveled and Reichsbank reserves were exhausted, Luther insisted that Germany's economic position was improving. But during this time, the Reichsbank lost another $10 million in reserves in a day, to the ire of the rest of the banking world. When Luther arrived in Basel, Harrison learned that Luther "had struck a snag" with their European counterparts for any new credits; it would now be impossible to turn to Harrison. Bankers in New York were frustrated by Luther's actions, and Morgan bankers claimed that Germany "was exporting [its] financial problems to the rest of the world," and saw the Brüning government as complicit.[67]

So, Luther traveled to London and Paris for urgent meetings. Through conversations with Norman, it became clear that Luther's resolution was only possible with *intergovernmental* support.[68] Harrison and Moret in France were constrained by governmental interests; no assistance from either foreign governments or central banks could be obtained without conditions. When Norman told Harrison about Luther's intentions to seek this billion-dollar loan, Harrison responded that such a large amount was not possible.

Governments and central banks in the former Allied powers could not agree on what ought to be done. The Hoover White House was drawn to the claim that this was a European crisis and not America's concern. But American private finance was deeply enmeshed in the problem. They were also caught between varying preferences of Morgan banks in the United States, London, and Paris, as well as the priorities of the British, French, and American governments over Germany's repayments of the Dawes and Young Loans.

Central bank leaders could not find a way around these political squabbles and preferred Luther turn to domestic exchange controls. Norman and Harrison pushed Luther to restrict credit to stem capital flight, but the banking collapse limited his room to move. France was the only European country that had enough gold reserves to help bail Germany out, so Luther had no choice but to turn to France for a long-term loan. But each entity in France had a different view on the German situation and demanded varying concessions from Luther.

The Bank of France demanded as a condition that the German government renounce its demands to reopen the reparations negotiations. They were concerned about the political situation in Germany. The French government's conditions were that Germany abandon its customs union with Austria, suspend the construction of "two new pocket battleships," raise rates to curb the flight of capital, "orient itself towards a policy of democracy and pacifism," and ban demonstrations by Nationalist organizations. François de Wendel and Édouard Alphonse James de Rothschild, the Bank of France's central bank's main regents, were "both resolutely anti-German."

Luther approached the Bank of France when he arrived on July 10, and lunched with both Rothschild regents, who immediately rejected his request.

He had no choice but to approach the French government, which was willing to extend Luther up to $300 million, but only upon suspension of the customs union with Austria, and other political and economic concessions. Luther could not agree to these conditions without consulting his government and returned to Berlin. Negotiations with the French went on for over a month and reached no conclusion.

Perhaps Luther went to the wrong Bank of France personnel when he first arrived in France. While Moret and Lacour-Gayet had some reservations in extending credit to Luther, their reservations were not as strong as those of the regents or of the government. Lacour-Gayet denied that these political concessions would stand in the way of assisting Luther. For the Bank of France, concessions demanded were more generally "certain things that must be done in Germany; among others, creation of a better political atmosphere," as the Nazi party were now increasing their political power in Germany. These same considerations were also imposed on the Austrian National Bank, as Austria's banking crisis also remained unresolved.

Clement Moret, governor of the Bank of France, was frustrated at Luther's bid for $1 billion and insisted that "he could not understand why the Reichsbank did not apply to him" directly for a credit. It turns out, personal considerations, that is, Luther's lack of trust and confidence in Moret, informed his reticence. Luther, "for fear of snub, would do anything rather than approach the Bank of France direct."[69] Luther did not trust that Moret would support a credit to Germany.

Because no one believed in the possibility of a quick recovery in Germany, Luther was forced to seek additional credits. The French government was his only hope, but they required extensive political concessions.[70] Harrison set out similar conditions for any additional support. Harrison believed extending any credits to the Reichsbank would be a mistake.[71] Norman and Harrison would not extend credits to Luther while the reparations issue remained unresolved as "granting further credits would be pouring good money after bad," and "increase German liabilities without resolving the political problem."[72] This approach marked a notable break from Norman's approach with Schacht. Despite the hyperinflationary concerns of the early 1920s and Germany's political and economic vulnerability at that time, such a fear did not dictate Norman's actions when he so generously agreed to fund Schacht's Gold Discount Bank.

Delays in negotiations and Luther's many failed efforts to secure any French assistance eventually turned the Bank of France's position and allowed political demands to override any central bank assistance. Lacour-Gayet suggested that if the BIS did not reach a "satisfactory interpretation of the guarantee clause" in the Hoover moratorium, France would demand repayment from Germany as they were coming due on July 15, even if it forced Germany to default.[73]

By this time, the crisis had spread across Central and Eastern Europe, unemployment was through the roof (by 1932, almost six million men were out of the workforce), and interest rates were raised to 15 percent to prevent further capital flight. The German banking system had completely collapsed, and industrial production was at an all-time low. French officials, at the central bank and in the government, grew increasingly concerned about the political situation in Germany, with the growing political power of the Nazi Party and Hitler. This political atmosphere darkened in Germany as the crisis continued and escalated across the continent.

Ultimately, failed efforts at securing a loan early in July were overshadowed by political caution in France; by this time, the Reichsbank alone could not support the case for a credit. Harrison and Lacour-Gayet believed that it may have helped if a few German government officials had gone "to Paris to discuss matters frankly as Dr. Luther had done" on his trip to Europe as the crisis emerged, to discuss the political situation and concerns among creditors.[74] Luther's position in the central banking world, as an outsider and no match to Schacht, his weak professional ties, and his inability to sway his government, impinged on his ability to manage the German crisis. Germany's position was so desperate that the monetary and political officials tried to sway Schacht to return as Reichsbank president, which did not happen until 1933.

The economic crisis continued to spiral as governments and central bankers squabbled and failed to cooperate to come up with any assistance to prevent Germany's move off the gold standard. France, now wielding more political and financial power in Europe, refused to concede its conditions on the customs union and on reparations. Central bankers were both unwilling and unable to avoid governmental and political interference in Europe and the United States. Germany was left to her own devices and eventually abandoned gold. It was decided that the French would ask the Germans to visit Paris. The Bank of France's next step was "to let the Germans sweat a day or two" and eventually turn to the British and American governments for conditioned assistance.[75] This assistance was much too little and came much too late.

In the cases of the Austrian and German crises, central bankers' efforts to coordinate and float credits to the ailing partners were fraught by their weak or poor personal relations. The impediments they faced were neither new nor distinct to the politically tenuous environment immediately after 1918. However, this new cohort of central bankers was unable and unwilling to circumvent these obstacles to preserve their autonomy and coordinate a financial rescue of the German and Austrian banking sectors. Instead, they caved to political preferences and squabbles that hampered any such rescue effort, and the crisis escalated and spread.

"The Old Lady Goes Off"

The British banking system was better insulated against the crisis than most other countries. But its fiscal situation was poor. Due to mounting deficits, its balance of payments position was in disarray. The collapse in international trade and the protectionist spiral in the United States and Europe meant that the earnings Britain relied on to finance its trade deficit—from financial services, interest earnings, and shipping—had declined so significantly that they could not cover the cost of its imports. Austria and Germany's decisions to freeze foreign deposits meant British deposits there were illiquid. As Britain's external position worsened, pressure grew on its reserves, leaving the Bank of England with little policy flexibility to manage payments and reserve pressures. Even painful policies and spending cuts by the new Labor government could not correct it.

Investors lost confidence in sterling's stability and Britain started to see capital leave its financial system. Firms and depositors held onto their cash, exacerbating declining demand and consumption and the shrinking monetary base. Sterling fell sharply after the DanatBank collapse. Within days, the Bank of England had lost $10 million in reserves. By the end of July, it had lost $56 million in gold. Britain seemed to be next in line to suspend gold standard operations.

To some, Britain's inability to recover from balance of payments pressures was because it could no longer credibly maintain parity due to the collapse of central bank cooperation. The domestic political climate hindered the government's ability to reduce deficits and made partner banks wary of assisting the Bank of England via credits. Norman's hesitation to increase interest rates to curb gold outflows had put the Bank's credibility, and therefore sterling, into question.[76]

This assessment underplays Norman's influence in Britain's monetary affairs. In 1925, Britain's return to prewar parity was engineered in a large way by Norman with the help of Strong in New York. The British government had been eager to meet this goal without relying on any foreign support. Nevertheless, Strong secured the support of the US Treasury and J. P. Morgan bank associates to float a large loan to Britain. Strong and Norman together circumvented political priorities and preferences. What changed in 1931?

Between June and September 1931, Norman's behavior and choices exacerbated the Bank's inability to credibly commit to gold and its willingness to participate in any credit arrangement. Norman became increasingly uncooperative with his own associates and his counterparts whose help was initially forthcoming. In a sense, during the second half of 1931, Norman's influence was as significant through his absence as it was through his outsized presence the decade prior.

In August 1931, Norman had a nervous breakdown and left Britain as the Bank continued to bleed reserves. In his absence, Ernest Harvey, the Bank's deputy governor, could not fend off government pressure to leave gold. Eventually, central bankers, including Norman, reluctantly accepted the inevitability that Britain would leave gold. But this did not arrest the crisis. Given that sterling and the Bank had been the linchpins of the gold standard system, Britain's departure from gold devasted confidence and stability not only in Britain but across Europe.

In June 1931, Norman's hesitation to raise interest rates challenged the bank's credibility to manage pressures and allowed the crisis to accelerate. It soon became clear that international help would be necessary to assist the Bank of England maintain parity. Richard Sayers, a historian of the Bank of England, notes that in early July, Moret was willing to extend credits to the Bank of England. Some of Norman's associates at the Bank of England, including Harvey, believed this show of cooperation might calm markets and render these credits unnecessary. Norman, in contrast, was stubborn about his views regarding sterling's troubles. He believed that sterling was not in trouble and sought to assure foreign partners the same.[77] So, he opted for a less cooperative route, and Norman chose not to take the French up on their offer.

Norman's belief in sterling's stability was quickly proven incorrect. In response to growing pressures on the Bank's reserves, Harrison and Moret were able to float a small loan, to the tune of $25 million, by the end of July, much like the modest forms of bilateral assistance that emerged early in the Austrian and German crisis. Both central banks were constrained by their governments in their abilities to extend more than these small amounts. It was far less than the reserve losses that the Bank of England faced, and not nearly enough to prevent the Bank from depleting its reserves in the following months. It failed to arrest Britain's crisis.

Even more, the use of these loans was not in accordance with what Harrison and Moret had agreed to with Norman. The Bank of England breached a spoken agreement with its creditors, perhaps a move he may not have made with Strong. In August 1931, the Bank suddenly suspended sterling support, to Moret and Harrison's dismay. Moret expressed his frustration as to why the credit had "so little psychological effect. He was even more puzzled to know why [Britain] had withdrawn exchange support."

There was much misunderstanding as to how the arrangement would be settled between Harrison, Moret, and the Bank of England. British officials believed settling the credit in gold would allow the line to remain intact, while Moret noted that he had not anticipated the agreement to be settled if that meant Britain would ship more gold to France.[78]

Difficulties in cooperation between the central banks of England and France were partly sourced in distant personal relations, which led to poor communication with Britain in discussing problems and coming to cooperative solutions together. Lacour-Gayet recognized the importance of personal relations, but had not established these ties with his British counterparts, Harvey and Harry Siepmann, to communicate on the terms agreed in the French credit to Britain.[79] This misunderstanding was exacerbated by Norman's poor communication with his domestic associates, many of whom he frequently, and famously, did not get on with.[80] Ernest Skinner, Norman's private secretary, was used to recurring "tense 'situations'" in Norman's personal relations with his deputies; "there were estrangements with them all from time to time." They wanted to be more than the deputy he felt he needed.[81] Norman's poor personal relations with his own Bank of England associates had severe consequences for the Bank and for Britain during the Depression, as he failed to fully convey his understanding with the French on the use of their credit to his Bank.[82]

Under pressure from the looming prospect of having to leave gold, Norman collapsed one day after leaving work early as he was "feeling queer." He had a nervous breakdown and left to convalesce in Canada on August 15, temporarily abandoning his duties.[83] His absence turned the Bank's functioning to Harvey and empowered the new MacDonald government.

The issue of how to support sterling had not gone away. However, given the misunderstandings that had previously risen between Moret and the Bank of England, the Bank of France was concerned about Britain's use of its previous credit. Now, it maintained that any additional support ought to be a longer-term line of credit. Even more, Lacour-Gayet had intimated to Harrison that such assistance could only be done together with the support of New York.[84]

Harrison told Lacour-Gayet that he received a loan inquiry from the British government (not the central bank), which he assumed Lacour-Gayet also received. Harvey believed that the French were not eager to assist the Bank of England. But from their communications with Harrison, it seemed they believed that Moret would be more forthcoming with assistance, if an invite was made to New York to simultaneously cooperate *pari passu*, that is, if credits would be floated on equal footing in Paris and New York. In London, they also believed that Morgan bankers in the United States would be called on to extend a credit of up to $300 million if the matter was settled with Paris.[85]

Correspondence between Lacour-Gayet and Harrison suggests a different story. Lacour-Gayet and Moret agreed in principle about the need for this loan, but now found it impossible, after their previous misunderstanding and sterling's growing troubles. Privately, Harrison and Lacour-Gayet believed that, while necessary, neither bank should participate in such a credit; sterling's troubles ought to be dealt with by private banks and not central banks. While Harrison saw this as urgent, Lacour-Gayet "figuratively, threw up his hands and said it was not possible" as they were not authorized by the French government to approach private banks and could not immediately do so.[86] This marked a break from the 1920s when Norman and Strong regularly went directly to private banks, and Strong could persuade Moreau to cooperate. This time, no adequate American or French assistance was forthcoming beyond a $20 million "transitional loan" with Morgan bank support. Norman's involvement was necessary to bring the Morgan bankers together.[87]

Norman's departure was followed by daily gold losses that continued to escalate, peaking at over $20 million in a day by mid-September. Harvey talked to Harrison about Britain's declining exchange position, noting that Britain had already used up most of its transitional credits. Both Harvey and Harrison agreed it was wiser to no longer peg sterling but "let it go its own way," at which point the Bank might regain some of its monetary policy discretion.[88] Harvey hoped that Harrison could hint at Washington's inclination toward taking an affirmative position on inter-Allied debts, which Harrison saw as unlikely. In Norman's absence, a special committee of directors was created to manage sterling, which opened weaker every day through August and September. The directors overseeing the situation were of Norman's bent and sought to keep the rate at $4.86 or higher.

Communication between Norman, Harvey, and Harrison remained patchy. Harvey and Harrison did not keep one another apprised on their banks' activities as Norman had done with Strong. Norman and Harvey also had little communication within the bank, which had bearing on how Britain's position was dealt with among international partners. While Norman was in Canada, he met Harrison, who informed Norman of the British government's budgetary program to reduce its deficits, which neither believed to be adequate.

Harvey and Harrison were less candid in sharing their assessments with one another. Harrison was more in the know about Norman's views and plans than Harvey, who was running the Bank's business. It was Harrison who informed Harvey of his communication with Norman, but not until weeks later. Given what Harrison had learned regarding Norman's view, when asked by Harrison whether he thought the government's program was satisfactory, Harrison found Harvey's answers to be unclear and unsatisfactory. This lack of open communication, as the Bank exhausted its transition credits, made Harrison wary of taking any chances on acting even "halfway," given the uncertainty over whether these actions would suffice.[89]

Sterling's position continued to deteriorate, and the Bank of England was unsure about its ability to manage their exchange situation. This raised a worrying prospect of a snap election. The Bank had exhausted almost all of its external credit as pressure increased on sterling. But the committee handling the situation remained fettered to the $4.86 value, provoking withdrawals from Europe and causing growing concern in New York. Washington would do little to help the situation. Harrison alone was incapable of steering the Board toward any sort of support to Britain. He also learned that Norman had now also changed his mind about Britain's commitment to stay on gold: it was "most important not to peg [sterling], that every peg in the past history had proved disastrous." Norman was to hurry back to Britain sooner than he was ready to see if he could handle the exchange situation more satisfactorily.[90]

On September 19, Harvey informed Harrison and his French counterparts that the government had come to the "definite conclusion, for which they saw no option, to suspend gold payments Monday morning," without explicitly stating that this would be temporary. He told Harrison that "it was only fair that [the Fed] should support sterling in order, if possible, to keep it over the gold point if we can do so with say one million pounds," as "they had reached the end of their tether and that so far as he could see there was nothing left to do."[91]

As Norman began his return to England, Prime Minister Ramsay MacDonald decided to suspend gold payments and go off gold on September 21, 1931. On his journey, Norman received a cryptic cable that "the Old Lady goes off on Monday," which he pretended to not understand as he returned to the Bank.[92] Until he arrived in Liverpool on September 23, some misguidedly believed he thought that his mother was going on holiday.[93]

In principle, Britain's departure from gold should have been an opportunity, opening new types of policy options when countries had devalued their currencies.[94] Instead, it ended in disaster in Europe, with Britain's neverending collapse. Neither the Bank nor the government had clear plans for their future, and much would depend on the next general election. Norman now wanted no external interference until sterling was returned to gold.[95]

Britain's crisis was met with inadequate and delayed assistance from its creditors and exacerbated by the government and central bank's inability to get its house in order. Credibility and cooperation collapsed. One key source of this collapse was Norman, who had chosen to take an uncooperative stance, within his bank and overseas, to exacerbate the political and economic impediments to cooperation and crisis management in 1931.

Tripartite Discussions, 1933

Schacht described the pound's fall in September 1931 as "a deathblow to trust and good faith in all international money and credit dealings."[96] Losses devasted the British Empire, its colonies and most of Europe, and exacerbated political disputes—Britain's leaders blamed the United States and France for Britain's crisis. Given Britain's central position in the financial system, many neighboring states lost millions in reserves and soon abandoned gold. Britain's neighbors and trading partners were severely affected by its abandonment of gold, creating pressures on the US dollar and capital flight from the United States and France to countries that had already abandoned the gold parity and devalued it. Britain's crisis had now been exported to its key creditors.

By 1932, the Depression showed no signs of ending—unemployment soared, and far-right politics were gaining ground in Germany and France. Clarke suggests that the devaluation of the dollar and of sterling "placed the gold-exchange standard under a cloud."[97] The BIS failed in its main goal of facilitating a resolution of the postwar reparations, and the Fed chose to make unilateral adjustments instead of participating in the BIS.[98] When Sayers asked what was discussed in Basel, Schacht replied, "Not very much—what you think about at a hen party—the only thing we ought to have talked about we never did—development help; the French were against that."[99]

In turn, the WEC was announced to be held in 1933, to manage "beggar thy neighbor" and isolationist policies and pursue currency stabilization in the post–gold standard 1930s, as one last gasp of international, multilateral cooperation to arrest the Depression. The conference was primarily an intergovernmental conference, with sixty-four nations attending.

By this time, important political changes were taking place, generating a new strong nationalist bent in state preferences. Hitler became the chancellor of Germany in January 1933. In France and Britain, economic despair from the Depression generated a push toward more nationalist politics. In 1932, Franklin D. Roosevelt's election added a new dose of ambiguity about US national preferences in international monetary affairs. In April 1933, Roosevelt announced that the United States would suspend gold convertibility while WEC delegates met in Washington, DC, to prepare for the conference in June. Roosevelt was focused on reflating prices to their pre-Depression levels and on dollar devaluation, which alarmed Britain and France.[100]

Because the WEC was a political conference, I do not go into the details of the meeting itself, which was ultimately derailed by incompatible national interests.[101] Reparations, debt, and currency stabilization were once again the key agenda items. Addressing these issues remained fraught as states continued to squabble over German debts, as well as their divergent monetary goals of reflation and currency stabilization. Any hope of success was dashed when Prime Minister MacDonald delved into the issue of debts in his opening remarks, as a breach of faith, considering he had told Roosevelt's government he would not bring it up.

During preparations for the WEC, Moret urged that the central banks ought to be dealing with the stabilization question. He proposed joint meetings between central banks and treasuries at the WEC, but initially was met with little support for this plan from Norman and Harrison, in another break from the past. Recall that following the Genoa Conference and during the Dawes negotiations, Norman seized the chance to hold private central bank meetings with Strong and Schacht. Expecting that little would be achieved at the WEC, Norman, Harrison, and Moret ultimately agreed to private central bank talks. Tripartite monetary talks began on June 9, right before the WEC, and ran parallel with the conference through June and July, aiming to reach some agreement over gold and currency stabilization.[102]

Unlike in the 1920s, central bankers this time were less able to circumvent, or influence, political obstacles and less willing to cooperatively resolve their diverging interests and economic constraints. Harrison could not overcome the hold of his government. Moret was similarly constrained in France. They now met an increasingly uninterested and uncooperative Norman, who had little hope of achieving anything at the Conference. It had become increasingly clear at the Bank of England that as long as monetary policy in the United States was determined by Washington, cooperation with the Americans was impossible.[103] And Britain's departure from gold gave the Treasury increased monetary authority vis-à-vis the Bank of England. Notably, Norman had faced a similar constraint before 1925, when Britain had not yet returned to prewar parity. However, that had not impinged on his willingness to circumvent governmental preferences. In 1931, Norman was unwilling to cooperate with his counterparts. By 1933, he was also unable to do so.

In preparing for the Conference, central bankers hesitated to discuss issues that were under the purview of governments, and vice versa. Harrison held that "it was of the utmost importance for the World Conference to avoid invading the central bank field and making any suggestions or instructions to central banks which might prove embarrassing." While they agreed in principle about the need for central bank cooperation, "it had not been settled what they were to cooperate about."[104] Their loss of autonomy stifled their efforts. As WEC proceedings and preparations began earlier in 1933, central bankers, it seemed, were largely kept in the dark. In May 1933, Norman "professed [to Harrison] to know little or nothing about the proposed procedure. He admitted many questions of central bank policy are on the agenda, but he had no way of knowing how they are proposed to be handled. He seemed disturbed at the whole setup and quite in the dark."[105]

They arrived in London not very hopeful, which made them not only unable but increasingly unwilling to push their boundaries as they had done in the past.

When asked what the WEC could achieve, Norman's response was "not a thing." The French felt similarly skeptical.[106] Norman's distrust of politicians clouded his hope of any progress. He believed that the French and British governments had already approached the United States about exchange stabilization through "devious channels" and was convinced that "there was little we [central bankers] could do" until it was clear what governments sought to achieve. In the run-up to the conference, Norman "didn't believe in any more conferences; especially hot air conferences of which there had been too many" when the meeting was first proposed and was largely disengaged from the effort.[107]

The tripartite talks began at the Bank of England on June 9, three days before the WEC. Very soon into the Conference proceedings, all eyes were more focused on the tripartite endeavors than the political meeting itself. During the WEC, in mid-June, the dollar also began to strengthen. To manage emerging fluctuations, monetary authorities quickly agreed in the parallel monetary talks to a limited six-week temporary stabilization period, pegging the dollar, sterling, and franc at their present values. Roosevelt, who had been supportive of currency stabilization, vetoed this proposal. Harrison was disappointed and sailed back to New York, unwilling to continue any efforts.

Harrison was replaced at the WEC by Raymond Moley, "the Man who controlled Presidents," known in US circles for his isolationist stance.[108] He was one of Roosevelt's closest advisers and assistant secretary of state to Cordell Hull. Moley made "every effort to appear as a loyal subordinate" to Hull, but no one trusted him.[109] The French believed he had the power to stabilize the US dollar if he chose to, issuing him an ultimatum: "Stabilize or we quit."[110]

Moley's delegation decided that the only way to resolve the situation was to issue a tripartite communiqué that some short-term agreement had been made. It was clear that the French were not going to get any commitment from the United States regarding "stabilization" per se, only a far more diluted wording that efforts would be made by non–gold bloc countries—Britain and the United States—to minimize currency fluctuations.[111] This communiqué would be shared with WEC delegations instructing them to work with their central banks over currency stabilization. He was so sanguine that Roosevelt would accept his proposal. But to Moley's dismay, Roosevelt rejected this plan, after which Hull told him "You had better go back home. You had no business here in the first place."

It was then that Roosevelt, on holiday on his sailboat, upended the entire Conference effort in his famous "bombshell" cable sent from his yacht on July 3. Roosevelt wrote that the failure of the WEC to address long-term economic problems was a "catastrophe amounting to a world tragedy." He opposed the "artificial and temporary" stabilization "on the part of a few countries only," which represented "old fetishes of so-called international bankers."[112] Roosevelt's words rendered any continued efforts at the WEC useless and threw the conference into an uproar.[113]

To save face, political and monetary leaders continued to find a way around ongoing currency wars for a few more weeks. In the end, all that they could agree to were rather empty statements affirming the "superiority of the gold standard over alternative monetary arrangements" but little as way of concrete steps on how to reestablish the system. Roosevelt's words had "consigned the World Economic Conference to failure."[114] The Conference was adjourned by the end of July, with no real accomplishments to show for it. Hull said, "Human ingenuity could scarcely have devised a more complete jumble and chaos of business and general economic conditions than those facing the nations and the conference when it convened."

"There are after all, only two ways of reaching international agreement" Hull said in his closing remarks at the WEC. "One is by imposing one's will by force—by war. The other is by persuasion—by conference."[115] But the most catastrophic impact of the WEC failure was that it made governments avoid further attempts at cooperation to facilitate an economic recovery. Instead, it reinforced nationalist and isolationist recourse, exacerbating debt disputes and currency wars, closing any opportunities to find a path off the road to war.

Although the 1933 meetings were a lost opportunity for strengthening Anglo-American monetary relations, bilateral Anglo-German cooperation was revived, in no small part, by Schacht's return to the Reichsbank that year. Even while Norman was unwilling to sway his government or the Bank's cooperation with Harrison and Moret during the Conference, he had returned to his ways of ad hoc, bilateral, and secretive interbank assistance with Schacht.

Schacht took over Germany's WEC preparations, and blamed American protectionism for Germany's debt distress. In May, Schacht threatened to default on American commercial debts that had been frozen in the Standstill agreement, but assured Hull and Roosevelt that he opposed moratoriums. Patricia Clavin shows that when Schacht returned to Germany, he announced that as of "July 1, 1933, the Reichsbank will discontinue making foreign exchange available for those obligations that existed at the time of the banking crisis on 15 July 1931," effectively denouncing Germany's Dawes and Young obligations.[116]

When the parallel central bank meetings began, Schacht used his influence with Norman to strengthen Germany's position. He took up talks with Norman and other British bankers in London. Roosevelt then learned that "British banking authorities [were] working closely with German authorities to develop further plans satisfactory to themselves" regarding German debts. It seemed to them that Schacht, a close friend of Norman, was favoring British bondholders over American bondholders. American authorities felt that Schacht "was being governed inordinately by considerations of the Bank of England."[117] Norman and Schacht arranged to renew the Anglo-German Standstill agreement, and had settled on their plans for Germany's debt payments to Britain and its suspension of US debts.[118]

Certainly, the crisis was not resolved at the Conference, and economic turmoil was increasingly heightened by growing political turmoil. But Norman and Schacht's arrangement had long-lasting effects for cementing Anglo-German monetary ties, encouraging Germany to continue favoring British over American financial interests, and strengthening British banks' support for Germany's commercial debt policy, which fortified the Nazi regime. As political and economic disputes heightened, Schacht wrote to Norman about their efforts through the troubled year:

> It seems to be that the world will still have to go through some more dark waters until we reach the shore and all that I hope and trust is that our mutual friendship will last during and after that time. I feel most strongly that, after the death of our New York friend, you and I have been the only two men who understood what had to be achieved. Let us not be discouraged by a passing setback and believe whatever may happen in the sincerity and friendship of Yours, thankfully and truly, Hjalmar Schacht.[119]

Death of a Banker

The years between 1928 and 1933 were some of trial, and mostly error, by politicians and central bankers. Friedman and Schwartz pin the responsibility for the Great Depression on central bankers, namely, the failure of the Federal Reserve after Strong's death.[120] Central bankers' inability to cooperate to arrest the 1931 crisis and during the WEC plagued international monetary affairs from 1929 to 1933 was "in no small measure a result of the internal struggle for power within the [Federal Reserve] System which followed the death of Benjamin Strong."[121] But it was not just Strong's death or Harrison that ought to bear the responsibility for the Depression. It was an entire cohort of central bankers that were at times unable, and often unwilling, to overcome structural, political, and economic obstacles to cooperation, bilaterally and through interpersonal channels, as they had done in the decade before.

Central bankers were now far more constrained by their governments, and no longer lived in a time "when each of the great central banks seemed to be personified by a single outstanding individual."[122] They also shared very different personal relations with their counterparts than their predecessors in the 1920s. This made it increasingly difficult for each of them to cooperate with their banking partners, and to act quickly and adequately in the face of rapidly growing crises.

With Strong gone, the US government and the Federal Reserve Board in Washington increasingly interfered in Harrison's New York Fed. Under Harrison, international considerations gave way to political involvement. Strong's death also dealt a blow to Anglo-American relations. Harrison was even limited in his ability to engage in international efforts, as an outsider to the BIS, and faced more restrictions on the New York Fed's international lending. While Norman's relations with Moret were not distrustful as they had been with Moreau, they were not adequate to pursue cooperative arrangements on the basis of personal trust and good will. However, Norman, despite added constraints on his own independence, was both willing and able to work with Schacht to renew the Reichsbank's Standstill agreement on its British debts.

A period of trade tensions and economic despair was followed by a modest and short-lived recovery from 1934 to 1937, with domestic policy tools. But each year after 1933 was marked by major diplomatic hiccups that escalated into war by 1939. The remilitarization of the Rhineland in 1936 by Germany violated the Versailles and Locarno Treaties (which were signed willingly by Germany), taking a sharp turn on the road to war. The only real recovery from the Depression came from the war effort, and more decidedly, at Bretton Woods in 1944, which also put in place institutions and resources for longer-term stability.

A few central bankers in the interwar years undoubtedly had a unique and outsized influence on their own banks and on international affairs. Others were less able to sway their banks and their governments as per their will. Central bankers' personal relations with their foreign opposites could also serve to bolster or constrain their individual power and their influence in monetary affairs. Interpersonal ties between central bankers in the 1920s and the 1930s could both help or hinder cooperation and crisis management.

Bankers' Trust is not a story of only Strong and Norman, or Schacht or Moreau. It is a story of the Normans and Strongs, the Schachts, and the Moreaus of the last century. Through their powerful personalities and unique interpersonal relations of trust, reciprocity, and goodwill, central bankers can determine the fate of the global economy in times of grave economic uncertainty. Next, I turn to the midcentury era to evaluate the creation of the central bank swap network in 1962, used to patch up the flailing Bretton Woods system.

3

SPRINGTIME FOR BRETTON WOODS?

Patchwork Governance in the 1960s

The power and influence that central bankers gained after the First World War was lost after the Great Depression and the Second World War. These crises altered the mandates, goals, and independence of central banks.[1] The Depression tested their credibility in preventing and resolving such grave crises. Midcentury central banks lost much of the autonomy from political interference that they held so closely in the interwar years. Now, central bankers were not primarily tasked with postwar reconstruction and development. Governments were in charge again, and central banks were relegated to being their de facto agents.[2] The Bretton Woods institutions—the International Monetary Fund (IMF) and the World Bank—were tasked with managing global finance and the gold-dollar monetary system.

After initial teething problems of this new governance architecture in the years immediately after the 1944 conference at Bretton Woods, the 1958–1971 period has been characterized as the heyday of the Bretton Woods era.[3] The international monetary system was bolstered by robust global financial institutions tasked to ensure the key pillars of monetary stability—liquidity, adjustment, and confidence—and postwar reconstruction and development.

But underlying this system were larger systemic fault lines, broadly captured by the Triffin dilemma: if the United States stopped running its balance of payments deficit, the rest of the world would lose access to reserve liquidity. At the same time, continually running a large deficit would hinder confidence in the reserve currency. Policymakers were once again faced with problems of adjustment and liquidity not dissimilar to those of the interwar period.

Most scholarship on this period in history has focused on the stability of the 1960s, the role of the IMF in managing the instabilities predicted by Robert Triffin, the collapse of the monetary regime, and the reemergence of global capital. These studies provide key insights into the stability and the breakdown of this monetary order, the gold-dollar standard.[4] Explanations privilege and prioritize the role of governments and international institutions in facilitating international cooperation to stabilize the system, and the power political, material, and ideational factors that contributed to the system's demise. This history has been thoroughly documented and analyzed, and explaining the collapse of the Bretton Woods system is not the goal of this chapter.

Instead, I show that, underlying these broader structural and ideational dynamics, bilateral cooperation for liquidity provision once again emerged from ad hoc experimentation facilitated by central bankers' interpersonal relations of trust and goodwill. The 1960s—viewed as the heyday of global financial governance, armed with institutional capacity, rules, and order—were in fact similar to the 1920s. Like the interwar years, central bank officials in the 1960s actively cooperated to generate innovative governance responses to cover up cracks in the system. They extended bilateral credits known as "swap lines" to one another to provide liquidity and maintain exchange-rate pegs under the gold-dollar standard. But this form of monetary management, although similar to the 1920s, emerged in very different economic and political environments in the 1960s.

This time, ad hoc and bilateral cooperation around the swap lines and credits emerged in a postwar economy governed by a different set of rules (the gold-dollar standard) and governance institutions (the IMF and World Bank). Crises in the midcentury period were also different: much less immediate and much more a feature of the monetary system of the time. Occasional flare-ups took the form of currency crises, mainly in sterling and dollar funding pressures, rooted in systemic disjunctures and balance of payments mismatches, encapsulated in Triffin's observation. And still, the outcome of interest—the policy and governance devices used to manage these pressures—mirrored those adopted in the interwar 1920s—bilateral, ad hoc, and innovative liquidity credits. Liquidity assurance came primarily from one central bank, the New York Fed, dubbed by Charles Coombs as "the bankers for all major foreign central banks," supplemented with help from the BIS.[5]

I show that central bankers' interpersonal trust networks enabled central bankers to enter into risky lending programs, without additional safeguards and conditionality, unlike IMF and other intergovernmental alternatives. Through these networks, monetary authorities could circumvent the institutional constraints now placed on their banks to put out fires by creating new and innovative policy tools.

Accounting for the changing global political and economic context of this time, I focus on ad hoc and bilateral central bank cooperation around the creation of the 1960s Basel Arrangements extended through the Bank for International Settlements (BIS), and the Reciprocal Currency Arrangements (RCA), which was the Federal Reserve's swap network arranged by the New York Fed to support the flailing Bretton Woods monetary system.[6] These arrangements, like the bilateral credits of the 1920s, were designed to support the US dollar and sterling exchange positions against fluctuations and speculative attacks, avoid drains on US gold holdings, enhance broader international monetary cooperation, and supplement IMF exchange arrangements. These efforts were made to provide central banks the necessary liquidity to pursue these goals in the long run and meet growing liquidity needs in the expanding global economy. Many European central banks also used these lines to support their currencies against fluctuations.[7]

Even more, by the 1960s, for the first time since the Second World War, the United States found itself in need of liquidity, and essentially, an international lender of last resort. But, as Daniel McDowell argues, in the context of an under-resourced IMF, which the United States had designed to push the burden of adjustment onto debtor countries, growing payments imbalances meant that the United States had become a debtor country as well, putting the US dollar's exchange and US gold stocks at risk.[8] The prospects of turning to the IMF were further hampered by the political and economic risks of the General Agreements to Borrow (GAB) mechanism, due to the slow negotiation process with multiple creditors, and the conditions attached to IMF assistance. In turn, the Fed swap program gave US policymakers an alternative liquidity mechanism, which was quick and responsive in a crisis, to provide countercyclical assistance with no conditions attached. The swap program was a response to structural inadequacies, supported by US power.

At the center of these arrangements was Charles Coombs, vice-president of the New York Fed's (FRBNY) Foreign Department at the time. In that sense, US power was vital to the American response to the structural inadequacies of the international lender of last resort mechanism through the IMF, harnessed and enacted on by Coombs. However, important parallel dynamics also influenced the creation of the Fed swap network, the RCA. First, on many occasions, especially in the creation and the expansion of the RCA, Coombs's actions were *not* representative of US preferences, and often did not represent the Fed's interests and preferences. Second, Coombs did not, and could not, act alone but relied on the support and cooperation of his close and trusted counterparts overseas. In fact, the initial ideas and mechanisms of the swap arrangement were engineered not by Coombs or other Fed officials but central bankers from continental Europe, first arranged through Basel.

The narrative presented in this chapter foregrounds the role of personalities and personal relations across national central banks, in facilitating the cooperative response to emergent crises. Alongside important structural variables such as state power in determining cooperation, these interpersonal and relational factors also helped shape the cooperative response of ad hoc, bilateral liquidity assistance during the heyday of the Bretton Woods era.

Central bankers' interpersonal relations, especially Coombs's friendship and mutual trust with his counterparts, were central to the Fed swap network. The influence of Coombs's friendly and trusting relationships, with various configurations of his counterparts, were especially prominent in signing the initial swaps. Key figures of this period included Max Iklé at the Swiss National Bank (SNB), Julien-Pierre Koszul at the Bank of France, Guido Carli at the Bank of Italy, Johannes Tüngeler at the Bundesbank, and Lord Cobbold and his successor, Lord Cromer, at the Bank of England. The case of British and American monetary relations, of slow and stalling cooperation, in part due to mistrust of Coombs among Bank of England associates, is particularly intriguing, given the otherwise close relationship between these two economies. I show that friendly relations between Cromer, William (Bill) McChesney Martin, chairman of the Federal Reserve Board in Washington, DC, and Coombs were key to overcoming this hurdle.

After providing a brief overview of the post-1945 period until current account convertibility was achieved in Europe, this chapter illustrates how these innovative governance efforts were activated through interpersonal cooperation among these central bankers and differentiated by the strength of these ties in their speed, amounts, and ability to limit political input into their activities.

1945–1958: After the War

As is well known, the United States had emerged out of the Second World War as a clear hegemonic power in the Western bloc and took the lead in European reconstruction. Under the Bretton Woods monetary system, the US dollar was pegged to gold at $35 per ounce; all other currencies in the system were pegged to the US dollar. The system was designed to "avoid the 'mistakes'" of the interwar years, achieve current account convertibility, prevent competitive devaluations, and promote economic growth.[9]

Through the late 1940s, the postwar global dollar shortage outside the United States was slowly reversed into a global dollar glut and a shortage in the United States, which now ran a small balance of payments deficit to flush the global economy with liquidity. The Cold War pushed the United States to exercise what the historian Gianni Toniolo calls "benevolent," or "consensual" hegemony over its allies in Japan and Western Europe after 1947.[10]

For the first dozen or so postwar years, payments adjustments and crises were addressed primarily by governments via intergovernmental arrangements and enacted by central banks. After the war, Europe and Japan were relatively weak and very dependent on US support. They benefited from narrow US balance of payments deficits, in exchange for dollar liquidity. The United States supported Europe's recovery through the Marshall Plan, and the European Payments Union (EPU) and the European Monetary Agreement were created to manage European currencies in a context of limited convertibility. With the help of Marshall Plan aid, European currencies were managed by the EPU.[11] The BIS played a technical role in facilitating multilateral cooperation among European governments and monetary authorities, moving away from bilateral payments.

Governments and monetary authorities were occupied with a series of financial pressures and new efforts aside from those of reconstruction and development in Europe as they adapted to the new currency system established at Bretton Woods. The creation of the Organisation for European Economic Co-operation (OEEC) helped create favorable economic conditions in Europe for both international cooperation and the strengthening of domestic institutions in Europe.

The EPU, deemed "a successful pioneering effort in economic and monetary cooperation," was the main instrument responsible for achieving current account convertibility by 1958 and facilitating the rapid liberalization of trade.[12] It was supported by intensive central bank cooperation and was terminated upon restoring convertibility in Europe soon after 1958. Similar efforts were less successful in the United Kingdom. Sterling, the second reserve currency in the international monetary system, had a bumpier journey to convertibility, facing several balance of payments shortages through the 1950s, resulting from significant deficits in overseas transactions, a lack of competitiveness, and the collapse of the British Empire.[13] The shortage of official reserves in the United Kingdom posed an added impediment to counter a run on the pound, necessitating assistance from the BIS.

Unlike in the 1920s, central bankers now were not only more constrained by governments and political interests, but many had also been nationalized after the disasters of the Great Depression and the Second World War. Right before the Second World War, most central banks became government agents of ministers of finance, "*de facto* if not literally nationalized until later."[14] Only the Fed regained its independence in 1951 and the Bundesbank in 1957. Most other European central banks regained their independence in the 1990s.

Central banks' primary tasks were to advise governments and the IMF, and implement their decisions, "but they did not take the lead."[15] As a result, the central banking profession itself also changed. In a climate of increasing state intervention, the financial governance system evolved in a way that required more bureaucratic work from central banks. Unlike the "lords of finance" from banking dynasties of the early 1900s, the goals, internal organization, and political influence in central banks led to the bureaucratization of central bankers.[16]

Postwar structural and institutional changes certainly created an environment more conducive to cooperation than the 1920s. This new context lends favorably to conventional explanations for cooperation: American hegemony, US dollar centrality, and Cold War alliances all shaped financial governance. International organizations played central roles in the global financial governance system, all while central banks were beholden to their governments.

With the establishment of the Bretton Woods institutions as key orchestrators in postwar reconstruction, the IMF played a greater role in managing international monetary affairs. Paul Einzig, an economic and political writer of the time, notes that the BIS had fallen out of favor with the US government and Treasury for siding with the enemy or for being "scrupulously neutral" during the war.[17] Many European governments also took an unfavorable position toward the BIS. Central banks were poorly represented at Bretton Woods, where it was even suggested that the BIS ought to be liquidated with the creation of the IMF.[18] Central bankers now operated in a world that had shrunk their previously outsized influence, tasked to simply guide the politicians and international organizations as they muddled through their postwar reconstruction efforts. And still, the troubles of the 1960s were managed largely through ad hoc cooperation, facilitated by central bankers' interpersonal trust and personal relations.

After 1958: The Heyday of Bretton Woods?

The system that was designed at the Bretton Woods Conference only became fully functional in 1958; it lasted until 1973, when countries began to float their currencies against one another after Nixon suspended the "gold window" in 1971. During this time, the Kennedy and Johnson administrations fought their political battles over European and British currency management through the US Treasury.[19] Central banks, still subordinated to the political preferences of their governments and finance ministries, cooperated extensively to support what Harold James describes as the heyday of Bretton Woods and the "golden age of capitalism."[20] A few central bankers, mostly those in charge of their foreign departments, collectively circumvented these institutional constraints to cooperate and innovate their way through the systemic fault lines.

Following extensive reconstruction and rebuilding efforts, aided by the United States through the Marshall Plan, the expansion of trade and economic growth in Europe and Japan shifted the balance of power toward these economies in the international system by the end of the 1950s. The increase in exports from Europe and Japan, combined with the United States's increase in military spending, rapidly expanded US deficits.[21] Now, US financing to rebuild Europe and Japan had created significant dollar shortages at home and a dollar glut overseas. But when central banks redeemed their dollars for gold, US gold reserves would fall to dangerously low levels.

It was this structural problem, and the implications of attempting to resolve it, identified and exposed by Triffin in 1960, that came to consume policymakers' attention through the rest of the decade. He predicted that if the United States corrected its persistent balance of payments deficits, the international community would lose its primary and largest source of reserves, which could not be sustained by adequate gold production at $35 an ounce. But if the United States continued to run deficits, its foreign liabilities would eventually exceed its ability to convert dollars into gold and erode confidence in the dollar.

No doubt, postwar cooperation, both multilateral and bilateral, benefited from the presence of a hegemonic power to play the role of an economic stabilizer.[22] But, the heyday of the Bretton Woods era was not the result of US hegemony alone. America's consensual hegemony in the 1940s and 1950s slowly eroded the political and economic conditions that had sustained postwar cooperation by the 1960s, while dollar centrality remained. European economies faced continued trouble managing their currency pegs, and the United States and the United Kingdom, who controlled the two reserve currencies, faced large and unsustainable deficits. Dollar funding remained a central issue for the entire system, and the United States relied as much on the support and cooperation of its partners as they did on the hegemon. As James reminds us, the United States and the United Kingdom "found their situations increasingly difficult" and had to resort to "expedients, devices, gimmicks and ad hockery to maintain their international position."[23]

The IMF and the BIS were important for cooperation and seen as central pillars of the governance architecture.[24] But the extent to which policymakers, including central bankers, saw the IMF and BIS as central to managing crises and financial pressures is intriguing. The IMF was indeed tasked with the role of acting as an international lender of last resort. To do this, it created important backstops and lending facilities to provide financial support in Europe—the GAB—in case, as the IMF's managing director, Per Jacobsson, said, "Borrowing could not really be improvised in a crisis: some advanced arrangements had to be made."[25] But the Bretton Woods system did not seem to rely on a robust, institutionalized governance framework. As the Triffin dilemma materialized, these institutions proved inadequate. Still, policymakers were able to prolong the gold-dollar standard for another dozen years.[26]

Setting aside the discussions and negotiations leading up to the GAB, I highlight monetary authorities' preference for improvised cooperation for bilateral liquidity assistance over such multilateral tools to avoid the cost of IMF assistance and the laborious negotiations with governments. I show that central bankers, with the help of their friends, spent the decade postponing the eventuality that Triffin had predicted. They engineered devices and gimmicks to find ways for surplus countries—Germany, France, Italy, and later Japan—to lend dollars to the United States and the United Kingdom to finance deficits. Liquidity provision in a crisis was once again up for innovation.

In the Bretton Woods system, central bankers played a largely subordinate and technical role.[27] Most leaders did not enjoy the same discretion and independence from governments as their predecessors. Given the bureaucratization and enlargement of central banks, individual leaders alone did not steer the global economy through the decade, as they had done in the interwar period. But emerging systemic problems and changes gave central bankers a new raison d'être: the financial system was rapidly evolving, with the emergence and growth of the Eurodollar market and the increasingly complex financial instruments used in private finance. With current account convertibility and the need to engineer improvised arrangements to prop up the dollar and pound, central bankers' technical expertise was invaluable. These emergent technical problems helped separate the central banking wheat from the political chaff.

Central bankers themselves were learning the ways of the growing private financial sector in real time, coming to grips with how the international monetary system was evolving. Coombs, at the New York Fed, wrote to Allan Sproul, a former president there, in 1964: "I can well understand your dismay at the growing complexity of the exchange operations reported in our last article. Sometimes I feel like we are trying to play half a dozen games of poker at once, although I am consoled by the fact that so far we have not wound up pursuing any busted flushes."[28]

As national economies grew increasingly interconnected, central banks' foreign currency desks and the BIS became a safe haven for their autonomy, at least in conducting their overseas operations. High-level staff and leaders in central banks' foreign departments played a key role in managing their activities, especially from their international desks and foreign exchange offices. From behind the scenes, a "new class of close-knit global technocrats" emerged.[29]

Per Triffin's 1960 diagnosis, endogenous mismatches in the system suggested that the collapse of the system was predetermined, and emerging imbalances were further complicated by the reemergence of global finance.[30] In response, central bankers took to extensive improvisation. Early in 1961, European central bankers, primarily Max Iklé in Switzerland and Cameron Cobbold at the Bank of England, created the Basel Arrangements through the BIS. Soon after, Coombs followed suit to arrange bilateral credits with his continental counterparts, starting with Iklé from Switzerland and Tüngeler at the Bundesbank. These early experiments laid the groundwork for a much larger effort: the creation of the RCA, also known as the Federal Reserve swap network. Together, these innovations kept the system going to maintain its external facade of stability.

These governing arrangements were generated and managed through extensive cooperation among central bankers. They worked to prop up the dollar, maintain exchange rate pegs, and provide liquidity to the global monetary system. But their success was short-lived. The balance of payments troubles that Triffin observed eventually culminated in the gold and dollar crises in 1971 and onward. Dollar convertibility was suspended that year, and with it came the demise of the Bretton Woods gold-dollar exchange rate standard.[31]

The Basel Arrangements

In 1961, a swap network created at the BIS emerged to support sterling. These came to be known as the "Basel Arrangements," the "Basel credits," or the "Bilatéral concerté."[32] They emerged following the revaluation of the German mark, Swiss franc, and Dutch guilder in 1961. These created what Coombs describes as a "burst of speculation against sterling" and the "dollar as usual was caught in the speculative backwash."[33] Emerging currency pressures led to a series of bilateral efforts by a few central bankers, namely, Coombs in New York, Tüngeler at the Bundesbank, and Iklé at the Swiss National Bank. Within months, these credits incorporated a handful of European central bankers through the BIS monthly meetings.

The Basel Arrangements and the Fed RCA network operated similarly: central banks exchanged their currencies for dollar credits from partner banks. The Basel Arrangements were provided by central banks to one another. They were used to boost reserve liquidity to fund exchange rate commitments and payments imbalances in 1961. These lines did not involve the high costs and supranational enforcement associated with IMF assistance. The Basel Arrangements were also specifically not created by BIS authorities. They were bilateral lines between central banks that just happened to first be arranged during the March BIS meeting in 1961. As an internal communication within the Bank of England shows, the press announcement of the Basel Arrangements would qualify "that this was only what the Press had come to call them and that the basic fact, viz. that it was Central Bank co-operation which had happened to have started at a B.I.S. Meeting came out quite early in the Article [the Bank Bulletin.]" to reflect the preferences of central bankers in Basel.[34]

Coombs was not directly involved in making these arrangements; they came about primarily between central bankers at the Bank of England and on the continent. However, Coombs's initial interactions with Guido Carli at the Bank of Italy, and Tüngeler, laid essential groundwork for these arrangements. Central to what soon became the Basel Arrangements were interpersonal ties of goodwill between Iklé and Coombs that led Iklé to approach his European counterparts to help offset pressures on US gold stocks to support Coombs. These initial interactions and informal bilateral conversations among friends at the BIS were the starting point for what developed into the Fed swap network in the following year.

Coombs Goes to Basel

Coombs recounts that when the German mark was being pressed "hard against its official ceiling in the exchange markets," the IMF approved the revaluation of the mark. This move was soon followed by similar moves in neighboring countries in the early 1960s. Currency revaluation on the continent triggered significant capital flight out of Britain toward Germany and Switzerland. At that time, the United States also faced gold losses, pushing important cooperative efforts between Coombs and Tüngeler. The Germans regarded this American assistance in 1961 as an important cooperative gesture and depended greatly on the trust and confidence shared among Coombs, Tüngeler, and Karl Blessing, president of the Bundebank.[35]

When these currency pressures emerged, and after the revaluation of the deutsche mark, the Bundesbank was flooded with speculative dollars, draining the United States's gold stock. Tüngeler called Coombs to discuss this issue and take decisive action to control the situation. Coombs "stopped off in Frankfurt and spent an evening at Tüngeler's home, drinking beer before his fireplace, and exploring with him ways and means . . . to check speculation against the dollar." Coombs highlights Tüngeler's "generous solution" to the problem, also noting, "Over the years, I have known no other central banker whom I have trusted more."[36]

Days later, Blessing, aided by Tüngeler, head of the Foreign Department at the Bundesbank, proposed a mark-dollar swap in the forward foreign exchange markets to Coombs. Coombs recalls the goodwill and friendship he shared with Tüngeler and Blessing at the Bundesbank. Blessing had watched the breakdown of cooperation in the 1930s from Basel, and now, as president of the Bundesbank, "with the mark entrusted to his care, he wielded his enormous authority with courage and discernment of his world financial responsibilities."[37] He played a towering role and was "an unfailing source of strength and morale in [all] Basel discussions." He understood "when to be helpful" and preferred bilateral cooperation to avoid long and complex negotiations involving governments.[38] Coombs described Tüngeler, with whom he developed a very close friendship, as a "courteous, easy-going German" who managed the bank's huge foreign operations "with highly professional skill and a remarkable sense of responsibility not only to his own country but to the outside world." But early that year, their "professional and personal friendship was just beginning."[39]

Tüngeler's suggestion was for Coombs to begin "forceful sales of forward marks" in New York, which would provide markets insurance against the risk of further revaluation. The problem was that the New York Fed did not own enough German currency to honor the ninety-day forward contract. Here, Tüngeler's ingenuity and goodwill came to Coombs's aid. If Coombs's bank could not honor spot purchases when the swap reached maturity, the Bundesbank would sell them marks for dollars at the same rate as in New York's forward sales. Because at the time the FRBNY did not have the independent authority to enter this agreement, Coombs sought the support of Robert Roosa and Douglas Dillon at the US Treasury, who authorized him "to conduct this pioneering experiment."

A previous, similarly experimental exchange just weeks before, between Coombs and Guido Carli, of "poor, war-torn, defeated Italy," had encouraged Coombs to consider these improvised solutions. Carli had been appointed as general manager of the Bank of Italy in 1959 and was promoted to governor in 1960. He was a man of few words but a "skilled economist, with finely honed analytical powers."[40] Carli had visited Coombs to discuss how to curb further gold losses in the United States, while the Bank of Italy "had a swollen dollar portfolio" that was legally convertible to gold at the Treasury. Any such conversion at the time would have posed a problem for the United States, given the extensive gold losses it was already seeing.

Carli enjoyed considerable authority among his foreign colleagues, "owing to his power of persuasion and also to the gold and dollar reserves on which he was sitting." His visit to New York came with an offer to sell $100 million of gold to the New York Fed to help maintain its gold stock when needed. Coombs and Carli's shared trust and friendship facilitated this generous offer, insofar as agreeing to make the transaction the same day that Coombs requested. Carli later recalled that it was in central bankers' informal meetings where the most significant decisions were arrived at.[41] Carli and Coombs developed a very close relationship with one another, where Carli "took over the role of [the New York Fed's] 'Italian Navigator.'"[42] Coombs's memoir, *The Arena of International Finance*, is even dedicated to Carli.

Creating the Basel Arrangements

While these early experiments between Coombs, Carli, and Tüngeler had proved successful, gold losses in the United States and hot money flows to Switzerland continued. At the Swiss National Bank (SNB), Iklé, who was in charge of banking operations, was quick to identify the same systemic threats that Triffin later exposed in 1960. Iklé was a lawyer by training who was "quick to acquire the necessary economic expertise."[43] He was personally very well connected with both Swiss commercial banks on Zurich's high street and his foreign central bank colleagues across Europe and in the United States. In the 1950s, he engineered small, short-term domestic swaps (which operated very differently to the international central bank swaps, but were similarly ad hoc) through the BIS to maintain fixed exchange rates in Switzerland.

As European central bankers grew concerned with increasing gold inflows and decreasing gold reserves in the United States at the turn of the decade, it was clear that the Bretton Woods system was under threat from short-term capital movements and speculation. At the time, the legal provisions governing the SNB meant that Swiss loans overseas could only be granted by the government. After 1959, a "radical transformation of this policy was then initiated . . . notably at the instigation of the imaginative Head of Department III, Max Iklé."[44] The domestic window-dressing swaps that Iklé engineered in the 1950s, and later, participating in international currency loans, were a significant break in tradition that Walter Schwegler, Iklé's predecessor in Department III, strongly opposed. Even under Iklé, the SNB Governing Board had declined a swap proposal from the BIS stating that "such a transaction would not be entirely compatible with the statutory provisions, and the bank currently has no need for additional income."[45] Iklé, acknowledging the legal restrictions, explained the high costs of exchange rate hedging, which Schwegler turned down.

So, Iklé took his ideas overseas, generating the earliest plans for swap lines with the New York Fed and the BIS to manage foreign exchange and provide liquidity assistance between central banks. In February 1961, Iklé first approached his counterpart in New York, Coombs, who managed the New York Fed's foreign currency transactions, when they were in Basel.[46] Here, he raised the idea of a Swiss franc-dollar swap to Coombs privately and "in lengthy letters and in personal meetings."[47] Iklé also shared this proposal of a Swiss franc-dollar swap with Roy Bridge at Bank of England and the SNB Governing Board, where he explained in detail the transaction itself, topped off with a list of its advantages for both Switzerland and the United States.

Iklé's moment arrived that March. The revaluation of the mark in 1961 had caused havoc in sterling markets and substantial gold drains in the US gold stock. When Coombs traveled to Switzerland during the 1960–1961 winter, he "had lengthy conversations with Iklé and had enjoyed the hospitality of his home," to find a solution to US gold drains and sterling's woes. During Coombs's visit, he recounts that Iklé "readily agreed" that as Switzerland had emerged as a "haven for hot money from all over the world" the SNB could no longer punish the US dollar "for buying gold with the proceeds of capital flight." Coombs was constrained and "irritated by the total lack on the American side of any technical facilities to deal with the problem. Here, Iklé's "good will was put to the test."[48]

It was this gentleman's agreement between a domestically constrained Coombs and Iklé to find a solution to the gold and dollar pressures in the United States that could circumvent institutional constraints on the FRBNY. To do this, Iklé turned to his European associates when they met in Basel the following Saturday. First, Iklé separately offered Bridge a three-month $310 million credit for the Bank of England over breakfast during the Basel weekend, on March 30, 1961. Bridge flat out refused at first. However, Cobbold, the governor of the Bank of England, a "genuinely apolitical" central banker, who championed the "we know how markets work" approach, got involved in Iklé's endeavors. Over the rest of the weekend, Cobbold actively worked to round up credits from continental central bankers, which "provided the all-important nucleus of a billion-dollar package" that soon came to be called the "Basel Arrangements." This weekend has been described by Frederick Connolly at the Bank of England as "a crystallisation point for the construction of a general swap network."[49] This "one stroke" cooperation among European central bankers, through the Basel Arrangements, saved both sterling and the dollar against immediate gold drains in 1961.[50]

The pressures triggered by currency realignment in Germany and Switzerland had been central to the inception of the Basel Arrangements, created primarily by Iklé and Cobbold, but also largely to honor Iklé's goodwill and reassurance to Coombs. At this time, however, a swap line between the New York Fed and the Swiss National Bank would have been out of step with the Governing Board of the SNB before Iklé took over the department. Iklé played a crucial role in changing the fundamental ways of his bank and recognized that his schemes overstepped the statutory provisions of the SNB, while the Fed and US Treasury were hesitant to enter such an arrangement without adequate cash reserves or any guarantee, which the SNB was not authorized to give. Iklé explicitly noted to Coombs that "such an operation, however, would mean throwing our tradition in respect of forwarding transactions overboard. We rather think that this would even go beyond the provisions of our banking law; all the same, the Board of Management of the Swiss National Bank would be prepared to assume full responsibility, provided an effective contribution toward the solution of the international monetary problem can thus be secured."[51]

To sidestep this hurdle, Bill Martin at the Federal Reserve Board suggested harking back to a central bank practice from the First World War to borrow foreign currencies via the Treasury and that this could be done by issuing a Treasury security in Swiss francs; Dillon and Roosa at the US Treasury agreed.[52] Coombs and Iklé engaged in swapping dollars for Swiss francs to "encourage the retention of dollar reserves" that August.[53] The success of the Fed's operations in German mark and Swiss franc markets "stimulated other European central banks to suggested similar experiments."

Iklé was also not the only central banker of that period to reshape his banks' international footprint. Coombs and the president of the New York Fed, Alfred Hayes, were also the first to break with the Fed's tradition of not participating in the Basel meetings when Coombs first attended a meeting in 1960, quickly becoming regular attendees.[54] This was an integral step for the Fed, and specifically for the New York Fed's leadership, to cultivate close relations with their European colleagues without which these informal discussions could not take place.

Personal visits and requests of this sort had become the modus operandi among Coombs and his friends. The success of the Fed's operations with the Swiss and the Germans had instilled a great deal of confidence in many Europeans about Coombs's plans. Monthly trips to Basel provided central bankers the ideal private and informal setting to discuss these requests. Later in 1961, in a similar private encounter at the BIS, President Holtrop of the Netherlands Bank approached Coombs saying, "Why don't you get together with my Foreign Department people and see if you can invent a way for me to avoid buying gold?" Coombs took on the request, arranging a cash balance at the Treasury to provide reserves for guilder operations in 1962.[55]

The "Basel" in the Basel Arrangements

Even though the Basel Arrangements were arranged at the BIS, they were not multilateral, institutional arrangements. After 1962, they provided an extension to the Fed's swap network to buttress its governance system with additional temporary measures, which could be arranged among European banks through Basel, without involving the Fed. These arrangements proved especially useful in overcoming several Bank of England associates' lack of trust in Coombs that I discuss ahead. Iklé was also keen to emphasize that these lines remained bilateral and between central banks. He "was worried about references to the 'Basle [Basel] Arrangements' saying, quite correctly, that the essence of the thing was a series of bilateral arrangements between Central Banks."[56]

Iklé's concern was part of a larger interest in protecting "the ability of central banks to extend such credits promptly, flexibly, and secretly, and affords a unique and potentially highly effective instrument of international financial cooperation."[57] Bilateral arrangements were generally preferred over having to resort to the IMF as a primary source of assistance. These ad hoc and "quickly mobilizable reserves" proved crucial for open market interventions by central banks, which were regularly arranged at the Basel weekends.[58]

The Bank for International Settlements in Basel offered central bankers a forum to regularly meet and get to know one another. Here, they had many opportunities to conduct their private, bilateral, or group meetings in a setting isolated and insulated from governmental and political interference. The Basel meetings were informal and were not institutionalized until 1964, when the monthly meetings officially became the G10 governors' meetings. The most valuable parts of the Basel weekend were the informal meeting and the governors' dinner, which was and remains by invitation only. Several Bank of England memoranda highlight that these meetings were "friendly and useful; most participants knew each other pretty well and a meeting of the minds was not difficult to achieve."[59] The camaraderie that central bankers developed in Basel was what attracted them to eagerly return each month. Louis Rasminsky of the Bank of Canada said that these visits were "an invariable source of pleasure" that also "served a therapeutic purpose."[60]

Central bankers also valued their visits to Basel for the private, bilateral meetings with their close friends, which "were in themselves worth the trip: they provided not only a quiet testing ground for new ideas and approaches but also an early warning system when things were beginning to go wrong."[61] One Bank of England official noted, "The unique character of the BIS made it possible to organize these arrangements with great speed, to employ flexible techniques & above all to maintain secrecy which was essential to combat the speculative forces which were at work. This essential need for secrecy, made it inevitable that a clear statistical explanation cd [*sic*] not be given at the time."[62]

The interests and goals of the BIS focused on managing the global financial system. Its operation depended greatly on who was present and the personal relations that they shared with their foreign colleagues. As already noted in the introduction to this book, Karl Otto Pöhl, a former president of the Bundesbank, had talked of the importance of close friendships, rather than financial resources, that are the real strength of the BIS. Indeed, changing personnel and personalities could mean a different BIS.[63]

The flexibility and informal nature of the Basel Arrangements were key factors in central bankers' preference to avoid the IMF. Central bankers in Europe disclosed "a very wide measure of agreement of the desirability of arranging that the first shock be taken up by ad hoc inter-Central Bank arrangements, the shape of which would not be in any way formalized, and that thereafter if the capital movements which these were designed to offset did not reverse themselves after quite a short period, the country losing reserves should go to the Fund for a drawing which it would use to repay Central Bank credits where repayment was desired."[64] When contracts could not or were not honored, central bankers would have to turn to the IMF, but the first port of call would be the bilateral network. Lord Cobbold wrote: "Our policy is to defer an approach to I.M.F. until later if possible, and then to use a drawing for some consolidation of Central Bank arrangements."[65]

Another key condition that facilitated these arrangements was secrecy over discussions and decisions. Operational secrecy was dearly guarded by central bank leaders across Europe; many of the earliest conversations leading to the creation of the Fed and the BIS swap networks took place in informal and private meetings. In 1961, Cromer wrote in his memorandum of the Experts meeting that December that his "instinct is that a written record, even of the figuring on balance of payments and even if it is confined to the participants of the management of the B.I.S. is, sooner or later, going to inhibit free discussion if that is the object of the exercise. I cannot escape the conclusion that if there is anything really serious that the Central Banks wish to tell one another, *the right channel is between Governors*."[66]

Sometimes this meant that not enough information was available to governments or markets regarding the proceedings of international transactions. But for central bankers, losing their autonomy and preference for secrecy was much too high a price to pay for increased transparency. It was essential for central banks to privately conduct their own dealings, which underpinned their cooperative arrangements of the 1960s.

While initial cooperative measures were being deliberated in Basel, the Bank of England's reports indicate that it was not alone in wanting to maintain this secrecy. It was repeatedly emphasized that "in the future, as in the past, secrecy must be paramount at a time when operations are in progress."[67] In discussions around the publication of the Bank's Quarterly Bulletin it was mentioned that "help was provided by institutions other than those mentioned. . . . [For your confidential information these were BIS and the Federal Reserve of the United States, both of which do not wish to be mentioned.] It may be asked which these institutions were, and the answer must be that this cannot be disclosed. It is of the essence of such operations that central banks participating should be able to do so without disclosure, if that is their wish."[68]

Even as the use of Fed or BIS swaps became more frequent and routine, keeping operations quiet remained a priority for central bankers. In 1964, regarding reports on the Basel Arrangements, a Bank of England report noted, "I think we could, if pressed, concede notification on the day following each operation, rather than the accumulation of a group of notifications; but even among friends there is something in operational secrecy and I do not think it should be easily conceded."[69]

The intimate setting of the Basel meetings and the regular personal travel and correspondence between central bank leaders afforded them a degree of privacy that they were accustomed to. Central bank operations also evolved in a manner that needed this cloister to arrange these transactions in an ad hoc and exclusive manner. Coombs characterizes them as "a major breakthrough in postwar international finance. At one stroke, European central bank cooperation had not only saved sterling but also had protected the dollar against heavy gold drains." The event also persuaded Fed officials of the need to "develop an active role in international financial markets" and encouraged Coombs in his monthly Basel visits "to explore new possibilities of transatlantic central bank cooperation," which emerged in the form of the RCA network in 1962.[70]

The Reciprocal Currency Arrangements

Differentiated personal ties among central bankers also influenced the scope and speed of cooperation. Among some, bilateral cooperation was seamless. Following Bridge's initial resistance to Iklé's ideas to collaborate with Coombs, further conversations took place exclusively among Coombs, Iklé, and Tüngeler. Coombs had "developed close and confidential relationships with his counterparts abroad."[71] He notes that he enjoyed "their full trust and confidence" before the Fed's network grew to include more partner banks.[72] The Fed swap network took a "hub and spoke" form, comprised of bilateral swap lines between Coombs and his partners. By 1971, the network grew eventually to include fourteen central banks and the BIS.[73] But the establishment of this program began with innovation that mirrored the 1920s programs, through bilateral central bank exchanges.

The earliest swaps that were taking off between the Swiss and the New York Fed, orchestrated intimately between Coombs, Iklé, and Tüngeler, laid the groundwork for the Fed's swap network in Europe. Coombs's account highlights the personal conversations and cooperation with his counterpart in France, crediting Julien-Pierre Koszul, the managing director of Foreign Services at the Bank of France, for designing that swap arrangement that evolved into the Fed's RCA.[74] Again, the swap arrangement between the Fed and the Bank of France emerged out of private, personal, and informal discussions between close friends. Coombs described Koszul as "a master of his profession" and a "quick-tempered French patriot, who nevertheless acknowledged some satisfaction in distant Polish and American ancestry," before these arrangements evolved into something more institutional and automatic.[75]

The conversation that led to the first swaps between the Bank of France and the New York Fed took place in private between Coombs and Koszul, when Coombs's thoughts turned to "the possibility of bilateral financing arrangements" with other central banks. In January 1962, he stopped by Koszul's apartment in Paris to talk over his ideas. He recalls that Koszul quickly "drove [his] problem into a corner and forced it to surrender the solution."[76] In doing so, he also offered the simplest explanation of how these swaps work, and how easily such ad hoc arrangements can be made: "Mon cher Charlie," he said, "it is very simple. We just do a swap of our currencies: we credit French francs to your account here in Paris against dollars to mine in New York. If you want to use your francs to defend the dollar in the exchange market, fine; if not, at the end of three months we reverse the transaction at the same rate, the money on both sides disappears, and everything is unchanged."[77]

It was very quickly agreed that the two banks would credit each other's accounts with an amount equivalent to $50 million in dollars and French francs. This agreement "became the prototype of all subsequent swap arrangements." Through this simple ninety-day loan arrangement, Koszul and Coombs were able to create an additional $100 million of international reserves "out of thin air."[78] This swap arrangement was much like the standing ninety-day transactions that Strong had arranged with the Bank of England in 1925, and so for Coombs, the FRBNY faced no legal obstacle, as it required no new legislation to undertake this task.

However, Martin knew that most of the Federal Open Market committee (FOMC) did not have any experience in international finance and would, as Robert Brummer highlights, "be reluctant to accept unfamiliar risks that might involve financial losses and new political risks."[79] While scholars have argued that the RCA was created and expanded with such ease because it served US interests, I highlight below that Coombs's persuasive role within the Fed, and his personal relations in Europe that helped facilitated this arrangement, were critical to getting the program off the ground.[80] The creation and expansion of this instrument went against the preferences of the FOMC and the Board to whom Coombs answered, who were wary of his experimental devices. Caution against this program included opposition from counterparts in Europe and hesitation toward the program by Martin himself. The arrangement faced similar opposition of Jacques Brunet, the governor of the Bank of France. As such, the informal and personal interaction between Coombs and Koszul that led to this initial agreement was especially important for the Fed-Bank of France swap line.

In May 1962, Brunet wrote to Cromer, who had just assumed the governorship at the Bank of England, that he "thought that the American idea of organizing swap facilities around Europe for large sums indefinite in time was wrong in principle" as it allowed the United States to avoid turning to the IMF to address the "deep seated difficulties" in the dollar.[81] Brunet was not opposed to central bank cooperation per se. He had cautiously suggested some cooperation among European central banks to pool resources in London gold markets, which was later visited to create the gold pool. However, Brunet, along with his government, grew increasingly frustrated with the United States for its dollar problems and exorbitant privilege that without Koszul the swap line arguably may not have come about. A line was also established, after much disagreement, with the Bank of England, once personal distrust and disagreements were overcome.

Following the success with the French swap, and a brief, speculative bout on Wall Street that sent money flowing back into mainland Europe, Coombs had "encouraging discussions" with Holtrop in the Netherlands, and Hubert Ansiaux in Belgium, and negotiated arrangements with the Belgians and the Dutch of $50 million each. But continuing dollar flows into Switzerland out of New York, and soon Canada, led Coombs back to Iklé, with whom he had taken on his earliest improvised efforts. Now, Coombs envisioned a swap of $200 million dollars, not the standing $50 million available to other European partners.

As Milton Gilbert, a former economic adviser to the BIS, describes, these swap lines were "imaginative tactical arrangements" created with great ease from informal and personal conversations rooted in "the spirit of trust and cooperation" that Coombs and his colleagues had developed through their "expertise and frankness."[82] Central bankers' ability to generate millions of dollars of international reserves inspired more ambitious plans in Coombs's mind. After his successful interactions with the French and the Swiss, Coombs spent the rest of the year in informal and private talks with his fellow central bankers in the rest of Europe and Canada. Walking in the shoes of Benjamin Strong, Coombs "embarked on a tour of European banks" to formalize these bilateral swap arrangements, which could be drawn by either party in the agreement, with little notice, and could be used for a wide range of purposes, such as propping up exchange rates or for liquidity provision.[83] By the end of 1962, Coombs had personally established swap lines with seven central banks in Europe as well as with the Bank of Canada, the Bank of Japan, and the BIS.

In doing so, Coombs was acting very much independently and not in line with the Federal Reserve Board. In a Joint Economic Committee Hearing in January 1962, Martin noted, the Fed "was not anxious to engage in this type of activity" and that these transactions needed to be "looked at on an ad hoc basis."[84] The FOMC, the main entity within the US Federal Reserve System tasked with all activities aimed at providing liquidity to the banking system, noted that these operations were "considered to be exploratory and experimental in nature." The committee found this arrangement to be "very new and radical." The Fed called on a Swiss witness to explain what it was doing.[85] In fact, on making these arrangements informally and privately, Coombs then had to convince the FOMC of their need and value.

In order to capitalize on this unique ability of central banks, it was important that central bankers could trust one another and have open discussions that facilitate such flexibility and informal assistance. Coombs recalls that through his visits to Basel and his own travel across Europe, he had got to know and trust many of his fellow central bankers. He recounts, "Officials of the German Federal Bank [the Bundesbank] had been quite explicit in indicating that they would not want a third party involved in the arrangement between the Bank and the Federal Reserve." These relations were important to maintaining a bilateral and ad hoc approach solely among partner central banks. As he told the FOMC, he also believed that this attitude "may have reflected in parts considerations of confidentiality and in part considerations of speed."[86]

For Coombs, the "professional understanding and personal friendship that quickly flowered" with his opposite numbers was what was so deeply satisfying in the "true camaraderie" of cooperation among central bankers.[87] It was vital for the New York Fed swap network that Coombs had created close personal relations with central bankers abroad and managed this system with the support of a small club of central bankers.[88] Even at the BIS, when discussing central banks' management of reserve assets, either through the Bank or even the IMF, central bankers noted the benefits of having different approaches and treatment of some countries, liking "the idea of a club of friends—'*on peut se permettre le luxe de certaines volies avec ces gen là* [we can afford the luxury of certain follies with these people].'"[89]

In the absence of a reliable and robust financial governance framework, these "*ad hoc* devices as central bank swap arrangements seemed to be patching up the world financial system with 'chewing gum and bailing wire,'" as described by many university economists who had little interest in the "ingenious scheme for creating world liquidity" engineered by central banks.[90] These arrangements grew into a large network of swap lines between the New York Fed and fourteen foreign central banks and the BIS, totaling $11.7 billion in foreign exchange reserves.[91] They resulted from "the close cooperation that has grown up among senior financial officials . . . supplementing older relationships through the IMF, and through bilateral contacts."[92]

As the supplier of the global reserve currency and therefore the primary transactions currency, bilateral financial assistance with the New York Fed was initially the primary form of cooperation. But it takes two to swap, and Coombs relied as much on his counterparts as they did on him and the Fed. This was because European currencies were only convertible to dollars and inconvertible to any other currency. As Coombs explained to Allan Sproul, a former president of the New York Fed, "The New York Bank has now become virtually the balance wheel of the international financial machinery."[93] Together with the BIS, the FRBNY stepped in to offer another option for liquidity and exchange rate management, facilitating an "array of short-term credit arrangements between central banks" to fend of speculative attacks on their currencies.[94]

Differentiated Ties: Distrust and Vouching at the Bank of England

Despite the ease of arranging bilateral swaps, and the low cost of these instruments to central banks, some central bankers in Europe were less enthusiastic about Coombs's scheme. Early on in Coombs's RCA endeavors, poor personal relations and a substantial lack of trust in Coombs and his swap program at the Bank of England hindered cooperation to arrange a Fed-Bank of England swap line. Where these ties were weaker or absent, such cooperation was more arduous, and arrangements significantly watered down. This was the fate of the Bank of England even though Britain and the United States had long enjoyed a special relationship, and the Bank of England was the New York Fed's closest foreign economic partner.

To offset the initial stumbling blocks in arranging a Fed swap with the Bank of England, the Basel Arrangements through mostly European central banks helped manage the pressures of gold and dollar drains on sterling. It was only later, when Cromer took over the Bank of England governorship that the Bank of England entered into a sterling-dollar arrangement to which they "agreed for the sake of good relations" with the Fed.[95] Still, a lack of trust and goodwill among other Bank of England staff and Coombs led to a much more limited swap line between the banks.

A closer look at the conversations and negotiations leading up to these arrangements highlights the conditions that allowed central banks to engage in such cooperation: trusted counterparts of Bank of England officials—Iklé and Tüngeler—who vouched for their successful interactions with Coombs to Cromer, and their trust in his plans, helped get a sterling-dollar swap line off the ground. Cromer played an integral role in overcoming the obstacles of poor relations between Bridge and Coombs, through his friendship with Alfred Hayes, president of the New York Fed, and Bill Martin, chairman of the Federal

Reserve Board. They emphasized the importance of secrecy in their interbank dealings, keeping their plans outside the political and the public view.

The Fed's emergence on the Basel scene had several Bank of England officials anxious, especially Bridge, who managed the Bank's international currency operations. Coombs and his European supporters, particularly Iklé and Tüngeler, helped push the idea of arranging central bank swaps between the Fed and partner banks at a BIS meeting in April 1961. Unlike Iklé and Tüngeler, with whom Coombs began his mission to engineer swap lines in Europe, the Bank of England was hesitant and turned down the offer. Bridge's lack of trust in Coombs delayed the Bank of England's inclusion in the Fed's swap network at its inception.[96]

Internal correspondence among Bank of England officials on the pilot sterling-dollar swap indicates that Bridge and his colleagues felt uneasy and threatened by the new American "arrival on the Basel and Paris scenes," which throughout 1961 and until 1962 highlighted Bridge's apprehension over Coombs and his plans.[97] In October 1961, Bridge wrote to his colleagues that the scheme "leaves little room for maneuver and could generate a lot of steam."[98] These concerns of overheating the economy and the artificial transactions engineered to manage sterling continued, as Bridge reiterated. He wrote to Maurice Parsons, then executive director at the Bank of England: "We ought to be reluctant to facilitate [the Fed's] using sterling in support of the dollar. . . . Coombs' proposal would produce an artificial increase to our reserve. . . . We do not want that."[99] And responding to Coombs's push for his swaps and gold schemes, Humphrey Mynors, deputy governor at the Bank of England, also expressed his own personal frustration at Coombs's agenda, writing, "As a bystander, I do not understand why so much attention is paid to the ideas of the unrepresentative and evanescent Coombs."[100]

But the unrepresentative and evanescent Coombs had interests much bigger than what his English colleagues anticipated. Coombs saw a need to arrange a reciprocal currency facility for last-minute emergency use and the best way to do this was a swap that "might conceivably involve an amount ranging up to $300 million."[101] Coombs met with Cromer in Basel and felt that the initial reception to his plan was "markedly sympathetic."[102] And when it came to arranging the line, it was Bridge who was sent to New York to deal with Coombs. Coombs mentions that "in British parlance" he "got a fairly dusty answer, not so much from Cromer as from some of his senior associates," sensing that Cromer's senior staff were suspicious of his plan despite his goodwill.[103]

This feeling is also evident in the Bank of England's records of the next Basel meeting, where it was noted that Coombs was "agitated at the lack of mutual trust between London and New York and cited some recent instances, including that the F.R.B.N.Y. were surprised that we did not like the form of the existing facility that they had given us [the Bank of England] and that they had accordingly reduced it by half thinking they were doing us a good turn."[104] At this time, Coombs learned that the British Treasury had "swung to much more ambitious schemes of converting the IMF into a largely automatic credit facility," which they had long seen as a last-resort option. And still, Bank of England associates deemed Coombs's swap proposal to be inadequate.[105]

In internal Bank correspondence, Bridge confirmed Coombs's assessment, explaining his reluctance in the matter to Parsons, saying he, Bridge, "had not yet come to trust" Coombs, throwing his plan off course.[106] Despite the long-standing political and economic partnership between the United States and the United Kingdom, and between their central banks, the lack of trust and friendship with Coombs at the Bank of England stifled the scope of cooperation through bilateral assistance between these bankers.

It was after "a certain amount of Anglo-American squabbling" that Bridge finally went to New York to discuss the swap. But the goodwill that Coombs counted on with his counterparts in Europe was missing. His hopes to arrange a swap of up to $300 million, which to many Bank of England associates seemed inadequate, was then negotiated down by Bridge to a much humbler $50 million.[107] Even this modest arrangement needed the supporting and vouching of Bank of England associates' trust partners on the continent. Ultimately, this swap line was not even drawn on when it expired in August 1961 and was liquidated and placed on standby.

What is especially interesting is that while senior associates at the Bank of England were so suspicious of Coombs's efforts, despite their success elsewhere in Europe, the Bank had entered into a similar agreement with Iklé in Switzerland in 1961—the one Bridge at first turned down. Once he had been convinced by Iklé of its merits after the revaluation of the German mark in 1961, the Bank of England was eventually "only too glad to accept" Iklé's offer of a three-month credit of $310 million.[108] Forrest Capie, a historian of the Bank of England, describes this moment as marking "the real turning point in central bank co-operation" for the Bank of England.[109] And given the SNB's initial resistance to Iklé's proposal to extend these swap lines, Iklé noted that he managed to get Schwegler's approval on a car journey from Zurich to Berne. Until then, Schwegler had been less enthusiastic about the SNB's engagement in international operations[110]

This agreement among the banks was first reached informally between Iklé and Parsons. Parsons wrote that "during the course of our conversation in Basel on Monday on the subject of the arrangement of a dollar deposit by the Banque Nationale Suisse with the Bank of England" Iklé had raised the question of "the free availability of these dollars" in the event that the SNB wished to call them. Iklé asked Parsons for some assurance that he "need have no fears that they will be blocked by Government action." Parsons responded that he was unable to give Iklé any "formal assurance on behalf of Her Majesty's Government." But in his view, "it was inconceivable that, short of the existence of a state of war between Switzerland and the United Kingdom, any action would be taken by Her Majesty's Government to interfere with [Switzerland's] rights to withdraw these dollars at any time you pleased."[111]

It was only then, following successful cooperation with the SNB, and on hearing affirmative words from Iklé and a similar vote of confidence from Tüngeler about their cooperation in the Fed's swap and currency intervention operations, vouching for Coombs and his plan, that Bridge and others at the Bank of England were swayed by Cromer to reconsider the Fed swap proposal. Cromer wrote to his associates, including Bridge and Parsons, "I ought also to record that both Iklé and Tüngeler in private conversation with me were insistent that their experience with the [New York] Federal in the matter of intervention. At no time had the Federal acted in the Market without advising the Bundesbank or the Swiss National Bank beforehand and, indeed, on most occasions had actually acted on the advice of the other Central Bank."[112]

Only then was Bridge convinced by Coombs's scheme and began to trust his word. In his memo on the "American Ideas for Strengthening the International Exchange Structure," Bridge closely evaluated how these "two-way credit facilities" were for use "in times of need."[113] In justifying the plan to his fellow associates, Bridge explained, "They have got arrangements of one kind or another lined up with the Germans, Swiss, Italians, and French. They now make certain proposals to us. . . . They stress however that while attaching—for obvious reasons—great importance to some arrangement with us they would not wish to press us to participate in any arrangement with which we are not in sympathy. I believe this protestation to be completely honest."[114]

Getting the Fed-Bank of England swap line off the ground was in no small part the doing of Cromer, and his predecessor, Cobbold, who left the bank "just after he had helped inaugurate the epoch of central bank co-operation through exchange swaps."[115] Cromer, who Coombs described as "enterprising and decisive," later suggested a "ten-fold increase" of the dollar-sterling swap to $500 million, in 1963, which Coombs "heartily welcomed" when the pound was again hit by heavy sales. But Cobbold before Cromer had not been convinced by this scheme. Cromer created support for the swap line among his colleagues by appealing to Iklé and Tüngeler. At that time, British financial relations with the United States had hit several rough patches and "increasing bitterness," due to the repeated sterling crises in the 1950s and 1960s and regular calls for American support.[116] Cromer played a key role in navigating these intergovernmental disagreements through his diplomatic connections in Washington, DC, before returning to London.

Still, the ease of arranging a swap as significant and sizable as Coombs had imagined had initially been hindered by the absence of closer friendship and goodwill between the foreign department leaders in London and New York. While the agreement did eventually get off the ground, once vouched for by Iklé and Tüngeler, the eventual agreement made was still much smaller than was necessary, negotiated down by Bridge from $300 million to $50 million.

In 1961, while Coombs was attempting to garner support for a Fed swap, British and American officials squabbled over sterling's woes. Eventually, the Treasury was forced to turn to the IMF to negotiate a drawing of $1,500 million to repay previous multilateral credits. But these early programs proved to only provide stopgap solutions to sterling's woes. The pound had come under crisis in 1961 following the revaluation of the deutsche mark and again in 1963. Both crises, as discussed above, were arrested with support packages arranged bilaterally with central banks.

From Cromer to O'Brien: Sterling Support, 1964–1967

At the Bank of England, Cromer's governorship similarly "covers the key years of central bank co-operation" in a way that proved hard to engineer in his absence.[117] Although this era was initiated by Cobbold just as Cromer assumed office, the close relations that Cromer had fostered in the United States were crucial for Britain's participation in the network of central bank support of the 1960s. Like Coombs and Iklé, Cromer's influence in facilitating the Bank of England's participation in the RCA was significant for many reasons. Most crucially, it was pivotal for maintaining sterling stability during the 1960s, when sterling faced repeated crises of confidence and credibility, especially between 1964 and 1967. Cromer's influence at the Bank, his ability to stave off political interference, and his close ties with Martin at the Federal Reserve helped secure financing to prop up the sterling peg. Capie suggests, "Perhaps Cromer's main contribution as Governor was his skillful use of central bank contacts in raising financial support when confidence in sterling was low."[118] Indeed, these efforts gave way to sterling's eventual devaluation in 1967, soon after Cromer left the Bank.

Cromer had spent much of his career in Washington, DC, where he developed close bonds with high-level officials at the Fed. It was fortunate that the apparently less personable Sir Oliver Franks, who had been offered the governorship to succeed Cobbold, turned down the job. Cromer was seen as "a congenial man, unfailingly courteous and considerate, and seemingly incapable of dissembling."[119] Cromer could and did capitalize on his personal relations. Cromer and Hayes in New York shared a "friendship that quickly developed" and was "communicated down the line, and cooperation between their two banks became the order of the day."[120] Franks, on the other hand, had a "rather cold personality" and did "not automatically exude bonhomie," which may have discouraged fellow bankers from talking freely with him. A close associate of the Bank called Franks "the dullest of dogs, a bum-faced purveyor of last year's platitudes."

After a brief lull in pressures on the pound, sterling came under fire again in 1964. Soon after, the Labor government was elected in 1964. Labor's election stoked fears of Britain's growing balance of payments deficits, and the Bank of England was slow to respond. There had already been talk of devaluation earlier in 1964, but it was not clear that such a policy would provide more than passing relief. These fears triggered a second sterling crisis that followed only weeks after the first. But the new government did not devalue. Instead, the 1964 sterling crisis was again responded to by Cromer and his counterparts through bilateral central bank arrangements. Cromer squabbled with Britain's new prime minister, Harold Wilson, who opposed any increase in the bank rate to alleviate speculative pressures. Wilson and Cromer did not like or respect one another. For Wilson, Cromer was "a right-wing reactionary in Labor circles, in the direct line of descent from Montagu Norman." Cromer called Wilson "slippery and unsound." Their antagonism did not help Britain's circumstances, and the crisis escalated quickly and peaked on November 24.

In the face of these troubles, Coombs learned that the Bank of England was losing reserves at "the rate of $1 million per minute" and that all credit facilities with the IMF and the Bank's swap line with the Fed had been exhausted. Cromer told the chancellor that the crisis was worsening because of a lack of confidence in the government's policies. All that time, Cromer had also been in constant communication with his counterparts across the continent and with Martin and Coombs. At 7 p.m. on November 24, a $3 billion rescue package of swap lines with eleven central banks was announced, which was achieved "largely at the personal initiative of the Governor" along with Coombs, who had similarly called on the support of his central bank contacts and had also managed to get the support of his own bank for this arrangement.[121] But Cromer knew this was a short-term fix and would not suffice in restoring confidence. He was right. Reserve losses recommenced and continued through to the start of the new year, followed by a few quiet months in 1965.

While the crises of 1964 had abated, fears of pressures on sterling, and concerns that the pound was overvalued, remained. That year, at the initiative of the government, the Bank took a range of measures, including exchange and investment controls. Cromer was not confident that these measures would work for confidence beyond providing moderate relief, nor was he confident that they would work in a crisis. And that crisis was only months away.

Cromer wanted to keep all options to discussions among central banks only and did not say anything to the chancellor or the government. In August 1965, Cromer told Martin in the United States that "things were not encouraging," and so Martin felt that something needed to be done to "reverse the psychological malaise in which sterling now found itself."[122] Martin broached the possibility that the Fed could float up to $2 billion with European assistance but without the possibility of renewal.

At this time, US president, Lyndon Johnson, expressed his frustration and lack of faith in the British administration to Martin, pushing him to "abandon sterling," "protect the dollar and let [the British] go their own way."[123] Martin had also lost confidence in sterling but did not share Johnson's ire toward Wilson and his government, and especially not toward Cromer. Johnson described the situation as "I have this feeling that just like a reckless boy that goes off and gets drunk and writes checks on his father, and he can honor 2 or 3 or 4 of them and finally [you] call him in and just tell him, now we've got to work this out where you live off what you're making . . . and if you don't I can't come to your rescue any more and he just goes on and ignores it and writes another one. Now the time is come that we've got to turn him down."[124] But while Martin shared Johnson's concerns, he was opposed to devaluation and sought to support Cromer.

Cromer and Martin, however, were friendly and trusted one another, as Cromer did with Hayes in New York. Together, while Johnson and Wilson's disagreement and dispute over sterling's troubles continued, Martin and Cromer devised the "Cromer-Martin Plan" to support sterling through central banks and the BIS. Cromer also requested an enlargement of its swap lines with the Fed and at Basel. Martin and Cromer were keenly aware "of the risks of political abuse of central bank credits" and were eager to limit cooperation to central bank support.[125] With the support of Henry Fowler of the US Treasury, all of the European banks and the BIS, who had participated in the 1964 sterling arrangement, once again sought to cobble together another round of sterling assistance. Coombs, Leslie O'Brien (now deputy governor of the Bank of England), and Bridge sought support from Iklé, Tüngeler, Carli, and others. It seemed that all were on board following a host of informal lunches and phone calls among the central bankers.

Once they all got to Basel in September 1965, it seemed as though many central bankers now found themselves at the end of their patience to support sterling yet again. In an acrimonious meeting, Coombs pressed his European counterparts to sign up for a new credit agreement to Britain.[126] But the Wilson government had interfered in the central bankers' plans, which had the effect of pushing prospective participants away. France withdrew, and others reduced their commitments to the sterling arrangement. The final arrangements were made largely by Coombs, who ran most of the negotiations with Europe. Cromer, Martin, and Hayes could not alleviate their counterparts' suspicions; Martin honored the Fed's share of the plan, and forthcoming sterling support was announced, with little information about who participated and overall amounts. It had the intended psychological effects, however, and funds flowed back into London.[127]

But once again, this temporary fix proved to be just that, and sterling's troubles were still not behind them. By the end of 1965, the next stage of sterling's crisis decade was brewing, and the Basel facilities available to the Bank of England were to expire in March 1966. By the middle of the year, when sterling was again under fire, Fowler tasked Coombs to put "together a $1 billion 'war chest to defeat a possible bear raid on sterling during September.'"[128]

Important leadership changes had taken place in 1966. This stage of the crisis was now under a new governor of the Bank of England. Cromer's appointment ended in 1966, and on July 1, O'Brien, who had been his deputy since 1964, took over. During his tenure, Cromer had reshuffled roles among high-level officials at the Bank in 1964. Humphrey Mynors, who had served as deputy governor with Cromer, retired. Prior to taking on the position of governor, O'Brien had been placed in charge of *domestic* issues, while Parsons had taken up the international front, which had important implications for when Cromer departed the Bank two years later.

Important political changes had also occurred. By the mid-1960s, Anglo-American political relations had soured, despite their deep economic and financial ties, as well as political alliance in the Cold War era. Monetary tensions between the United States and United Kingdom in fact exacerbated emerging political tensions that eroded this traditionally special, interstate partnership.[129] Wilson and Johnson parted ways over the war in Vietnam and heightened economic tensions as the United States supported sterling through its troubles early in the 1960s. Still, it was very much in the American interest also that sterling was not devalued, as the two international currencies (the other being the dollar) were deeply interconnected.

When O'Brien came into office, talk of the prospect of sterling's collapse had grown in the public and in the media. The *Observer* reported, "The sooner sterling topples, the better."[130] All through July 1966, the Bank lost almost $1 billion in reserves, some of which it secretly financed with its Fed swaps and Basel credits. Bridge wrote to O'Brien two weeks days after he took office: "The smell of the start of another crisis—like November 1964 or March or July/August 1965—is unmistakable."[131] O'Brien was also opposed to devaluation, as was Cromer before him. But it seemed as though the mood was changing among higher-ups in the Bank that its possibility ought to be promoted from an "unthinkable last resort" to an "explicit possible policy."[132]

O'Brien took up Cromer's efforts to secure cooperative assistance from Martin and his counterparts in Europe. Fowler supported O'Brien's effort to secure $3 billion, and "talks with Fowler . . . got off to a good start." He was favorable to O'Brien's plan, which was essentially a repeat of the Martin-Cromer plan from 1965. Fowler advised Johnson that the risks of devaluation to the United States were just too great, and devaluation was "desirable only if the devaluation were modest, if others didn't follow, if Wilson was also able to keep up his military commitments overseas, if the government didn't fall and, finally, if inflationary pressures didn't undermine the impact."[133]

But O'Brien could not muster up the support of central bankers in Europe, who had now refused to even hold guaranteed sterling. Instead of providing bilateral credits, they prescribed that O'Brien went instead to the IMF's GAB for the full $3 billion standby arrangement. This would use up most of the IMF's coffers, making it difficult for the United States to borrow anything before sterling was finished. But before both US or British Treasury officials, "who negotiated vigorously" with central bankers and the IMF to secure an arrangement, Wilson decided on November 13, 1967, that sterling would be devalued. The US Treasury officials, who now feared a speculative attack on the dollar would follow, amped up their efforts with the support of British civil servants to "persuade continentals to cooperate in securing something" in the days that followed. After an arduous four days, it seemed as though a short-term credit was in sight, with support from Italy and Germany. But this agreement came too little too late, and by the evening of November 17, it was announced that sterling was to be devalued from $2.80 to $2.40.

Under Cromer, the Bank could resist political pressure, and instead put pressure on governments by warning or threatening them over their policy decisions. He saw great value in the short-term central bank credits and the flexibility of having them available on standby. These views were important for garnering support for the swap network among his colleagues.[134]

On Cromer's departure in 1966, the intense ad hoc cooperation in which the Bank actively engaged "began to fade" when he was no longer around to manage market and political pressures on sterling and the currency system.[135] Sterling's crisis and eventual devaluation occurred alongside political disputes at the intergovernmental level between Britain and the United States, and each crisis was progressively worse than the previous. But there was nonetheless also a remarkable difference in the Bank of England's ability to secure support for sterling under Cromer and O'Brien, suggesting again that leadership changes can contribute to changes in outcomes of liquidity assurance through ad hoc and bilateral assistance in times of crisis.

The Patchwork Frays

Midcentury central bank cooperation was both a reflection of central bankers in the past and a glimpse into the future. The Basel Arrangements and the Federal Reserve swap network are reminiscent of the cooperative efforts of the 1920s. These improvised efforts to create money out of thin air were already part of central banks' toolkits in the post–Second World War era. Central bankers relied on their personal relations with each other to support partner banks in maintaining currency pegs and provided liquidity to do so. IMF facilities were decidedly last resort options which central bankers actively sought to avoid. They turned instead to ad hoc arrangements to maintain stability and prolong the life of the Bretton Woods system.

Although most central banks were not independent during this time, key practices and methods from the interwar days remained intact. First, central bankers' informal and personal relations, correspondences, and interactions greased the wheels of the global financial system. Second, their distance from politics affected how some central bankers viewed their professions, duties, and their colleagues. Finally, aided by the privacy of the BIS, central bankers continued to cooperate with one another on a personal level, behind closed doors and outside the public eye.

Central banks used instruments that mirrored the bilateral and ad hoc credits used all through the 1920s, but in a different international monetary system under the gold-dollar standard. It was therefore not entirely certain that these instruments would work similarly and as effectively in this new postwar climate, as Martin and other central bankers highlighted early in the 1960s. Thus, although bilateral swaps and credits had not left central banks' toolkits since the interwar period, central bankers understood this as a policy innovation.

At the heart of the Basel Arrangements first created in 1961 were important trusting, trust-building, and reciprocal relationships between Coombs in New York and his counterparts Carli and Tüngeler in Italy and Germany. Iklé played a crucial role in laying the foundation of the Basel Arrangements network, which was only possible with his and Cobbold's support. Soon, these lines expanded to incorporate the New York Fed. To make these arrangements, it was essential that Coombs was able to circumvent restrictions on the Fed's ability to enter these arrangements.

Where personal affinities were less trusting and friendly, and central bankers did not share interpersonal relations of trust and goodwill, swaps were harder to arrange and were ultimately watered down as well. This was the case of cooperation between Coombs and the Bank of England, where several associates distrusted and were wary of Coombs's endeavors in Europe. As a result, the initial swap line between New York and London took longer to get off the ground and was ultimately much smaller than Coombs had hoped. Interestingly, Iklé's proposal, of a much larger credit, while initially rejected was quickly taken up in the proposed capacity the year before.

In joining BIS meetings, Coombs broke with the long American tradition of not officially participating in the institution. Iklé similarly broke with tradition of the SNB in staying out of such policy areas as his predecessor, Schwegler, had done. Moreover, the BIS played a critical role in providing central bankers privacy and insulation from political interference to undertake their operations, even when many central banks did not enjoy statutory independence from governments and treasuries as they had in the past.

All in all, the troubles of the Bretton Woods era were patched up using ad hoc efforts, which were short-term fixes (and viewed to be such). Ad hoc governance innovation that emerged through interpersonal channels played a meaningful role in shaping outcomes of bilateral and ad hoc cooperation throughout the 1960s to delay the inevitable demise that Triffin had predicted.

Eventually, however, the international monetary system succumbed to the absence of any fundamental remedies for its underlying fault lines and imbalances. In 1967, sterling's devaluation was not welcomed in the United States, and as predicted, gold sales and speculative attacks made their way to the dollar. Within weeks, the United States suffered "the most severe monetary crisis" that it had faced until then in the postwar period.[136] Devaluation also did not end Britain's financial problems, or its difficulties in fending off speculative attacks. Instead, the sterling crises evolved into larger and more severe dollar crises after 1968. Persistent uncertainty and speculative attacks in the years that followed impaired central bank cooperation and ultimately led to President Nixon's unilateral decision to close the gold window on August 15, 1971, prompting the collapse of the Bretton Woods system and a pivot toward a new system of fiat currency.

Why the system collapsed has been documented and thoroughly debated in a large scholarly literature.[137] Explaining the collapse of the Bretton Woods monetary system is not the goal of this chapter. Instead, I have demonstrated that to cooperatively kick the Triffin dilemma can down the road, Coombs at the New York Fed relied on his personal relations with his European counterparts, as did European central bankers in Basel with each other.

The Hardy Perennial

The years immediately after the Nixon shock were some of unprecedented volatility. The 1970s were marked by energy crises, stagflation, and conflict. The economic boom of the early 1970s stirred up enormous inflationary pressures in the United States and elsewhere in Europe. Inflationary pressures came alongside the end of decades of growth and expansion after 1945, bringing on a period of stagflation across much of the West.[138]

As is well known, these economic troubles were exacerbated by war and oil politics when Arab oil countries that made up the Organization of Petroleum Exporting Countries (OPEC) announced an embargo on countries that supported Israel during the 1973 Arab-Israeli War and raised oil prices, further increasing inflation by 1974. The first energy crisis was shortly followed by the second oil shock in 1979, after the Iranian Revolution, and further aggravated with the Iran-Iraq War in 1980.

The oil shocks triggered grave crises as oil-importing countries accumulated debts that they could not pay, and oil exporters accumulated large amounts of dollars. These petro-dollars were recycled through foreign banks, which were then loaned to governments especially of oil-importing countries to finance their payments deficits. Much of this financing was used to buy oil and pay for other imports, perpetuating this recycling. Many of these countries were seen as good loan prospects in the 1960s and 1970s. By the early 1980s, the governments of Mexico, Brazil, Argentina, and many others started to find that they could not service their debts.

The Latin American debt crises were followed by another decade of crisis in emerging markets, including the Mexican peso crisis of 1994 and the East Asian crises in 1997. As discussed in the introduction to this book, I do not deal with these crises because the types of evidence necessary to identify a link between interpersonal relations of trust and the likelihood of ad hoc lending (versus multilateral options), such as records of correspondence between central bank leaders or firsthand interview accounts, are unavailable or insufficient.

As Kindleberger observed, financial crises are "a hardy perennial"; they are an inevitable part of economic life.[139] The road to the global financial crisis (GFC) was peppered with crises, now largely in emerging and developing countries. The East Asian crisis was followed by a currency crisis in Russia in 1998, a debt crisis in Argentina in 2001, and the bursting of the dot-com bubble just a few years before policymakers in the United States, Europe, and soon most of the world were once again put to the test, when the GFC began in 2007.

4

THIS TIME IS DIFFERENT?

Crisis and Cooperation in the Twenty-First Century

In 2008, the global economy faced its worst crisis since the Great Depression. The crisis began in 2007, and soon, global markets were on the brink of a repeat of the crisis of the 1930s. In response, the United States Federal Reserve (the Fed), stepped in as an international lender of last resort (ILLR), injecting nearly $600 billion in emergency liquidity into the global economy through a selective series of central bank currency swaps with fourteen partners. The European Central Bank, the Bank of England, the Bank of Japan, the Swiss National Bank, and the People's Bank of China followed suit, albeit at a much smaller scale, and largely localized (with the exception of China). These efforts were critical in providing liquidity to prevent another Great Depression, a crisis that was "at its core a failure of central banking."[1]

Swaps are bilateral currency exchanges between central banks; but implicitly, the Fed was providing dollars to partner banks. The Fed itself did not *need* euros, pounds, or any other currency; its counterparts needed dollars. Fed swaps were essentially the highest-quality loans available, at very favorable terms: no conditionality. These lines emerged rapidly, to bolster domestic rescue efforts, and provided critical fixes for the inadequacies of the global financial governance system.[2] The global swap network has since evolved into a key feature of the global financial safety net (GFSN), and five of the Fed's fourteen swap lines were made permanent in 2013. Fed swaps again proved to be a vital liquidity backstop in March 2020, to manage the financial fallout of the COVID-19 pandemic.

The series of banking failures that began in August 2007 emerged in a manner that threatened to emulate its 1930s predecessor. But unlike the Depression, this crisis catalyzed a concerted response from central banks that some economists suggest "generated one of the most notable examples of central bank cooperation in history—the large swap lines set up between a number of central banks."[3] As one financial journalist, Neil Irwin, described it, "Over two continents, five years, thousands of conference calls, and trillions of dollars, euros and pounds deployed to rescue the world's financial system, central bankers would take the primary role in grappling with the global panic that began in earnest on August 9, 2007. They would act with a speed and on a scale that presidents and parliaments could never seem to muster. Over the next half decade, Jean-Claude Trichet, Ben Bernanke, and Mervyn King would create the world to come."[4]

Why and how were central banks able to cooperate to avert a second Great Depression following the banking panics in 2007, a task that seemed out of reach in the 1930s? In this chapter, I explore the individual and interpersonal dynamics underlying this unprecedented central bank cooperation. Once again, interpersonal trust guided central bankers toward cooperative solutions to manage the crisis. The Fed swap network emerged alongside a slew of domestic unilateral rescue efforts, as well as multilateral interventions and coordinated policy adjustment. The emergence of the swap network within this broader realm of rescue packages, however, was seen as most surprising and unprecedented. It is this unexpected outcome that this chapter explains.

I examine central bank cooperation during the crisis and problematize the manner in which the Fed swap network emerged to manage liquidity pressures. I argue that key central bank leaders and their personal relationships played a central role in facilitating the creation of the Fed swap network, an outcome that was neither automatic nor obvious. Understanding how these arrangements emerged and evolved into critical crisis-management tools today is essential for deepening our understanding of the robustness and durability of the global financial safety net.

We meet a new cast of characters who found themselves at the center of the financial crisis. A key figure in this story is the chair of the Federal Reserve Board, Benjamin S. Bernanke, working alongside the vice chair Donald Kohn, and after 2009, the president of the New York Fed, Timothy Geithner. Their counterparts in Europe—Jean-Claude-Trichet, president of the European Central Bank (ECB), and Mervyn King, governor of the Bank of England—as well as Masaaki Shirakawa, governor of the Bank of Japan, played central roles in the coordinated financial rescue efforts deployed by central banks. I also introduce Davíð Oddsson, governor of the Central Bank of Iceland, as well as central bank leaders in emerging market economies, such as Guillermo Ortiz Martínez of the Bank of Mexico, Duvvuri Subbarao at the Reserve Bank of India, and Henrique Meirelles at the Central Bank of Brazil, among other key players.

Because central bankers' communications today take place via the phone or email, I cannot rely on evidence from central bankers' personal and formal exchanges during this period. Instead, I offer new, firsthand insights on the crisis-management and cooperative effort from these leaders. I present evidence collected through elite interviews that I conducted with former leaders of major central banks during the global financial crisis (GFC), including Bernanke, King, Shirakawa, Trichet, and Subbarao, along with several deputies and central bank associates and staffers. I also provide interview evidence from central bank and finance ministry officials in Indonesia, Singapore, Brazil, and Iceland, who wish to remain anonymous. I triangulate this evidence with transcripts of Federal Open Market Committee (FOMC) meetings and journalistic reports during the crisis.

Using this novel empirical material, I join the extensive debates in economics and political science to explain patterns of cooperation during the crisis. As in the historical chapters, conventional accounts of interstate economic and financial ties, economic power and significance, cooperation through international institutions, and shared policy preferences and economic beliefs provide important baseline explanations for this outcome of crisis management. However, as I show, several questions around the Fed's selection of swap recipients remain unanswered.

Next, I describe the economic and political context of the GFC and provide a brief primer on the crisis from its outbreak and the domestic crisis management efforts in the United States that followed. I then turn to the relational dynamics underlying the creation of the Fed's swap network among a few advanced economies. Here, I show that bilateral cooperation among central bankers in the Global North, while less surprising, emerged through interpersonal and informal channels first, rather than through formal institutional channels, as they quickly but quietly arranged the earliest swap lines in December 2007. I also show that stronger and weaker personal ties in part explain variation in liquidity assistance available to countries that requested swaps from the Fed, with a focus on Mexico, with brief discussions on Brazil and Singapore. I also draw attention to Iceland, India, and very briefly Indonesia, whose swap requests were denied by the Fed.

Global Finance in the New Millennium

The crisis emerged in an economic and political context very distinct to the interwar and midcentury years. This was not a world of postwar reconstruction and rehabilitation, although the United States was engaged in its own wars in the Middle East, which shaped public spending, deficits, and debt. The means chosen to finance the US military buildup for the Iraq and Afghanistan wars fueled an economic boom and a housing bubble that eventually burst.[5] But the aughts were not marred by reparations battles and efforts to rebuild the global economy after a global war.

The collapse of the Bretton Woods gold-dollar system in 1971 brought on the current fiat money system of mostly floating exchange rates. The US dollar remained the key global reserve currency. Access to dollar liquidity therefore remained a primary concern for the rest of the world. The system's functioning is shaped primarily by the United States and a handful of Western European economies. But the world had changed in ways that distinguish the contemporary era from the past. First, the arrival of a unified Europe with a common currency, the euro, and the European Central Bank. And second, the rise of new major players—China, India, Mexico, Brazil—has brought about a consequential shift in the global balance of power. Financial globalization and market integration had increased both interdependence and vulnerability of national economies to pressures overseas.

The global economic governance system, the rules that regulate the global economy, and the institutions that enforce them had evolved and expanded. Today, the task of large international financial institutions (IFIs) is to coordinate global action.[6] Since the 1980s and 1990s, many central banks have gained de jure independence from governments to avoid short-term political interference in monetary policy decisions.

The central banking profession has also changed. John Singleton notes, "Central bankers in the early twentieth century knew little, if anything, about economics." This could not be less true today.[7] Central bankers today tend to be trained academic economists. How they engage with their counterparts, and how frequently they do so, has also evolved. They have moved away from the detailed and personal letter-writing of the past. However, technological advancements in travel and telecommunications mean that it no longer takes days or hours to communicate, but seconds. Central bankers are now in more frequent and instant contact than their predecessors.

Together, these changes make for a context very different to that of the gold standard or the Bretton Woods years, and were consequential for the outbreak, nature, and resolution of the GFC. Troubles in one part of the world, and especially in the United States, are even harder to contain to national borders today than in the past. International pressures called for an international response. Fortunately, the speed with which policymakers could communicate and the frequency with which they met facilitated rapid and coordinated responses from central banks as the crisis broke.

The Crisis Unfolds

Early in 2007, New Century Financial Corp., a company specialized in mortgage lending to cash-poor homebuyers in the United States, disclosed that many of its borrowers had started defaulting on payments. By March, its stock price had collapsed to $3.21 (from $15 earlier that year, which was already down by half its value). The company had declared it would stop making new loans, and it was now in need of emergency financing. In April, New Century Financial filed for bankruptcy. In the following months, large numbers of private-label mortgage-backed securities were downgraded to high risk and several subprime lending companies closed up shop. Dropping demand for housing fueled speculation of further house-price declines. Many subprime borrowers could not sell their homes to pay off their mortgages.

On August 9, 2007, a large French bank, BNP Paribas, suspended withdrawals from three investment funds that it managed. These funds were deeply invested in US securities markets, especially in mortgage-backed securities. In the next month, German banks faced collapse and were rescued. Bank failures in Europe peaked when Northern Rock PLC, a mortgage issuer in England, faced a cash crunch, as mortgage securities markets had become toxic. These bank failures were also associated with investments tied to the US subprime mortgage market.

As troubles emerged, central banks, governments, and monetary authorities were once again faced with a host of policy options to resolve immediate, local pressures and bank failures unilaterally, as well as through multilateral policy coordination.

The ECB was quick to intervene as a lender of last resort in the euro area. The Fed, eager to signal that it was on the same page as the ECB, released a statement that it was prepared to provide the necessary "liquidity to facilitate the orderly functioning of financial markets."[8] The central banks of Canada and Japan also intervened to manage liquidity pressures. The Fed cut interest rates just ten days after the BNP Paribas episode. On September 13, the Bank of England announced emergency support for Northern Rock, and the next day, depositors withdrew £1 billion, triggering the largest bank run in England in a century. Northern Rock was eventually nationalized, and the government took steps to guarantee depositors' savings.

The problems faced by European banks soon returned to their place of origin. In Europe and the United States, large financial institutions such as UBS, Citigroup, and Merrill Lynch announced losses and exposure to bad debts, all associated with subprime mortgages. By the end of January 2008, a credit crunch had hit the world's richest countries and global stock markets faced their largest falls since September 11, 2001.

The crisis was punctuated with an onslaught of emergency financial packages and unilateral measures across national economies to rescue domestic banking sectors. These interventions came from central banks, with support from their governments.

Beginning in September 2007, the Fed and the ECB established a slew of bailout programs and began cutting interest rates dramatically. The Fed lowered the funds rate for its lending facilities by three-quarters of a percentage point to 3.5 percent, its largest rate cut in a quarter of a century. On March 7, 2008, it announced the release of $30 billion in a twenty-eight-day credit facility on March 10 and 24 through the Term Auction Facility (TAF), a new method to help sound banks acquire funds that they could lend on to consumers and businesses, which had been established in December 2007 and lasted through March 2010.[9] This facility was established alongside the first round of central bank currency swaps with the ECB and the SNB.[10] Until March 2008, the Fed tried to keep liquidity in financial markets, lending $200 billion to bail out bond dealers, who were stuck with toxic mortgage-backed securities and collateralized debt obligations.

The toppling of big banks culminated with Bear Stearns's collapse in the United States and was declared functionally bankrupt.[11] And although it was not regulated by the Fed and did not have access to the Fed's emergency assistance, its collapse would devastate financial markets. As a result, the Fed invoked its emergency authority under the Federal Reserve Act 13(3) to provide liquidity to "any individual, partnership, or corporation" in "unusual and exigent circumstances."[12] It then further lowered interest rates to 2.75 percent, halving the Fed funds rate within a six-month period.

After what seemed like a lull in the crisis, and signs suggesting that the worst was over, troubles hit Fannie Mae and Freddie Mac, two federally backed mortgage companies, in mid-2008. Both institutions continued to suffer large losses and were placed into conservatorship amid the subprime mortgage crisis. Large British banks such as HSBC and HBOS revealed sinking profits, and house prices across the United Kingdom fell rapidly. The financial system that had been breaking down slowly now crumbled all at once. By the autumn of 2008, Lehman Brothers felt the pressures that had got to Bear Stearns some months before; on September 15, 2008, when the Fed had no legal way to hand over money to save Lehman, Lehman filed for bankruptcy.[13] The same day, Merrill Lynch was purchased by Bank of America.

Amid the uncertainty, an excess of toxic assets and a systemic credit crunch, global dollar liquidity continued to collapse (see figure 4.1). Banks found it difficult to lend to one another. Worse, they could not lend to ordinary people.[14] Banks' assets were now considerably less valuable, if valuable at all, than when they had bought them. So, the Fed and US Treasury created a series of programs

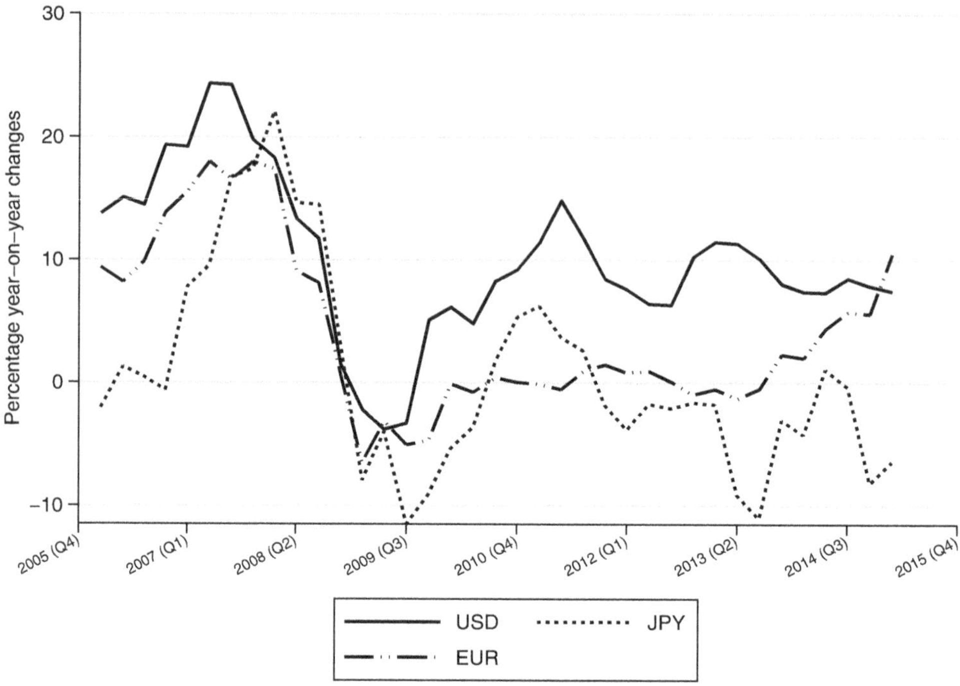

FIGURE 4.1. Global Liquidity Indicators (Quarterly), 2006–2014. Percentage year-on-year changes, in Euro, Yen, and US dollars. Source: BIS Statistics.

to strengthen domestic market stability and enhance market liquidity. That December, the Fed announced it was to lower its benchmark interest rate further to zero for the first time since the Great Depression. But, as central banks exhausted their monetary policy discretion, they could no longer lean solely on their go-to unilateral tools.

This was no ordinary credit crunch. The collapse of money and credit was systemic and had made its way abroad. Dollar funding strains became significant problems in Europe, the United Kingdom, and Japan. Norway had moved to protect its domestic banking system, while the highly leveraged Icelandic banking sector was inches from collapse. The problem was a lack of capital. They all needed help. For governments, arranging large packages was politically difficult to justify. And even had that not been the case, they would have still taken weeks to arrange. Across the world, national economies needed money to free up lending.

As the crisis worsened, Daniel Drezner argues that "despite initial shocks that were more severe than the 1929 financial crisis," the global financial governance system of formal and informal rules and institutions "responded quickly and robustly." In other words, the system worked.[15] International organizations such as the International Monetary Fund (IMF), the Group of 20 (G20), and central banks were revitalized to respond in an "effective and nimble fashion."[16]

Others argue that the role of this system is exaggerated—the IMF's resources fell short, and the G20 did little to bolster the Fund's capacity to meet the global demand for loans at the worst point of the crisis.[17] Two of the most significant rescue measures emerged out of international cooperation between central banks. One is the first ever coordinated interest rate cut in October 2008. The Fed, the Bank of Canada, the ECB, the BoE, and the Sveriges Riksbank (in Sweden) all cut their primary lending rates by half a percentage point. The Swiss National Bank also cut rates. The Bank of Japan publicly endorsed the move. This coordinated rate cut gets the most attention as an act of unity among central bankers and made front-page news the day after it was announced. Despite this fanfare, the move had at best a modest effect on calming markets.

A more significant cooperative step was extension of liquidity swap lines by several major central bankers, led by the Fed. These steps were unprecedented in their amounts and their coordination.[18] This program was neither an automatic nor an obvious policy response but rather symbolized the adage that situations of such gravity called for "outside the box" thinking.[19]

The largest swap network was established by the Fed, which extended bilateral currency swaps to a select fourteen central banks and is the focus of this chapter. The Fed essentially expanded the size of its balance sheet to deploy this program, and it was the institution's single largest crisis-fighting effort during the GFC.[20] The first lines were set up in December 2007 and continued through 2010, peaking with the largest swap amount of USD$170.93 billion to the ECB on October 2008. The Fed alone injected over half a trillion dollars of liquidity using these instruments. The Bank of Japan also extended dollar swaps to a few partner economies such as India or Indonesia, who experienced dollar shortages but did not receive a swap line from the Fed. South Korea received dollar swaps from both the Fed and the Bank of Japan. A euro network and a Swiss franc network also emerged. Of course, euro-denominated loans outside of the euro area were far fewer than those denominated in US dollars. Euro-denominated reserves made up about a fourth of world reserve holdings as opposed to two-thirds of world holdings being denominated in dollars.[21] Poland, Hungary, and the ECB received SNB swaps.[22] The People's Bank of China swap network emerged in 2009 and has since proliferated in its size and global reach. Using these swap lines, central banks injected trillions of dollars and euros into the global economy during the GFC between 2007 and 2010.

My study focuses on the swap network provided by the Fed, setting aside other central bank swap networks, such as those provided by the ECB or China. This is because, as was the case for the crises of the 1980s and 1990s, the kind of evidence

TABLE 4.1 Federal Reserve bilateral swap agreements, 2007–2010

SWAP REQUEST	INITIAL SIGNING	TERMS
European Central Bank	December 2007	Unconditional
Switzerland	December 2007	Unconditional
Canada	September 2008	Unconditional
United Kingdom	September 2008	Unconditional
Japan	September 2008	Unconditional
Australia	September 2008	Unconditional
Denmark	September 2008	Unconditional
Norway	September 2008	Unconditional
Sweden	September 2008	Unconditional
New Zealand	October 2008	Unconditional
South Korea	October 2008	Limited
Singapore	October 2008	Limited
Mexico	October 2008	Limited
Brazil	October 2008	Limited
Chile	—	Denied
Dominican Republic	—	Denied
Iceland	—	Denied
India	—	Denied
Indonesia	—	Denied
Peru	—	Denied
Turkey	—	Denied

necessary to illustrate and support my argument—interview accounts from recipients of ECB swaps, or real-time transcripts of the ECB's negotiations and decisions to extend these lines—as I provide in the Fed case, are unavailable.

At least seven central banks that requested a swap line from the Fed were denied one (see table 4.1). Even more, while these lines are largely viewed as unconditional, the terms of these arrangements vary between swap partners. A select few countries were given unconditional drawing authority, without further need for authorization from the Fed once a line was agreed to. For the four emerging market economies, limits were placed on the amounts and use of these instruments. Limits were presented as "additional safeguards," and "lines could not be drawn on without further authorization, and individual drawings would be limited to $5 billion."[23]

These liquidity lifelines were arranged *bilaterally* between the swap-issuing central banks, here, with the Fed, and the recipient counterparty. Again, these lines emerged in an experimental and ad hoc manner and proved essential to bolstering the rescue measures undertaken by central banks and governments, providing critical measures to patch up the inadequate governance system. To many central bankers at the time, it was not initially clear that they would succeed.

By extending these liquidity lifelines, the Fed played the critical stabilizing role of ILLR. However, per Walter Bagehot's principle of "lending freely against good collateral at a penalty rate," the Fed as an ILLR did not lend freely. Additionally, the collateral in a currency swap is the foreign currency being swapped, and the currency risk was assumed by the Fed's counterparty. But the risks of financial or currency collapse, and so the failure to honor the agreement, were systemic.[24] In other words, *there was no good collateral*. Now, central bankers' discretion was paramount, especially in providing liquidity sans good collateral under conditions of uncertainty, and not risk, where the "probable distribution of outcomes itself is unknown."[25] This is evident in the ambiguous, differentiated and arguably preferential application of the Fed's criteria in selecting swap recipients. Fed officials at the front line even recognized that the crisis was a period of radical uncertainty.

By mid-2007, before the worst of the crisis was upon them, FOMC officials cited concerns about unquantifiable uncertainty, not risk. In a June 2007 meeting, Jeffrey Lacker noted, "There is a vast range of uncertainty out there about which we can't help markets and they can't help us."[26] In the September meeting that year, Donald Kohn, the Fed vice chair, found that the range of outcomes were "just too wide, and there's very little central tendency in it. So, I'd be very uncomfortable with a statement saying that I kind of thought the risks were balanced."[27] By the end of the year, just as the Fed was about to extend its first swap lines, Kohn explicitly stated in a December FOMC conference call that financial institutions were protecting themselves "against a true Knightian uncertainty that they can't price and don't know how to protect themselves against."[28] Fed officials found themselves in an environment of radical uncertainty as they entered the new year. Conventional metrics were no longer reliable, and policymakers had to rely on subjective reasoning as they worked to put out the fire.

Who had access to these swaps and who did not was certainly influenced in important ways by the structure and balance of economic power in the global financial system. Still, although these conventional accounts can explain our baseline expectations, the Fed made some puzzling choices as to who would or would not have access to these conditionality-free arrangements.

To explain the Fed's selection of swap recipients, the international political economy field turned to interstate and interest-group politics. Of course, interstate economic ties create an interdependence and thus credibility that actors will avoid defaulting on loans or cooperate to minimize mutual harm.

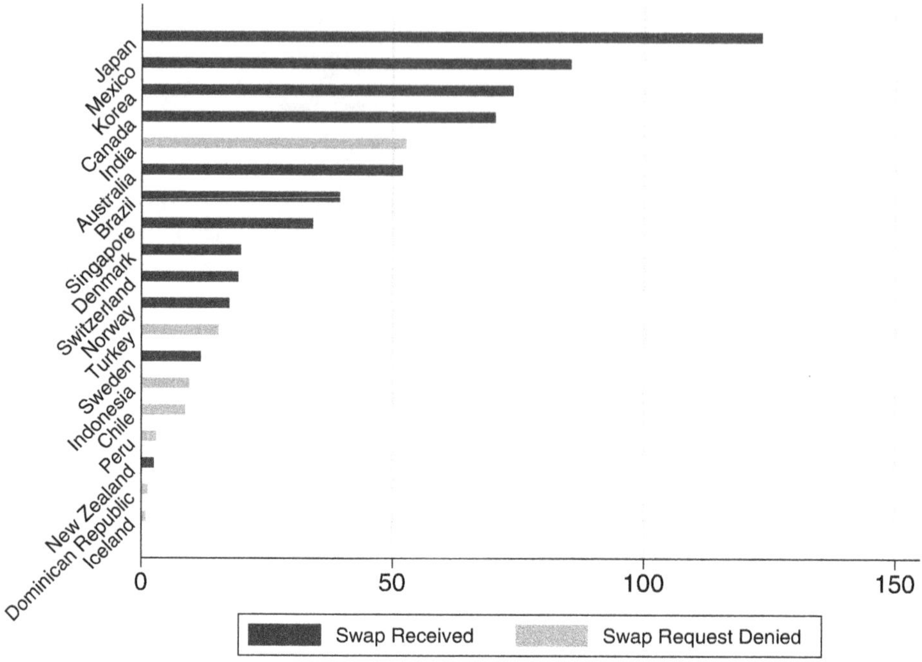

FIGURE 4.2. US Bank Exposure, 2007. This figure plots US bank exposure overseas for all countries who requested a swap, measured as the percentage of the consolidated claims of US banks in a foreign economy (in USD billions) as a proportion of total of the global consolidated claims of US banks as of December 2007. I exclude the UK and EU, which have the largest bank exposure, for space considerations.

And obviously, Fed officials had an incentive to assist foreign countries to protect the US banking sector and financial interests from overseas pressures; not doing so would imply that Fed leaders did not do their job.[29] Unsurprisingly, per our baseline expectations, a key predictor of receiving a Fed swap is the exposure of US banks to an overseas economy.[30]

Although US bank exposure and dollar shortages did motivate the Fed, a few cases stand out (see figure 4.2).[31] Bank exposure in India was far greater than in several swap recipient states, while New Zealand, whose banking ties with the United States are among the lowest of all swaps requested, received a $25 billion swap. Among the fifteen economies facing the largest dollar shortages, such as Chile, Iceland, India, and Turkey, who requested swaps, were denied.[32] Emergent market economies (EMEs) were undoubtedly disadvantaged in their international competitiveness and faced higher barriers to accessing this conditionality-free safety net.

We also know much less about *how* these lines came about and who was present at discussions and negotiations. As this book has shown so far, understanding the origins of such governance arrangements allows us to assess their robustness and their durability in the global financial safety net. In the rest of this chapter, I explain these outcomes discussed above and identify and illustrate the manner in which the Fed swap network emerged to highlight the interpersonal dynamics underlying this international cooperative response to the crisis.

The Inner Club

In 2007, a new cohort of central bank leaders found themselves at the front line—Bernanke, King, Trichet, and Shirakawa. In 2008, *Newsweek* ranked Bernanke, Trichet, and Shirakawa the fourth, fifth, and sixth most powerful people in the world who "could determine whether the global market avoids calamity."[33] They entered the crisis with "different backgrounds, temperaments, and intellectual proclivities." They did not agree on the causes of the crisis and held different views on how to resolve it.[34]

Armed with the backing of their institutions, they took extraordinary, innovative, and improvised measures to tackle the crisis. They played crucial roles in the negotiations over international liquidity arrangements and managing financial instability at home and internationally. In the broader professional community of central bankers, a handful of central bank leaders were deeply enmeshed in the central banking fraternity; some were more deeply embedded in interpersonal ties than others. These relationships were integral to managing relations within central banks that today are far more decentralized than they had been in the past.

A central figure in this story is Bernanke, who himself is an expert on the Great Depression. His work with Mark Gertler explored the "expertise, information, and relationships" based on which banks made decisions to lend. Along with Simon Gilchrist, they later developed the concept of the "financial accelerator" that identified how economic shocks were transmitted through credit channels from the economy into the financial system in the 1930s.

In my interview with Bernanke, he noted, as he has also written elsewhere, that on assuming the Fed chairmanship, "an early priority was forging cordial working relationships with international policymakers."[35] He already knew King when he took up the post. Bernanke and King both began their careers as academic economists. They first met when they shared an office suite at MIT in the 1980s and had a reunion lunch soon after Bernanke took office. While scholars would argue that this shared educational background lends itself easily to consensus and cooperation based on shared beliefs and preferences, that was not the case for Bernanke and King. Bernanke viewed the crisis as a "deeply intertwined set of risks to the banking system and the overall economy."[36] King saw these problems and fault lines as less severe, viewing the crisis as a corrective for the long bout of banking excess.[37] Neither anticipated that they would be responsible for the world's most important currencies during the worst crisis since the Depression.

King also had a similarly old connection with Trichet, when they met at the other Cambridge—Cambridge University—decades before. Trichet was a lifelong bureaucrat who had studied Latin and the classics before beginning his civil service career. He "saw his profession as a central banker as being about something much bigger than economics."[38] King and Trichet first met when Trichet was visiting Cambridge for his studies on the British tax system. Despite this old, academic connection, they too, like King and Bernanke, diverged on what caused the crisis and disagreed on the best approach to resolving it. Trichet initially viewed it as a one-off problem of banking panic and market uncertainty. And despite their divergent career and education backgrounds, Trichet and Bernanke saw it as essential to act quicky and assertively. King, on the other hand, saw regulating banks as messy and legalistic and found Trichet and Bernanke's initial response as an overreaction.[39]

Certainly, international institutions, such as the Bank for International Settlements (BIS) or the IMF, provided central bankers a space in which they could meet and build their professional and personal relationships with their foreign counterparts. Bernanke first met Trichet in New York during an IMF meeting. This is also where he sought to forge relations with his counterpart in Mexico, Guillermo Ortiz Martínez, when he first assumed the chairmanship during his visit to New York for an IMF meeting.[40]

Shirakawa, governor of the Bank of Japan, had been a part of the central banking world for decades and had spent time representing the Bank of Japan in New York earlier in his career, acting as general manager for the Americas in New York City. When he took up the governorship, he made the move from a faculty position in public policy at Kyoto University. Shirakawa is known for his unconventional and innovative ideas. But he also preached cautionary monetary policy and, throughout his term, resisted governmental pressure to take a more aggressive stance. He believed that a loose monetary stance would encourage "unchecked government spending and runaway inflation" and believed that it was the government's responsibility rather than the central banks' to "encourage economic growth through structural reforms and other growth policies."[41]

In interviews, several central bankers mentioned that they had developed close personal relationships of trust and goodwill with one another before the crisis through both their private and formal meetings and frequent correspondence and had developed long-standing personal familiarity with one another.[42] Certainly, they did not share the intimate friendships of their interwar predecessors. But despite their different priorities and philosophies, they did share close relations of trust and goodwill, which helped them to converge on a plan to establish swap lines.[43] It was crucial that they could work together and have free and frank debates around their disagreements. It was also important that disagreement and criticism among central banks would only occur in private.[44] This was especially so for building trust that distinguished those central bankers who, like King or Bernanke, view themselves first and foremost as *not* politicians, from those with closer professional and personal ties to the political sphere.[45]

Kohn noted that bankers today work within stricter institutional and legal constraints and do not share the deep and detailed letter-writing traditions of their predecessors. However, regular contact and correspondence allow them to build similar personal and social relationships with one another that give them added insight to their personalities.[46] Shirakawa also noted that technological advancement in communication has allowed them to maintain very private and regular contact both formally and informally.[47]

Charlie Bean, then a deputy governor of the Bank of England, talked of the long-term personal relationships that some central bankers develop with one another over their careers.[48] But many central bankers noted that within the central banking club, there is an inner circle.[49] Others noted that institutions, especially the BIS, play a crucial part in fostering reciprocity and trust between central bankers.[50] The Global Economy Meeting and the BIS dinner allowed for a free and frank exchange of views over the goings-on in markets.[51] The dinner is particularly important. Its closed, exclusive, and informal setting facilitates free-flowing conversation. The strongest interpersonal relations are cultivated in this confidential environment. Several central bankers noted that the exclusiveness of these dinners also generated strong personal ties between those who were regularly invited than those who often remained outsiders.[52]

And although international financial institutions have routinized day-to-day cooperation and institutionalized intergovernmental credit facilities, once again, as in the past, the crisis decisively showed central bankers' preferences for bilateral and ad hoc strategies to meet liquidity needs.[53] Institutions mattered in the GFC, but primarily in their role in providing opportunities for face-to-face interactions and communication among monetary authorities, such as at the BIS. But rather than turning to these long-standing institutional liquidity facilities, a handful of central banks sidestepped traditional avenues for intergovernmental lending for ad hoc, bilateral alternatives.

Unconditional Swaps

In a crisis, history counsels cooperation; its absence in the 1930s had disastrous consequences. During the GFC, advanced economies shed available strategies through the IMF or G7 accords to go their own way. Given that the crisis first erupted and spread across European and American banks, the ECB, the Bank of England, and the SNB were obvious recipients of Fed swaps. However, even among these more highly interconnected economies, the initial discussion and negotiations over swap lines were facilitated by favorable individuals and interpersonal ties that were conducive to early and rapid, ad hoc, and bilateral cooperation among these few banks.

In interviews, central bankers acknowledged and emphasized the importance of personal relationships and reciprocity among friends in facilitating such cooperation during the crisis, even though, as one interviewee said, "It's not the traditional point of emphasis for most researchers."[54] Unlike epistemic communities, where policymakers need not meet formally or informally, in the context of cooperation during crises, it is important that individuals tasked with crisis management know one another personally.[55] It was also vital that they had opportunities to interact and discuss problems in private outside the public view. Of course, many of these individuals were also part of a broader and more diffuse community of economists, or central bankers, sometimes trained in similar traditions, and may have crossed paths in previous academic professions too. But these central bankers were not all career technocrats, nor did many of them share educational credentials. Instead, in the uncertainty of the crisis, relations of personal trust and reciprocity were essential in order to facilitate cooperation around new and experimental approaches to crisis management.[56]

The origins of the Fed swap network were in a meaningful way grounded in relationships of trust and goodwill shared among a handful of leaders, which facilitated rapid bilateral cooperation early in the crisis. No doubt, most central bankers talked of the institutional and legal constraints on their discretion, the influence of domestic concerns, and the international economic and political climate on their foreign operations. But despite central banks' large institutional apparatuses and operations within legal and institutional frameworks that outlive individuals, leaders' influence increases in a crisis.[57]

Swaps were typically arranged following a request from one central bank to another, usually the Fed. Agreements were reached over bilateral phone calls or emails, with personal appeals from governor to governor.[58] Initial conversations and informal agreements were made primarily at the leader level. Leaders often discussed these arrangements with their foreign counterparts *prior* to seeking their own banks' support and approval.[59]

Trichet referred to this cohort of central bankers as a "collective brain," noting that the ties binding them together were not just professional but personal. He talked of how their easy and immediate personal relationships "of extraordinary confidence and intimate knowledge" were critical for generating collective solutions to the crisis, especially since they entered the crisis with differing views of both its causes and how best to resolve it. This is evident in that domestic crisis management policies varied across the world.[60] As central banks were exhausting their monetary policy discretion, one former central bank official suggested that in finding solutions to the crisis and making final decisions, leaders had the final word.[61]

Bean noted in an interview that while things do ultimately "get done," under conditions of uncertainty, such facilities are difficult to rapidly get off the ground in the absence of personal relationships and trust.[62] Indeed, as Jonathan Mercer notes, "If observers attribute cooperation to the environment rather than the person, then trust cannot—and need not—develop."[63] Despite the ease and low cost of assembling swap lines, central bankers faced with the same crises have not been guaranteed the same privileged access to ad hoc liquidity assistance through swap lines. It soon became apparent that emerging economies were disadvantaged in their international competitiveness and faced higher barriers to accessing this conditionality-free safety net.[64]

Generally, where central banks cooperated, it was not entirely surprising, but some cases can be identified where the necessary liquidity assistance did not occur. Requests from some central banks of systemically important or highly financialized economies, such as India and Iceland, were denied; others that did not unambiguously meet the Fed's stated criteria, such as Brazil or Mexico, were granted one.[65] Lending central banks suggested that liquidity shortages determined swap access. However, four of the fifteen economies facing dollar shortages—Chile, Iceland, India, and Turkey—that requested a Fed swap were denied.[66] Swap requests from the Dominican Republic, Indonesia, and Peru, which were not facing as severe dollar shortages, were also denied.

That the core, Western economies received the first unconditional swaps is not entirely surprising. These economies shared close banking and financial ties, and many were G7 members and fixtures at the BIS meetings and exclusive dinners. They interact regularly to incrementally build trust, goodwill, and familiarity over their careers.

Some non-US central bankers noted that Bernanke strongly favored showing a unified front among major central banks.[67] In previous studies, scholars have similarly emphasized Bernanke's pivotal role in pursuing the swap lines during the crisis in contrast to the nonaction or wrong action by central bankers in the 1930s.[68]

How these swaps were arranged, however, is intriguing. Central bankers initially disagreed on how to manage the crisis, and such cooperation was not automatic. Before even getting to my questions, in an interview, the first thing that one former Fed official said was "You want to think about personal relationships. It is important that you can get your counterpart on the phone."[69] They went on to say that, essentially, the earliest conversations and informal agreements were made privately at the leader level, often without knowledge of these discussions among their own central bank associates. Of course, they did indeed later consult with senior associates, who would be involved in executing these functions alongside partner banks.[70]

But initial cooperation occurred outside traditional institutional avenues, through leaders' interpersonal exchanges. When a solution was found, it was crucial that central bankers trusted one another to honor these agreements. The risks associated with the swap lines were mitigated by only extending them to trusted counterparties.[71] When decisions had to be made quickly, institutional trust depended on interpersonal trust and reciprocity among leaders.[72]

Some European bankers noted that Bernanke strongly favored showing a unified front among major central banks. Bernanke, an expert on the Great Depression, said to me that he had taken two technical lessons from that crisis. First, to not let the money supply collapse; and second, to ensure the availability of credit in the system. Second, he had also learned that in a powerful position, with powerful tools, a central banker ought to be "cautious, conservative and careful" in normal times. In contrast, in a crisis, it is often necessary to be bold and innovative, in consultation with colleagues and within political and legal constraints.[73] Caution and conservatism had prevented central bankers from managing the collapse of credit and the money supply a century ago. As discussed in the introduction of this book, Bernanke recognized the role of central bankers in the Depression and assured the audience of preventing a repeat.[74] Several of Bernanke's domestic and foreign colleagues who I interviewed suggested in interviews that this mantra undoubtedly informed his activist approach to the GFC.

Early on in the crisis, as discussed previously, central bankers were not unified in their agreement on how to manage it. So when a solution was found, as one central banker noted, it was crucial that central bankers knew and trusted one another to honor these agreements.[75] Much of the risk associated with these lines was mitigated by only extending them to trusted counterparties.[76] When decisions had to be made quickly, institutional trust depended on interpersonal trust and friendly relations among central bank leaders.[77] Early in the crisis, trust lay at the heart of the swap lines.

While some characterize the swap arrangements as *unilateral* defense mechanisms, motivated by the goal to protect US power and financial interests, they are *bilateral* arrangements.[78] Bernanke and his Fed associates depended as much on the trust, goodwill, and support of their counterparties as they did on the Fed. In many cases, not unlike Coombs's experience in the 1960s, Bernanke's counterparts initiated swap agreements even as pressures had eased.

In the summer of 2007, dollar funding pressures were growing in Europe; as David Wessel notes, European banks "couldn't easily find [US dollars] in malfunctioning markets." At the time, "key players at the Fed and at the ECB, for different reasons, were reluctant to make what seemed the obvious move," which was extending swaps.[79]

As pressures increased later in the year, it seems the tone was shifting. Interviews and FOMC transcripts show that the swap lines with central banks in Europe had been discussed and prearranged privately and informally between central bank leaders, prior to seeking their own banks' approval.[80] In the FOMC meeting of September 18, 2007, on the question of dollar swaps and an auction facility, Bernanke shared that in "some conversations [he] had, in particular with President Trichet of the ECB, [they] came up with the possibility of combining these two things, essentially having auctions simultaneously in the United States and Europe, and then using the swap markets to provide the dollars to the extent that the ECB would like to have them." They had arrived at a similar plan with the Swiss National Bank.[81]

Across the Atlantic, European central bankers, initially resistant to the swap proposal, later expressed, as Adam Tooze writes, that they "didn't expect to have any difficulty getting hold of dollars" from the Fed.[82] ECB officials noted that Trichet and Bernanke had discussed these arrangements privately. Both leaders then had to gather the support of their banks, which they would generate in internal meetings to get consensus support, so as to not go back on their word. The internal deliberations over predetermined settlements were therefore essentially pro forma, as central bank leaders had already informally agreed to these arrangements, grounded in interpersonal trust and reciprocity.[83] By making these agreements informally, leaders had great discretion over their banks' decisions.

Unlike Bernanke and Trichet, King viewed the crisis as a corrective for banking excess and was eager to avoid a moral hazard problem from bailing out banks. Earlier in 2007, he strongly opposed any intervention for liquidity support as he believed it "encourages excessive risk-taking and sows the seeds of future financial crises," which explains why the Bank of England did not join its European counterparts in proposing swap lines with the Fed.[84]

But when talking about the lead-up to and decisions made to arrange a swap, King emphasized people and personal relationships between central bankers mattered. He was close with Kohn's predecessor, Roger Ferguson Jr., with whom he had arranged a dollar swap with the Fed on September 12 and 13, 2001, immediately following the attacks on the World Trade Center in New

York City. King suggested that the 2007–2008 swaps emerged in a similar manner. In an interview, when I asked King how these lines first came about, he said, "If you trust your counterpart, for temporary and emergency purposes, you can give the Fed a call."[85]

Paul Tucker, who assumed the deputy governorship at the Bank of England in 2009, was close with Kohn at the Fed. He suggested that friendly and informal relations with Kohn, developed largely in Basel, helped facilitate discussions on how to collectively address liquidity pressures. Kohn similarly said that he and Tucker "had developed a close working relationship that was very useful when [their] economic and financial systems were under stress."[86]

The possibility of coordinated action was broached in broad terms between Tucker and Kohn in South Africa when walking to a formal dinner. Tucker sensed an appetite in the Fed to take joint action. They had a very long, free, and frank conversation ("there's something about a good walk and talk"), where they could discuss the need for coordination or cooperation in ways that would demonstrate "joinedupness" to the world while each central bank tailored its actions to its own particular circumstances. This personal, informal discussion between Tucker and Kohn helped lay the groundwork for official follow-up discussions between the Fed, Bank of England, and others. When, a few weeks later, a handful of central banks announced new measures, the *Financial Times*'s front-page headline focused on the coordination.[87]

The first lines were extended in December 2007. By September 2008, the Fed's swap network encompassed the ECB, the Bank of England, the Swiss National Bank, and the Scandinavian central banks.[88] And in September 2008, when Japan sought out a swap, following an extraordinary meeting in the middle of the night, Shirakawa notes that "the arrangement was up and running in a matter of a few days, without any information leaks before its launch. It reflected a strong mutual trust among central banks."[89] When recounting this cooperative effort in an interview, Trichet claimed that the collective brain was "equipped with the appropriate synapses," opening the possibility for an early, quick, and cooperative response to the crisis.[90]

The crisis generated unusual circumstances for central bankers. With conference calls occurring at unusual hours, as Shirakawa writes, "to negotiate and hammer out practical solutions with overseas counterparts, sometimes without sleep," knowing people well, and knowing how to talk to, negotiate, and reason with them was essential.[91] King talked of his extensive interaction with Kohn, with whom a US-UK swap had already been discussed informally. Interestingly, these plans for collective efforts between the United States and United Kingdom ran counter to King's initial refusal to lend to the system.[92] But central banks could not rely on governments for large amounts of liquidity, nor could they arrange swaps publicly. Confidentiality and trust were crucial, and reciprocity and personal relationships mattered fundamentally for cooperation and as traits that are a mark of central bankers who work closely together.[93]

Some central bankers note that in the earliest days, these huge agreements that central bankers entered into, often overnight, were arranged solely on the word of central banks' leaders.[94] Given the uncertainty around the success of crisis management efforts, the earliest and largest swaps between major central banks were grounded in their governors' personal trust. Almost nothing about their outcomes was known ahead of time. In his memoir about the crisis and its aftermath, Bernanke recounts his worry that early swaps may not have sufficed in Europe: "This may not work. I don't want to oversell it," [Bernanke] told the FOMC. "If we do it, we are just going to have to give it a try and see what happens."[95] This worry and uncertainty around the success of these policies was echoed by several central bankers.[96] Through these swap lines, the Fed's lending to central banks reached almost USD$600 billion between 2007 and 2010, peaking at $170.93 billion in an overnight swap to the ECB on October 15, 2008.[97] When later asked by Alan Grayson, a Florida Democrat, during a congressional hearing, which foreign banks were lent the money by the Fed, Bernanke answered, "I don't know."[98]

Since the announcement of these lines, the use of these tools has been seen as extremely problematic in the public and political spheres. Gerald O'Driscoll, formally of the Dallas Fed, called out the New York Fed for undertaking this effort in a manner that is "troublesome in a democracy" and for using its authority "to bail out European banks."[99] Others have criticized the Fed for extending swap lines during the crisis that were issued without either approval or oversight from Congress and from the White House.[100] Even those who acknowledge the Fed's need to play the role of an international lender of last resort are concerned with the potential risks and public costs associated with these arrangements in their current form.[101] And, by 2010, the FOMC itself came to recognize the political risks associated with these measures, especially, as Michelle Smith, the Fed's communications director warned, anything that they were "keeping secret" that would fuel speculation in Congress.[102] But in its earliest days, keeping these efforts behind closed doors, between just a few, apolitical central bankers, was essential.

Neil Irwin writes that the Fed's extensive but "hidden liquidity support measures" were "a closely guarded secret even by the standards of the always secretive Fed." During the panic, "information about the Fed's lending was so closely held—and had it been known publicly, so potentially explosive—that only two people at each of the dozen reserve banks were allowed to access it."[103] The FOMC meetings in which swap lines and other programs were finalized were followed by "closed meetings" with the Board, which published no transcript, only "very summary" minutes released two weeks after the meetings. The information provided was "very general—something like there was a discussion of means to address money market issues."[104]

Throughout the crisis, central bankers had taken to innovation and improvisation, somewhat departing from convention of caution in favor of what Bernanke and others refer to as "blue sky thinking."[105] Central bank staff had been working on a wide range of proposals that were circulated to Bernanke, Kohn, Geithner, and Kevin Warsh. Deliberations over these "pre-decisions" took place in closed meetings. Fed Board meetings are subject to "sunshine laws": formally, a meeting is made public and informative, which Bernanke observed in his book, was "not a great venue for blue-sky thinking and strategizing." And some interviewees noted that the Fed's legal team could make exceptions as to what constituted a meeting.[106]

Smaller meetings of fewer than four Board members did not trigger this open-meeting law, and because Geithner was not a Board member at the time, these meetings were exempt from the sunshine requirement. Because such a setting was more suitable for blue-sky thinking, these group meetings were often kept exclusive to these four individuals, while Bernanke tried to keep other Board members not in attendance at these informal meetings "apprised of developments through one-on-one lunches and frequent email exchanges."[107]

The Bank of England also chose not to announce major policy decisions and actions, not only to the public, but to politicians as well. Arranging swaps and the coordinated rate cut would have been "impossible to do publicly" given their immediate impact on markets and the widespread effects of interest rate changes.[108] Other central bankers also alluded to the ambiguity over what counted as a meeting in their banks—whether three people in an elevator or conference calls with foreign counterparts was a meeting was debatable.[109] But it was these private, closed door environments that created the space for sensitive decision-making, especially where expectations could impinge on the markets.

The first swap agreements expired in February 2010 just as liquidity pressures slowly began to ease. When pressures mounted in Greece early that year, the Fed did not have a swap line in place with the ECB despite the possibility of contagion via European banks.[110] But the Fed did not rush to reactivate or enhance them. The Eurozone crisis had not quite begun; problems of drying up liquidity in the United Kingdom and Japan eased. Still, Trichet, King, Shirakawa, and Bernanke sought to reopen their swap lines that had just expired. These steps could not have been taken in the absence of interpersonal connections between Bernanke and the rest.

In an impromptu conference call that interrupted FOMC officials' Mother's Day celebrations on May 9, 2010, Bernanke broached the idea of reopening these swaps with the ECB, the Bank of England, and the Bank of Japan: "Yesterday Jean-Claude Trichet called me and made what I would characterize as a *personal appeal* to reopen the swaps that we had before. This morning I have gotten, again, *personal calls* from Mervyn King, of the Bank of England, and Masaaki Shirakawa, of the Bank of Japan, also asking us to reopen the swaps."[111]

Bernanke went on to say that this exchange with Trichet followed an ECB Executive Board meeting where they came to "very significant decisions" that Trichet shared with Bernanke on "a highly confidential basis."[112] In acknowledging the extraordinariness of these steps, Bernanke reemphasized that Trichet's call was a "personal appeal" and that Trichet "feels it is very important for us to support him, and he understands [the Fed's] concerns."

King and Shirakawa's appeals carried a similar personal tone.[113] And in interviews, where I discussed this moment in the crisis with King and Shirakawa, they both echoed Trichet and Bernanke's sentiment. Shirakawa noted that at the time, the sentiment expressed by the Fed was that there was no need for a swap; on the ground, Japan was not affected by the emerging European crisis. To request this new swap from the Fed, it was helpful that Shirakawa had a close personal relationship with Bernanke, which made broaching the topic and agreeing to reopen the lines much simpler.[114] King's account of this decision was similar, adding that these central bank leaders' reciprocal and cooperative manner of working was facilitated by goodwill and interpersonal trust between himself and Bernanke.[115]

In sum, interpersonal ties of trust and reciprocity played a crucial role in facilitating bilateral and ad hoc cooperation, even among the core Western economies during the crisis. These relationships were especially important in renegotiating these lines when there was no longer a need for them. Moreover, the swap network emerged through private, informal, and personal discussions during the crisis, rather than formal, institutional channels.

What Would Bair Do?

In interviews, a constant theme from central bankers from a range of countries was Bernanke's expertise on the Great Depression as vital to the Fed's global activism in the rescue effort. In that vein, many interviewees raised a hypothetical scenario of what the crisis response would look like had the Fed not been under Bernanke's watch, all indicating his distinct influence in the GFC. In a Federal Reserve Oral History interview, when asked how a "Volcker-Corrigan team, dealing with crises or their potential could have looked very different from the Bernanke-Kohn team," Kohn talked of Volcker's skepticism toward financial innovation, especially that he would have been more skeptical of the innovation in the 1990s and 2000s. Another former central banker discussed the notion of a different Fed leader, say, someone who focused more on concerns of moral hazard. Some even proposed a provocative counterfactual of an alternative world in which Sheila Bair at the Federal Deposit Insurance Corporation (FDIC) was in Bernanke's position as Fed chair during the crisis.

Entertaining this counterfactual raises the plausibility of alternative outcomes in the global crisis management effort under a different leader. Note that interview accounts specifically did not intend to criticize Bair in any way, and interviewees emphasized that they hold her in high regard. Rather, they simply suggested that she, and perhaps anyone else, may likely have approached the crisis with a different focus, such as minimizing moral hazard concerns, and so, would likely have adopted a different set of policy responses. Moreover, this is a *hypothetical* counterfactual inference to simply speculate what *might* have been, drawing on a combination of speculative interview discussions and character descriptions from published works, as an exercise in conjecture.

In *The Courage to Act*, Bernanke's assessment of Bair gives us some insight on his perception of her and policymakers' experiences of working with her. He describes Bair as "a prairie populist, [who] inherently distrusted the big Wall Street banks and the government agencies charged with overseeing them." He goes on to write that Bair "could be turf-conscious and hard to work with," but he also "grudgingly [admired] her energy, her political acumen in pursuing her goals, and her skill in playing to the press."[116]

Given Bair's concerns about moral hazard and distrust in big banks, one might conclude that a Bair Fed may not have adopted such an activist approach or experimental approach to the rescue effort. In interviews, other central bankers suggested that actions taken by Bair or someone else in Bernanke's position would have been shaped by their philosophical bent in banking. In fact, Bair's views were more akin to King's beliefs and initial reluctance to take forceful action, as they both viewed the crisis as a corrective to banking excess. She found that the Fed's domestic rescues had created too much moral hazard. King similarly had expressed, about the Fed's early swap lines, that "the provision of such liquidity support . . . encourages excessive risk-taking, and sows the seeds of future financial crises."[117] A Bair-King pairing leading the Fed and Bank of England may have approached the crisis from a different philosophical bent, which could easily have generated a very different global crisis management effort than the Fed swap program. Perhaps a Bair Fed would have gone to Congress sooner in the crisis than Bernanke and Paulson did, in orchestrating the domestic rescue.

Jean-Claude Trichet, on the other hand, had been critical of the Fed for letting Lehman fail and believed it could have been avoided. Presumably, a Bair-Trichet combination may have responded very differently to how Bernanke and Trichet approached the crisis effort, influenced by Bair and Trichet's limited combined appetite for extensive innovation and ad hoc liquidity provision.[118] Even looking to the past, while the need for experimentation was a closely held view by the Fed's leaders during the GFC, this belief was not shared by their Fed predecessors such as Volcker, suggesting that the Fed's own approach to the crisis may have significantly diverged under different leadership.[119] In other words, without Bernanke at the helm, this time *might* have been different.

Differentiated Ties

In 2008, four EMEs also benefited from US liquidity assistance: Mexico, Brazil, Korea, and Singapore were granted a Fed swap in 2008. With the exception of Mexico, this was the first time that emerging markets were included among the Fed's swap recipients. Fed officials reasoned that these are four of the largest and systemically important emerging economies. Each of these central banks was offered up to $30 billion for three months.[120] Studies show that the Fed's criteria in selecting swap recipients were not applied unambiguously to the emerging markets that requested a swap to access this conditionality-free option.[121] Instead, geopolitics and diplomatic ties facilitated this cooperation.

Although some suggest that these instruments are used to exert leverage against risky partners, I argue that these geopolitical motivations are not motivated by leverage but by *favoritism*: by assisting those with whom Fed leaders shared close interpersonal relations of trust and goodwill.[122] Fed leadership mitigated substantial risks incurred in these agreements by excluding those with whom they did not share strong personal ties of trust and goodwill and assisting only those central bank leaders they did trust, to show a united front.

By focusing on the case of Mexico, I show that arranging a swap agreement with EME central banks relied on central bankers' relationships of interpersonal trust, goodwill, and reciprocity. But where relational ties differed, so did access to dollar liquidity. Conversely, the absence of such personal affinities between bank leaders hindered India's chances at receiving a Fed swap. India matched Mexico and Brazil on the Fed's criteria for a swap, especially regarding the Fed's key justification for their swaps of having a GDP of over $1 trillion. Yet it was unsuccessful in its bid to acquire a Fed swap during the crisis.

Limited Cooperation: Mexico

Unlike advanced economy swaps, arrangements with Brazil, Mexico, Singapore, and South Korea were conditional and limited. The configurations of trust sources here are more mixed, as these countries varied in their financial centrality and systemic importance. Mexico and Brazil also performed less well on indicators of sound economic management, such as CBI, inflation, and reserves.[123] The risks that these measures of economic soundness signal suggest that material considerations and conditions of cooperation were less favorable for these countries.

I focus primarily on Mexico to show that close interpersonal relations could overcome concerns about institution- and country-level credibility to grant a swap. I show that the Fed used material as well as social and personal reasoning to grant Mexico a swap and signal support and trust in the governor of the Bank of Mexico (Banxico). However, these concerns were hedged with limits and conditions in how these could be used.

Although the exposure of US banks overseas undoubtedly influenced the Fed's selection of its swap recipients, this, and other objective economic criteria against which the Fed vetted swap requests, does not satisfactorily explain the selection of its swap partners.[124] As discussed in chapter 3, Mexico already had a standing swap with the United States through the North American Framework Agreement (NAFA).[125] Concerns of economic soundness and risk calculations were apparent in these discussions, citing fears that these banks may default on this dollar-denominated loan, not make whole on the swap, or face severe depreciation.

Within the FOMC, several officials were eager not to grant any EMEs a swap and preferred that they turned to the IMF for a credit line. Charles Plosser, then president of the Philadelphia Fed, said in a 2008 FOMC meeting, "I'm worried about other central banks ganging up on us as a group, saying that they have to have this. I would prefer that even large countries use some combination of the IMF facility plus their own reserves to meet these needs."[126] Plosser added that most major banks in Mexico, barring Banamex (belonging to Citi), "are foreign owned—EU banks, Spanish banks—those banks clearly have access to dollars through the ECB swap line."[127] Moreover, in contrast to the advanced economy swap recipients, Mexico, and indeed Brazil, experienced high inflation, even greater than India, Chile, or Peru, whose swap requests were denied.

Other FOMC officials strongly supported helping the Bank of Mexico. At the FOMC meeting in October 2008, Nathan Sheets justified this swap noting that Mexico, Brazil, and Korea were large, systemically important economies with a GDP of around $1 trillion.[128] When the emerging market swaps were voted on, Richard Fisher of the Dallas Fed noted that Mexico had "a sophisticated central bank" and that Guillermo Ortiz Martínez was a "very good central banker." In fact, Ortiz Martínez "had been [in the United States] to visit and had already approached" Sheets about a swap in addition to what was in place through NAFA.[129] Before and during the crisis, Sheets had served as the director of the Division of International Finance and had worked closely with his central banking counterparts in Mexico and elsewhere. His FOMC associates noted in interviews that he had developed a close personal and professional relationship with Ortiz Martínez and other officials at the Bank of Mexico.[130]

Other FOMC and Fed officials also noted their preexisting friendships and trust in Ortiz Martínez before the crisis.[131] I talked to FOMC officials about the interpersonal and social considerations made by the Fed over the EME swaps that are evident in the FOMC meeting transcript. Bernanke noted the importance of trust and reciprocal relations with central bankers of these economies as important to instilling confidence in these transactions.[132] Several other interviewees stressed the importance of their friendships and trust in Ortiz Martínez as a necessary facilitator for cooperation with Mexico.[133]

One New York Fed ex-officio involved in the crisis management effort and the swap arrangements, and focused on the emerging market lines, explicitly noted that there is "absolutely no substitute to interpersonal trust in issues of cooperation, especially in times of stress." Their experience of the crisis taught them that these lines in particular, as opposed to more costly or conditional assistance, would have been difficult to arrange in the absence of these strong personal relations among bankers in both institutions.[134] When I asked former central bankers in interviews why some central bankers at the Fed did not want to put Mexico through the stigma of IMF facilities, considering its financial position, a minimal need for a swap in 2008, and opposition to the line with the Fed, another former FOMC official said, "That's what you get when you go to dinner parties," highlighting how friendly ties can facilitate interpersonal cooperation.[135]

Similar language was also used around Singapore: FOMC officials thought it would be "beneath Lee Kwan Yew's dignity" to go to the IMF. Meanwhile, Brazil was seen as "the dodgiest of the lot" with whom Fed officials had a unique negotiating history. A former leader of the Central Bank of Brazil, who was not involved in negotiating these lines, expressed some surprise that Brazil was awarded a swap line from the Fed in 2008, given its perennial problem of high inflation and recent crisis, and that its central bank was not formally independent. Moreover, Mereilles did not have an economics PhD like some of his counterparts. But he had spent a great deal of his career in US financial institutions and had been close to high-level financial and political elites in the United States prior to taking up the central bank presidency. They surmised that

Mereilles's connections in US financial circles must certainly have helped him form closer ties with Fed officials to open up a conversation about a swap in 2008.[136] Despite concerns around Brazil's financial position, Fisher and others emphasized in the 2008 FOMC meeting that it would be "an insult to these four parties" not to give them a swap as they had already negotiated these arrangements with some safeguards.[137]

Swap lines were granted to just four emerging market partners with fundamentally different policy preferences to the United States. But to hedge against risks, they were limited in their terms. These four swap partners were offered up to $30 billion per central bank in 2008.[138] However, rather than using swaps to exert leverage over one another as other scholars suggest, reciprocity and goodwill, with the added goal of helping trusted friends, avoided the stigma and conditionality of going to the IMF. In extending these swaps, given the risks of the arrangement, Bernanke and others noted the importance of trust and reciprocal relations with central bankers in these economies as important to instilling confidence in these transactions.[139] Even though material considerations in Mexico did not unambiguously call for a swap, the FOMC discussion around granting Banxico any assistance showed a sense of obligation, sympathy, and trust toward the bank and its governor. FOMC officials employed social and personal considerations to balance against less clear material justifications for a swap. However, it was important that this swap came with additional safeguards attached in drawing limits and stipulations to seek authorization for any drawing.

Noncooperation: Iceland

Unlike the rest of Europe, Iceland's multiple swap requests were unsuccessful. The Fed deemed the Icelandic economy too small and not systemically important to warrant a swap. New Zealand, also at the margins of the Fed's criteria, in terms of size and US banking ties, received a $25 billion swap. As central bankers and economists highlight, although a "tiny country of 330,000 people in the middle of the Atlantic Ocean," Iceland was nonetheless systemically important. Its banking system had become "so large and heavily exposed to foreign liabilities" by 2008. It was an early victim of the financial crisis and a generator of systemic risk; several large European and US banks were heavily exposed to Iceland's crisis. To put the scale of the Icelandic financial crisis into perspective, scholars note that Iceland's bank failures would place third among the largest bankruptcies in US history, only behind Lehman Brothers and Washington Mutual in 2008.[140]

But the "wild ride" of dealing with Iceland, as Stefan Ingves, then governor of the Swedish National Bank, called it, was exacerbated by Davíð Oddsson, governor of the Central Bank of Iceland. Oddsson entered office in 2005.[141] Before that, he had been Iceland's longest-serving prime minister and later foreign minister. Unlike many of his counterparts, he was not a trained economist and was seen as a central bank outsider.[142] Here, I illustrate why the loss of trust in Oddsson and his bank hindered Iceland's access to the Fed's liquidity assistance.

Early in the crisis, Oddsson made multiple unsuccessful Fed swap requests, writing to Geithner in New York that "the perception of strong allies" was important and a swap with the Fed would be of monumental significance.[143] But following several incidents both before and during the crisis, one former Icelandic public official suggested that Iceland's closest Nordic central bank allies, as well as King in Britain and Geithner in New York, had lost trust in Oddsson.[144] They further shared that Ingves wrote that they had lost trust in Iceland's central bank under Oddsson and thought that Oddsson and his bank did not appreciate the risks at hand. Although Iceland could access dollars from its long-term Scandinavian partners, Sweden initially rejected Iceland's request to draw on it. These lines were "designed as an IMF program without the IMF . . . because [Ingves] used to work at the IMF."[145] They required banking reform and could only be drawn with approval from their creditors. When the Swedish central bank approved Iceland's drawing soon after, Ingves notes, what "really upset us was that the whole thing was signed and the Icelandics delivered nothing, zero on it."[146]

An Icelandic official also mentioned that King declined Oddsson's request for help because he did not trust him. King was adamant that Oddsson clarified how any swap arrangement would be used and indicated his concerns of an imminent banking collapse during the 2008 IMF spring meetings. He would only help Oddsson collectively with other G10 bankers, which he had informally discussed with Ingves and "would request a discussion at [the BIS] dinner."[147] But it soon became known that Icelandic banks had been funding themselves through the ECB, off the books. On this revelation, Trichet called Oddsson, furious. Now, Oddsson's closest economic partners had lost his trust and his closest economic partners in Europe could not vouch for his trustworthiness.[148]

Simultaneous to these developments during the summer of 2008, Geithner had also been in contact with his European counterparts. He reportedly had doubts about the success of an Icelandic swap. One Icelandic official noted that it was hard to justify loaning Iceland billions of dollars on the word of a man whose role as prime minister and central bank governor sparked nationwide protests on revelations of fraud and negligence.[149] Trust between Oddsson and his counterparts was missing, with little else to facilitate cooperation. When the Fed announced its Nordic swap arrangements, Iceland was not included. Oddsson wrote to Geithner that he felt Iceland had been left in a lurch and asked him to reconsider.[150] After his request was declined, Iceland's three largest banks collapsed in October 2008. The government was forced to sign an IMF agreement on October 24, 2008. Only then did Ingves in Sweden allow Iceland to draw on its swap line, as the IMF was now "involved in keeping an eye on things staying on track."[151]

Noncooperation: India

In the October 2008 meeting, when the Committee was making its decision as to where to draw the line and which emerging markets they should assist, Sheets recognized at an FOMC meeting, "Wherever you draw the line, there is going to be somebody who is just a bit away from the line that says, 'I am very similar to those folks.' . . . In my mind the next one for which you could make a case would be India."[152] Sheets also argued, however, that India was not as integrated in the global financial system as the others. But like Brazil, Mexico, and Korea, India was also a large and systemically important economy with a GDP of over $1 trillion, a criteria that was used to justify the EME swaps. Still, with the exceptions of these four EMEs, Kohn announced that he was "in favor of very strongly encouraging other countries to go to the IMF."[153] In the case of India, material considerations and economic necessity alone did not suffice to justify a Fed swap with the Reserve Bank of India (RBI). However, interpersonal trust between the RBI governor, Duvvuri Subbarao, and Shirakawa did facilitate a Bank of Japan-RBI dollar swap.

India matched and even outperformed Brazil on many of the Fed's criteria for a swap but failed to cross the Fed's boundary line to receive a swap.[154] In an interview, I asked how Fed officials adjudicated the distinction between these two economies, and why officials saw Brazil as warranting a swap but not India. One former Fed staffer who was involved in running these operations exclaimed, when I asked this question, "Who gives a shit about Brazil? They're corrupt, they were quite closed up at the time, and most of their banks are state owned. I don't know why they got a swap, and I doubt anyone on either side would be willing to say more on the matter."[155] But given the FOMC's concerns about lending to EMEs, it raises the question then of why they drew the boundary line where they did.

Why was India treated so differently to the other large EMEs who received a swap? For some central bankers outside the United States, this was surprising. In a recent book, Paul Tucker recalls learning about India's swap denial and proclaimed, "But India will be a power!"[156] Another former central bank governor outside the United States and India observed the absence of trust relations between Subbarao and Bernanke and other Fed officials. These relations were not fraught, but they lacked the familiarity and personal bond that would otherwise facilitate friendly and open discussions around this possibility. Others suggested that this key trait of perceiving one's identity as above politics was not shared by Subbarao as he had previously held the position of finance secretary prior to assuming the central bank governorship, which kept him outside the inner central banking circles.

One US central banker talked of general negotiating difficulties in the absence of familiarity between interlocutors, which could hinder cooperation. Another interviewee found this to be the case between the United States and India. Several central bank officials emphasized in interviews the importance of personal relationships and the implications of their absence for accessing swaps. Some central bankers outside the United States suggested that the absence of a close relationship between Subbarao and Bernanke stacked the odds of getting liquidity assistance against India.[157]

In my interview with Subbarao, his very first comment on his time as governor of the RBI was that he was not a career central banker. He noted the distinct type of personal relationship among his colleagues that he saw as especially unique in their importance and influence in policymaking.[158] Being an outsider to the central banking world and more connected to the political arms of international finance hindered Subbarao's ability to develop closer personal relations with his foreign colleagues.[159]

Subbarao himself mentioned that the United States had been sheepish for being the epicenter of the crisis. Moreover, at the BIS, although there was a formal EME meeting, the advanced economy dinners were specifically informal, exclusive, and invite-only. This served to reinforce personal ties and hierarchies among those in the inner club, while those not invited did not have the opportunities to build friendships and trust with their counterparts. Often, prior to many international meetings, a handful of G7 leaders had usually met and preagreed on key decisions, which were presented to all participants as a fait accompli.[160] One central banker outside India and the United States even suggested to me that that a close read of Subbarao's memoir calmly and subtly shows his frustration for not being granted a swap during the crisis with no clear explanation for why.[161]

It was fortunate, however, that prior to and during Subbarao's tenure at the RBI in September 2008, monetary and economic relations between Japan and India were strong. Relations between Japanese and Indian central bankers were also strong, professionally and personally. Shirakawa spoke highly of Subbarao and his predecessor, Y. V. Reddy, and of his personal relationships with them, which they had developed through official and informal interactions. The personal trust and reciprocity that was missing among Subbarao and Fed central bankers was strong between Subbarao and Shirakawa and helped India avoid having to turn to the IMF.

In an interview, Shirakawa said about Subbarao, "I like him, and he's extremely intelligent."[162] Subbarao said that he interacted with Shirakawa far more frequently and closely while at the RBI than with any Japanese representatives while he was finance secretary.[163] Both of them, and their foreign colleagues, acknowledged the mutual respect, trust, and reciprocal relationship that Shirakawa enjoyed with Reddy and Subbarao, which made establishing a Japan-India *dollar* swap an easy solution to arrive at.[164] In this agreement, the Bank of Japan took on an even greater risk in extending a line denominated in dollars and not yen, even though the rupee was not a convertible currency, which is a significant mark of Shirakawa's trust in Subbarao. This swap also opened up the possibility for the RBI to avoid the costly policy adjustments tied to drawing on the RBI's foreign exchange reserves or requesting IMF assistance and gave India access to a dollar swap from the Japanese. Subbarao and Shirakawa's trusting relations were important to showing a united front and facilitated arranging the Japan-India swap in 2008.[165]

As a brief aside, similar interpersonal distance and the absence of personal relations with Fed officials similarly hindered Indonesia's efforts to secure a swap. A former Indonesian policymaker talked briefly about approaching Geithner and Bernanke during the crisis, to seek a swap line.[166] They noted that they, alongside their central bank and finance ministry associates from Indonesia, approached Fed officials during IMF and G20 meetings during the crisis to open up a conversation about a swap line. These conversations were not fruitful. As some Indonesia policymakers saw it, their swap request was brusquely dismissed by Geithner, who told them to first get their house in order.[167] Of course, Indonesia's case did not quite fit the material criteria for a swap, as they were not as large or systemically important as the other emerging markets in consideration for a Fed swap. As such, this policymaker was not entirely surprised their request was rejected, but they noted the dismissive nature of Geithner's rejection of this request. They went on to say this was not a typical manner for central bankers to engage with one another and lacked the openness and frank discussions they were used to.

They also highlighted the interpersonal aspect of broaching these conversations with a comparison to their interactions with Janet Yellen a few years later, when she took the helm, after the 2013 taper tantrums that hurt many emerging markets. In particular, the leadership change at the Fed, with Yellen assuming the chair, changed the Fed's engagement with its emerging market partners. They found that Yellen listened more attentively to their concerns during central bank and other official meetings. Yellen's Fed was more receptive to understanding the influence of Fed policies on emerging market positions and having open discussions about the Fed's relationship with various emerging market economies. Of course, this was not at a time when Indonesia needed or requested a Fed swap, and I do not claim that Yellen's Fed would have extended a swap to Indonesia during the GFC. But we see that leadership changes can help thaw cool relations and foster more collaborative environments for bilateral cooperation and exchange.

Material considerations alone did not guarantee cooperation around liquidity assistance between central bankers. Rather, interpersonal trust ties remain integral to greasing the wheels of this type of central bank cooperation, most crucially in moments of crisis and uncertainty. These case studies show that differentiated personal relations are marked by preferential access to less costly, conditionality-free liquidity assistance. Interpersonal trust made it possible for some central bank leaders to approach trusted colleagues and secure lower cost liquidity through swaps. Where interpersonal ties were absent, such arrangements could not get off the ground.

A Standing Bazooka

In 2008, Bernanke was keen to get temporary authorization to use swap lines during the crisis, "so I know I've got my own bazooka here." And the crisis demonstrated that this bazooka had proved vital to the global crisis-fighting efforts. And so, in a 2009 FOMC meeting, Sheets presented a memo proposing the establishment of standing swap lines with the Bank of England, ECB, Bank of Japan, and the Swiss National Bank. These standing lines essentially now provided these partner central banks with a more permanent backstop to dollar markets abroad. Technically, the Fed could still prevent the use of these lines, but now, these large financial centers would be less reliant on ad hoc arrangements than they had been in 2007 and 2008, without having to go through the difficulty of renegotiating these lines in the event of a crisis.

Here, I provide new details on how the Fed deliberated and came to establish five standing swap lines with the United Kingdom, Canada, Japan, Switzerland, and the ECB. The focus here is less on the interpersonal aspects of this decision-making, as the FOMC transcripts suggest that the push for these permanent lines largely came from the Fed itself and not from a partner's request. However, deliberations in the Fed's initial conversations in 2009, and the eventual authorization of these permanent lines in 2013, highlight two important political- and individual-level dynamics: First, the Fed recognized that where it drew its line was a sensitive, political question, which had implications for its relations with partner banks. Second, Sheets was no longer at the Fed in 2013 when the FOMC established these standing lines, and the considerations of who ought to be included in this group changed, with the notable absence of Mexico.

The "standing" swap lines proposed by Sheets in 2009 would be limited in their amounts and in partner banks' abilities to draw on them. These lines would effectively be reauthorized annually when the FOMC is reconstituted each year.[168] Sheets proposed including Canada and Mexico's lines through NAFA in this group, as "not enhancing the lines might strain [the Fed's] relationships with them."[169] In response, James Bullard, then president of the St. Louis Fed, asked about the "difficulty of having to, as you say, renegotiate and set up the details, as you did this time," for discontinued lines, and the implicit likelihood that these partners may not get a swap in the future.

Sheets's response to Bullard shows that central bankers thought about the individuals involved in negotiating these lines making decisions, and consequently about how personnel changes could affect crisis management in the next crisis. Sheets was less worried about scaling up a program than of the difficulty of going "from zero to four" lines, and not from four to fourteen "if the world blows up . . . eight or ten years out." Why? Because "ten years from now, the folks in New York who did all the work may be onto other things or in other positions, and just as was the case in this last episode, we had to run around and pretty much figure these things out from scratch."

Sheets also questioned the assumption that countries that had received a swap in the GFC ought to get a temporary swap again, saying, "Now, the flip side of this is that we gave them a swap line once, and if things get bad, we're going to give them a swap line again. I think that is a very reasonable presumption if a crisis erupts in a year or two years. But if the next crisis is eight or ten years out, there is a lot of water under the bridge. The world looks a lot different, and it's not clear to me that there is the same presumption." It may end up that the FOMC, in the event of this later crisis, may choose to give the same partners another swap line, but he did "not think there would be as strong a presumption *as if* they actually had a swap line with us."

Sheets wanted to arrange standing lines only with the United Kingdom, Europe, Switzerland, Japan, and potentially Canada and Mexico. To him, there was a qualitative difference among these six parties, in terms of their economic size, and in the case of Mexico and Canada, their proximity to the United States. On that point, Bernanke joked, "The North American location is hard to change." Janet Yellen, then president of the San Francisco Fed, and later Fed chair, and Eric Rosengren, then president of the Boston Fed, pushed for a larger set of standing swaps.

The FOMC debate illustrates the committee's concerns about managing their relations with partner banks, stigmatizing those that were not granted standing swaps, and geopolitics. Rosengren worried about the unintended consequences and the risk that the Fed's reasons for limiting these standing lines might be misinterpreted. A swap line with Mexico would imply that the Fed was "comfortable having them as a counterparty." By not expanding the network, Rosengren was concerned "about stigmatizing the countries like Mexico and Korea and other countries that want potentially to be a counterparty in part for the signalling benefit." Yellen agreed and was concerned about the economic consequence of excluded parties' potential reactions if the Fed then told, say, "Korea . . . well, we are not putting you in the same category as before."

FOMC members found it was necessary to delineate those in and outside this standing network by some clear metric. But what that metric would be was a sensitive question. "Size" would pose problems for justifying these limits to exclude Asia, as Bullard observed: "When I say Swiss, 'It's a small country, come on. This is an old club that you guys have been fostering for years.' And 'You just don't like us because we're in Asia.' I can imagine that that is sort of the attitude."

No decisions were made in 2009. But the FOMC recognized the utility of having standing lines, that "coordinating policy decisions with foreign central banks has the potential to be complicated and time consuming, so it's preferable to have as many as possible of these decisions negotiated in advance." They also noted that "the swap lines have been a powerful symbol of central bank cooperation." This proposal was discussed occasionally in the years that followed and five standing lines were established in 2013, with the Bank of Canada, the Bank of England, the Bank of Japan, the European Central Bank, and the Swiss National Bank.

There is little evidence of how the Fed's negotiations with its counterparts went in 2013, but the FOMC discussion to create these permanent lines that year was quick and notably different to the previous one. Specifically, Sheets, who had been a key architect of the GFC swap lines, especially in emerging market lines, had left his position at the Fed. Relatedly, the current discussion was whether to convert temporary lines with the Bank of Canada, the Bank of England, the Bank of Japan, the European Central Bank, and the Swiss National Bank, into permanent ones. Mexico, whose 2008 swap had expired, was no longer included in conversations alongside Canada. In 2013, FOMC members were more willing to differentiate between Mexico and Canada without including the NAFA lines that both countries had.

Some FOMC members wanted to at least inform their Mexican counterparts ahead of time about the Fed's decision to establish its standing lines. Fisher expressed concern that Mexico was not included and not given advanced notice of this decision. Some other FOMC officials, however, noted that it was not typical to provide counterparty banks any advance notice about these decisions, in the October 2013 FOMC meeting. Fisher noted, "They're highly sensitive, and, again, it is part of NAFTA, and with any differentiation between Canada and Mexico, I would suggest politely that we let them know at the earliest opportunity, and before others, if possible."[170] But barring that minor debate, the discussion around this standing facility was short. Five permanent lines with the Fed were unanimously approved in October 2013, without including Mexico, as Sheets had initially proposed in 2009. These lines proved vital in 2020 with the outbreak of the COVID-19 pandemic, as I will discuss in the conclusion.

What's Past Is Prologue

Even though central bankers today do not operate with the same free rein of their 1920s counterparts, when the worst crises emerge, the discretion and decision-making power of individual leaders and high-level personnel is substantially heightened to facilitate quick action to arrest emerging troubles. Bernanke, King, Shirakawa, Trichet, and their international and domestic associates walked in the shoes of Strong, Norman, and their international colleagues by responding to the GFC with extensive intervention to provide liquidity in the drying up global economy. In periods of crisis and uncertainty, especially when time is short, and the trajectory of current problems is unknown, central bank leaders lean on a range of heuristics and personal judgments in their decision-making. These assessments are shaped not only by institutional relations and economic signals but also by individuals' personal relations of trust, goodwill, and familiarity with their counterparts.

With each passing decade, central banks, governments, and other policymakers have invested endless resources and countless hours in creating, building, and strengthening the rules and institutions that govern the global economy with the goal of establishing a robust and reliable global financial safety net. And still, when the global economy faced an imminent crisis in 2007, monetary authorities and central banks sidestepped this system to take the ad hoc route.

Insofar as monetary authorities avoided a second Great Depression in 2008, yes, the system worked. But as the crises emerged and escalated from 2007, just like their predecessors experienced in the 1920s and the 1960s, central bankers once again took to ad hockery and governance innovation to stem liquidity pressures around the globe. While these tools had been used before, it was still unclear whether they would work at all this time or how far they would go to mitigate the crisis.

Once again, the crisis was resolved by a handful of central bankers who decidedly sidestepped this system of preexisting and institutional forms of intergovernmental lending and opted for a more ad hoc approach to crisis management. In the absence of this trust, the personal appeals that central bankers made to their friends in the United States may not have had the same sway. Many of their initial discussions around arranging swaps, and agreements over these decisions that were made informally, over dinners or on long walks, may not have been possible.

CONCLUSION

> **A system of this kind . . . is really a system of rule by men and not by law and is extraordinarily dependent on the particular personalities involved.**
>
> —Milton Friedman (1962)

The conclusions of this book are simple but consequential: in managing the global financial system, individual central bank leaders and their personal ties with one another matter. In short, in a crisis, interpersonal cooperation greases the wheels of international cooperation. This is especially the case with bilateral and ad hoc liquidity assistance among central banks.

In March 2020, as the world went into COVID-19 lockdown, businesses shut up shop, and governments imposed travel bans, it was clear that financial troubles would follow close behind. As states, markets, and businesses braced for the economic shocks brought on by the health crisis, people everywhere wanted governments and policymakers to deploy their crisis management toolkits and do something, anything, to ease the blow of the oncoming economic downturn. The global crisis called for an international response. To manage the economic shocks brought on by the pandemic, financial experts and journalists called on the Fed to "to dust off an old, 2008 crisis-era tool of dollar liquidity management" and "bring back dollar swap lines."[1]

In response to these calls for the Fed to re-up and expand these lines, others asked whether Jerome Powell, at the time the chair of the US Fed, had the capacity and clout among his international counterparts to carry out this task. The central bankers who helped forge the global financial crisis (GFC) swaps had by now left the offices they occupied over a decade prior. While Powell had been "forging collaborative relations" with his international colleagues, those relations had not been "battle tested—yet."[2] Unlike most of his Fed colleagues, Powell was somewhat an outsider in the central banking world when he first joined the Board in 2012. He was trained as a lawyer, not as an economist, and "spent his career toggling between two worlds: government service and private-equity dealmaking."[3] Since his arrival at the Fed, Powell had been wary of the distorting effects of Fed interventions on credit markets.

The concern that these lines would be difficult to negotiate in the future had been considered by the Fed. In a Federal Open Market Committee (FOMC) meeting in November 2009, Nathan Sheets proposed establishing standing swaps with the Bank of England, the European Central Bank (ECB), the Bank of Japan, the Swiss National Bank, as well as with Canada and Mexico. Standing lines would essentially provide these partner central banks with a more permanent backstop to dollar markets abroad without having to go through the difficulty of renegotiating these lines. Sheets was less worried about scaling up a program than the difficulty of renegotiating them from scratch in a future crisis. As discussed in chapter 4, a large part of this apprehension was rooted in the effect of changing personnel at the Fed, as those who had done the work during the GFC would likely no longer be in office during the next crisis.

In 2013, five standing lines were established with the ECB and the central banks of Canada, the United Kingdom, Japan, and Switzerland. So, in 2020, it mattered much less whether Powell was an "insider" or not. It also mattered less whether he shared collaborative relations with his counterparts abroad. That was the purpose of the Fed's standing swaps: to mitigate any obstacles to using these crisis-era tools under different leadership. Sheets had been right that it would be easier to scale up these arrangements than to start negotiations from scratch. In addition to the standing swaps, on March 19, 2020, the Fed announced temporary swap lines with the remaining nine central banks that it had assisted in the GFC.

Fed swaps have become a central pillar of the global financial safety net since the GFC. However, historical experience cautions against betting that swaps are here to stay, as some have suggested.[4] The use and endurance of the Fed's standing swap network is not a certainty, as technically they are reinstated every year when the FOMC is annually reconstituted.[5] The reasoning for this comes down to central bank leaders' preferences: the role and existence of Fed swap lines in the global financial safety net relies on the Fed chair's discretion. In 2020, Powell's Fed made the choice to preserve and utilize the Fed's standing swap network. In 1996, Greenspan's Fed dissolved the standing swap lines that Coombs had created.

Even though these lines have repeatedly proved effective in managing systemic financial pressures, their central role in global financial governance brings with it a host of political conundrums. On recapping the key takeaways of the analysis and argument presented in this book, I return to discuss the implications highlighted in the book's introduction.

Key Findings

Bankers' Trust was motivated by the question of why some crises are arrested through ad hoc and bilateral central bank cooperation while others are allowed to escalate. It addressed the related problem of access to the global financial safety net by highlighting a channel through which inequalities emerged between national economies over who benefits from access to easier, flexible, and lower-cost foreign exchange liquidity, and who is excluded: bilateral central bank cooperation. To understand why outcomes of cooperation vary in their form and scope over time, it is essential, first and foremost, to understand how these outcomes come about and who creates them. The patchy and inequitable record of monetary cooperation in times of systemic crises calls for a better understanding of why central banks are more willing to cooperate with some than with others to create ad hoc and innovative methods of crisis management.

To explain these patterns, this book closely explored the decisions and discretion of the principal providers of global liquidity: central banks and those who run them. In a crisis, central bank leaders have a distinct and significantly increased influence and are the ultimate authority over their banks' crisis management policies. Whether and how they exert their heightened influence is less well understood.

The central claim of this book is that central bank leaders' personal relations matter. They can influence the types of liquidity assurance strategies available to their banks when they face financial pressures. I provided a framework that helps us distinguish the influence of individuals and interpersonal relations in international monetary affairs from structural and material factors. I found that leaders can and do influence their banks' willingness to enter experimental crisis responses, such as ad hoc credits or swap arrangements. This willingness and ability to enter these cooperative arrangements is influenced by leaders' personal relations with their counterparts.

At important moments, leaders could determine the choices and approaches of their banks. In many cases, they went against their institutions' preferences or changed the way they operated. For instance, Norman's approach to returning sterling to prewar parity in 1925 went against the preferences of the British government and Treasury. In the 1960s, Coombs and Iklé similarly circumvented institutional constraints and preferences of their central banks in the arrangement of the earliest swap lines. In moments of uncertainty, leaders and high-level officials tasked with important crisis management goals can determine how their bank pursues various policy options.

More importantly, individual leaders, through their personal relations, are crucial to filling the gaps of the global financial governance system in times of crisis. In the absence of a robust financial governance framework, where monetary authorities and policymakers cannot rely on means that are automatic or mechanic, or even adequate to meet current needs, they often resort to ad hoc measures for liquidity provision. But to come to these arrangements, it is essential that leaders, in participating in the agreement, trust one another. Central bank leaders' personal ties can influence the types of monetary transactions available to them to manage liquidity and financial pressures. When central bankers enjoy favorable personal relations of trust and goodwill, they are more likely to engage in ad hoc, bilateral cooperation to manage financial pressures. In the absence of these ties, central banks will have to turn to more costly measures.

Central bank leaders' ability to engage in extensive bilateral cooperation relies on and is indeed facilitated by leaders' independence from their governments. While this autonomy is protected for many central banks around the world today, statutory political independence is a relatively recent development in much of the world. The case of the 1920s highlighted the deeper historical origins of this idea and institution, as championed by Montagu Norman and Benjamin Strong in the 1920s. They secured their de facto independence through secretive and opaque policymaking, especially in the context of international policy. Moreover, they proselytized this idea to their foreign counterparts through their international lending practices, favoring independent banks and bankers in liquidity assistance programs and often requiring autonomy as a condition for bilateral credits. As such, central bank cooperation has evolved in an interpersonal, secretive and opaque manner, which has persisted since the days of Norman and Strong, and continues to the present day.

This dynamic of interpersonal cooperation was crucial in the interwar 1920s. The Norman-Strong partnership functioned primarily on this personal and relational level, where the two regularly went out of their way to help one another in managing their financial troubles. They also extended such graces to their friends elsewhere: Hjalmar Schacht in Germany, and Junnosuke Inoue in Japan, benefited similarly from bilateral and ad hoc assistance in the mid-1920s to finance their debts and stabilize their currencies.

One might suggest that this practice of central banking was only possible and unique to the institutional, political, and economic climate of the early interwar years. However, I have shown that despite changing and increasing institutional and legal constraints on central banks after 1945, the relational side of central banking has remained alive and well. In the 1960s, Charles Coombs's personal relations, friendship, and shared trust with Max Iklé, Johanes Tüngeler, and Guido Carli, underpinned Coombs's European efforts that led to the New York Fed's swap arrangement. These themes reemerge in the creation of the Federal Reserve's swap network with the outbreak of the GFC in 2007. When central bankers had little idea of the trajectory of the crisis, or the likelihood of success of these policies, they swapped hundreds of billions of dollars, overnight, to partner banks. The initial lines were made in no small part on the word of central bank leaders participating in these agreements. Strong's observation that "in none of our business relations has the personal relation played so large a part as in banking" still echoes in the corridors of central banks today.

Differential personal ties also shape access to foreign exchange liquidity programs and outcomes of crisis management. Central bankers implicitly or explicitly distinguish among their foreign colleagues. When leaders do not enjoy the personal trust and goodwill of their counterparts abroad, they must turn to more costly and conditional crisis management and liquidity policies. For instance, in chapter 1, loans to the Polish central bank extended for the purpose of currency stabilization were extended not through bilateral credits but instead multilaterally. These loans came with limits and political conditions attached to protect creditor banks who were engaging with colleagues some of them had never even met.

The effects of a lack of trust and close personal relations among central bankers were most prominent early in the Depression, following the sudden death of Strong, and leadership changes elsewhere in Europe. As bank runs engulfed Central Europe, Hans Luther was not found to be the "right" type by Norman and was disliked by influential figures in the Bank of France. As a result, the Reichsbank had to resort to politically charged governmental assistance from France, which required large political and economic concessions and multilateral, conditional assistance from central banks through the Bank for International Settlements (BIS). The dismantling of the tight personal networks that Norman and Strong had cultivated hindered the international central bank response to the 1930s bank runs and the Great Depression.

Once again, this pattern of differential ties leading to differential monetary transactions is not limited to the interwar period but has persisted through the decades after. In the 1960s, due to the absence of personal trust among British central bankers in Coombs, in New York, Britain initially had to resort to central bank assistance through the BIS, as well as International Monetary Fund (IMF) loans, to manage sterling pressures. It was only when the governor of the Bank, Lord Cromer, and his European associates could vouch for Coombs to Roy Bridge that Bridge settled on a scaled-down swap line with the Fed.

Differential personal ties also helped determine the dividing line among the largest emerging markets as to who got a swap during the GFC. We see that some emerging economies—Mexico and Brazil—were able to secure a Fed swap, while India, which outmatched Brazil on the Fed's swap criteria, was unsuccessful. Where Duvvuri Subbarao (in India) did enjoy the trust and goodwill of Masaaki Shirakawa in Japan, they arranged a bilateral dollar swap between their two banks, and India could avoid the costly conditionality of multilateral assistance.

The close personal connections, and the confident and friendly environments that they generated, allowed central bankers to act on the trust of their colleagues in an atmosphere of grave uncertainty. Close personal ties were especially crucial in facilitating experimentation and innovation in the tools that they could deploy. Leaders who enjoyed the trust and goodwill of their partner bankers could more easily circumvent costly forms of liquidity assurance and adopt more rapid, flexible, and ad hoc solutions for their financial troubles.

Extensions and Limitations

This book has shed light on the distinct role of leaders and their interpersonal relations in the context of international finance and crisis management. My findings suggest that in issues of crisis management and cooperation more broadly, interpersonal relations among individuals can help us better understand decisions and policy choices in areas outside of international monetary relations. This book thus calls for further exploration of the role of relational dynamics such as interpersonal trust, in questions of cooperation, bilateral and otherwise, in crisis and uncertainty. The crises of the 1980s and 1990s, mentioned in chapter 3, present important test cases for my argument and also highlight a key scope condition that interpersonal trust facilitates cooperation among states within material and economic boundaries and can sway decisions on the margins. Trust alone will not carry countries not meeting key economic criteria over the boundary line.

Because central banking is a unique policy arena in several important ways, there are additional scope conditions for my argument. These aspects suggest that the theoretical framework would need to be adjusted to suit a broader set of policy areas outside of money and international finance.

First, central banks are unlike most independent agencies in that they are domestic institutions with a large international reach. The deeply interconnected nature of global finance makes states and national markets vulnerable and exposed to fluctuations and volatility overseas. Central banks' mandates, to secure domestic financial stability, imply an interest in supporting financial stability in markets to which they are most closely connected. As such, the actual jurisdiction of central bank mandates is far less clear. Any other policy arena in which such dynamics may play a similar role would have to be similarly situated on the domestic-international boundary. One issue area that might fit this scope condition is that of climate governance. Climate crises do not emerge only or correspondingly in locations, say, where carbon emissions are the highest. One state's choices and problems can and have quickly become everyone's problem. As such, the climate policy space similarly negotiates this tension of local problems wanting global, cooperative solutions.

A second scope condition is the level of technical expertise that central banking and financial policy demands. The arena of international finance is especially technical, and esoteric, and maintains a high barrier around those in the know and those outside, pushing the activities of central banks into what Culpepper calls "quiet politics."[6] Much of central banks' outsized power is sourced in this feature. Other policy areas in which individual and interpersonal dynamics are strongest would be those that share similar qualities to those of central banks. Again, climate cooperation and especially innovation to find solutions to the climate crisis require a high level of technical expertise in climate science. Cooperation over nuclear proliferation, deterrence in the security space, or nuclear energy policy also share a similarly high barrier to entry that can keep policymaking exclusive to a relatively small and insulated set of decision-makers, which is similarly undertaken in secret and behind closed doors. Given that conflicts of interests among parties in the security space are more severe than among central banks, this may limit the scope of affective ties in influencing cooperation relative to costly signals. These policy areas may provide fertile ground to further test the scope of the framework.

A third scope condition is that this theoretical framework is particular to the context of crisis and uncertainty. In more certain times, routine cooperation through traditional institutional or intergovernmental channels generally suffices. The need for interpersonal trust is especially heightened in situations of radical uncertainty, when conventional metrics and signals are less informative and system trust is compromised. Moreover, decisions in crises need to be made quickly and agents will not have the time to undertake long and arduous negotiations and deliberations. So, leaders and policymakers will instead rely on subjective reason, informal channels of cooperation, and interpersonal trust.

That is not to say that the argument will seamlessly travel outside of the monetary realm without adjustment. Many of the early-twenty-first-century crises are not limited to one issue or policy area alone. As we move into unfamiliar territory, such as the recent pandemic, and escalating climate crises, the unknowns will be far greater. What about when financial crises emerge from nonfinance sources? The COVID-19 health crisis once again reminded us that nonfinancial crises can have grave financial repercussions. Fortunately, central bankers during the GFC had put into place precautionary backstops to protect against this possibility.

Even when out of the central banking world, in situations of war and uncertainty, these interpersonal ties, and the unique frankness and openness among central bankers, have proved effective in addressing financial pressures. When the war in Ukraine began early in 2022, European policymakers were initially worried that Russia might get wind of looming US sanctions, anxious to put them in place, while Janet Yellen, a former Fed chair, and at the time US Treasury Secretary, "pored over the fine print." But at this time, Yellen found herself working alongside Mario Draghi, former ECB head, then the prime minister of Italy. While sanctions agreements were slow to come about, the president of the European Commission, Ursula von der Leyen, asked Draghi to work out the details with Yellen: "We were all waiting around, asking, 'What's taking so long?'" recalls an EU official. "Then the answer came: Draghi has to work his magic on Yellen." By the evening, agreement had been reached.[7]

While these outcomes bode well for the prospect of future crisis management, it is not guaranteed that the right instruments or people will be in place in future crisis, especially those with nonmarket roots. To better understand the prospects for crisis management warrants further exploration of the role of leaders and relational dynamics among policymakers in crisis-prone, technical issue areas outside of the monetary realm.

Implications

My findings illustrated how monetary leaders negotiate structural, material, and institutional variables in shaping world politics. The narratives and analyses in this book highlighted the sensitivity of financial governance, crisis management, and policy innovation for navigating crises. But historical experience, namely the Great Depression, suggests a cause for concern when thinking of the prospects for the future of financial governance. The lasting personal connections that central bankers built were crucial in facilitating a collaborative crisis response from central banks in times of stress. But when these relationships fail to emerge or leaders are replaced, collectively navigating crises has been a more tortured effort, with devastating consequences. My study thus highlights the implications of the concentration of power in global financial governance.

Two broad theoretical implications emerge from my argument. The first is the need for further individual-level and relational analyses into the role of interpersonal trust in international politics to better understand the origins of important governance institutions and instruments. The second is to further our understanding of how political agents can and do shape and reinforce global hierarchies through their personal relations with their foreign counterparts.

Leaders in International Monetary Affairs

A key theoretical implication of this book is that monetary leaders matter, especially in conditions of crisis and uncertainty. Leaders matter in two meaningful ways: first, their own individual discretion and influence in international monetary affairs is apparent in their ability to influence the policy disposition and preferences of their bank. Second, they can influence patterns and outcomes of crisis management and bilateral cooperation through their interpersonal relations with their foreign counterparts.

In addition to leaders' influence in shaping domestic policy, leaders also influence how their banks engage with foreign entities and in their disposition toward risk-taking and experimentation. The power and influence of Norman and Strong in shaping the trajectory of the monetary system, through the 1920s and for decades after, is indisputable. Strong's singular influence in US banking circles and his ability to maintain the New York Fed's independence is evident not only in his lifetime but also in his death. Coombs, Iklé, and Cromer were central players in shaping their banks' practices and policy choices, willing to go off message from their institutions' traditional practices or their home governments' interests. Bernanke and Jean-Claude Trichet's leadership and persuasive negotiating capabilities were integral in fostering a united front among some of the world's largest central banks to manage the crisis.

The unique influence of central bank leaders is also evident in how leadership changes were followed by policy changes and a change in access to liquidity assistance from partner banks. Leaders' individual influence thus cannot be overstated, especially in the relational context. We therefore cannot be sure that every next leader will adopt the same policies, share the same personal ties with foreign partners, or enjoy access to the same types of liquidity assistance.

A deeper understanding of global economic and financial governance would result from exploring individual-level influences, not only in the management of financial crises but in the specific conditions and contexts in which leaders have shaped governance innovation and cooperation in other areas of the international political economy. After all, the first ideas for the BIS emerged in Norman's personal conversations and correspondence with Strong and Schacht.

The origins of this most crucial institution for financial management are as much rooted in very particular personalities and personal relations as in structural determinants or a convergence of ideas among policymakers. The swap network created in 1961 has a similar origin story. Informal and personal interactions between friends influenced the liquidity provision strategies that central banks adopted to meet their foreign exchange funding pressures in the 1960s.

Historians have suggested that "such a climate of trust, a blessing as far as cooperation is concerned, is a curse as far the historian's work is concerned."[8] I could not agree more. Disentangling the role of trust from broader material and ideational variables is murky and complicated. But understanding the importance of trust in cooperation underscores a need to identify it and better incorporate it into our explanations of various types of cooperation. Understanding the origins of these crucial financial governance innovations can deepen our understanding of the past, present, and future of the global governance system. There is therefore much value in further exploring the individual and relational dynamics among leaders, not only in financial crisis management but also in governance and policy frameworks in all areas of the international economy and in global governance more broadly.

This book made a case for further exploring the role of leaders in a broader range of issue areas. Leaders' influence and interpersonal relations may also play a crucial role in crisis management in conditions of uncertainty outside finance. It also highlights the need to understand the conduct of international monetary affairs from the perspective of leaders themselves. The firsthand insights demonstrate that we cannot understand outcomes and decisions in international politics as distinct from the policymakers who shape them.

Hierarchy in International Relations

The patterns of crisis and cooperation discussed in this book highlight a second theoretical implication: financial crises and international crisis management can create and reinforce hierarchies and inequities in the international monetary system. The GFC once again brought the Fed into the position of an international lender of last resort. This significantly expanded the reach of the Fed's powers, responsibilities, and influence far outside its borders, in a way that it could impinge on economies and publics to whom it does not answer. The crisis illustrated that the Fed's role, capacity, and power in financial governance today far exceeds that of the international financial institutions that comprise the governance system. Even many central bankers acknowledge these problems and their own discomfort with how the system operates. Donald Kohn, who was vice chair of the Fed during the GFC, recalled that the Fed's swap program "put the FOMC in the 'uncomfortable' position of being an 'arbiter of the soundness of other countries' policies, the liquidity requirements of their banks, and their systemic importance.'"[9]

As scholars have argued, in determining crisis management policies to save the world, central bankers are saving some more than others.[10] I have shown that this is not only in the case of protecting private finance domestically but also in terms of international central bank assistance and international crisis management: crisis resolution efforts can also perpetuate the existing hierarchy and inequities in the global economy. As illustrated in chapter 4, frustration over these powers of the Fed was felt by foreign central banks, especially those in emerging markets who undoubtedly faced a higher bar to accessing swap lines but depended on the Fed for assistance. Most emerging and developing economies lacked the international clout and competitiveness to give them access to lower-cost, conditionality-free liquidity through the Fed swap network.[11] Instead, they were forced to turn to the IMF and other costly channels.

Similar patterns emerged in the twentieth-century crises. Through their close personal relations with Schacht and Inoue, Norman and Strong solidified banking connections and Germany and Japan's positions in the core of the global economy. Of course, these ties were further supported by broader economic and political relations, reinforced over time. But as the 1920s show, central banking and monetary relations offered another channel to construct and cement these hierarchies.

The differentiated nature of central bank assistance between the core central banks and those outside this community served to further distinguish states within the hierarchical order. Specifically, currency stabilization in Eastern Europe was decidedly multilateral, contingent on political conditions, and ultimately sought by France. Distrust and personal differences between Norman in Britain and Émile Moreau at the Bank of France hindered Norman's participation and willingness to lead multilateral credit support for Poland. France, which eventually took the lead, took on a more politically charged effort in Poland. Indeed, a similar pattern emerged in these stabilization efforts in Romania and Bulgaria, and elsewhere in Eastern Europe, separating these states from those that received extensive, bilateral support from Norman and Strong alone.[12]

These hierarchies have been entrenched since the GFC, with the establishment of the standing swap lines, and the Fed's response to the emerging pandemic. Powell's Fed went even further in its domestic and global crisis interventions in 2020. On the international side, in addition to re-upping GFC-era swap lines, on March 31, the Fed also announced a temporary repurchase facility (repos) for foreign and international monetary authorities (FIMA), which was also more widely accessible than the swap network. Through these lines, FIMA account holders could borrow US dollars in exchange for their US Treasuries holdings in the New York Fed. These more expansive lines gave a larger number of emerging markets access to dollar liquidity and were likely created because the pandemic was far more global and generated an economic environment very different to that of the GFC.[13]

However, the Fed's broader-ranging liquidity arrangements once again reinforced hierarchies in the global financial system. Major central banks' ability to access larger amounts of dollar funding dwarfed that of smaller central banks using the FIMA repos. The Fed's varying foreign facilities, the standing swaps, the temporary swaps, and the FIMA repos, each less attractive than the previous, represent the same concerns that the Fed had discussed in 2009—that by excluding, say, Mexico or Korea from the standing arrangements, or continuing to exclude other large emerging markets from the swap network at all, the Fed signaled to these economies that they were not seen in the same category as those that could access the larger and unlimited dollar liquidity arrangements, as discussed in chapter 4. Parallel to the Fed's GFC interventions, its pandemic interventions, although broader, once again reinforced global hierarchies and perpetuated inequities in the existing global finance governance system.

Differential personal ties have worked to differentiate between states in the core and the periphery in international monetary relations. Through their personal, informal channels, bolstered by preexisting institutional and resource-based hierarchies in global finance, central bankers can shape and reinforce system-level hierarchies and inequities among states.

These theoretical implications highlight two key political and policy implications. First, the management of systemic financial crises inevitably relies on ad hoc and experimental efforts, and monetary leaders regularly seek to sidestep the existing governance system. This pattern of cooperation calls into question the legitimacy of independent central banks at the domestic and international levels. Second, the global financial safety net is riddled with gaping holes. This suggests the institutional setup of central bank independence should be rethought while protecting their necessary emergency powers for crisis management.

The Politics of Central Banking

The post-GFC years have highlighted the extent to which central banks and central bankers influence our daily lives. These crises remind us of the outsized power held by unelected policymakers in politically independent agencies. From this realization has emerged widespread and even bipartisan backlash against central banks across the world. At the heart of the influence of these powerful individuals lies a tension between central banking and the core principles of democratic governance—accountability, representation, and transparency.[14]

In the last century, if not longer, central bank cooperation has been shrouded in secrecy, and leaders have relied on closed door conversations and substantial opacity in undertaking these operations. This practice of secrecy took hold in central bank practices under Norman and Strong. Central bankers regularly met in private and often did not publicize their travels to see one another; they even travelled in disguise and under false names, and to all in these circles, this was not unusual. Norman even kept his dealings quiet within his own bank.

Undoubtedly, this ability to arrange liquidity support in the face of shortages and financial pressures, quickly and without any political interference, is essential for crisis management. Even more, in undertaking experimental and innovative policies, as tends to be the case in the gravest circumstances, a confidential environment, proved to be necessary. Crucial conversations took place in private, informal settings, in a "walk and talk," a "fortuitous happenchance" or a gathering in an elevator. This allowed for productive brainstorming, sharing of ideas and proposals, and keeping one another informed of important developments, without causing market reactions. However, this secrecy in central banking has generated a transparency deficit for central banks, who are now facing increased pushback for their policies and opacity.

The crisis also drew attention to the international layer of the contradictions between central banks and democratic governance. Central banks' foreign lending practices are yet another mechanism (in addition to domestic policies) through which they protect the interests of private finance: they can choose who to rescue in a crisis, both domestically and internationally. In doing so, they delegate more powers to foreign central banks to decide who will benefit from these liquidity lifelines overseas. These cooperative liquidity programs can also serve to influence the policy decisions and preferences of foreign partners who participate in them.[15]

This is not a new concern. These practices of independence and cooperation are rooted in a longer history, dating back until at least as early as the interwar period. The institution of central bank independence was declared in Norman's 1921 central bank manifesto, where he wrote that "autonomy and freedom from political control are desirable for all central and reserve banks" and that it was upon conforming to this principle that cooperation was also a desirable policy.[16] Moreover, central bank autonomy strengthened the personal ties among central bankers internationally, which allowed banks to access liquidity assistance from partner banks. Creditor central banks privileged more independent banks, creating an incentive for this institutional setup to be widely adopted.

The nature of such policymaking is at odds with key democratic norms. The case study of interwar financial governance identified the origins of such practices, the personal and interpersonal dynamics of central banking, and how they influenced and institutionalized central bank independence and cooperation. In the 1920s, these practices were developed in a context of little political accountability, limited political representation, and outsized amounts of autonomy for leaders to shape the way their banks evolved and the activities they undertook.

After 1945, when central banks became answerable to governments, these practices became increasingly embedded in the normal operations and institutional structures of central banks. International organizations, especially the BIS, and the technical knowledge required for their work, offered them a safe haven outside political influence. Through their foreign operations, central banks in the 1960s could expand their jurisdictions and shape policy choices overseas through their personal encounters, conversations, and agreements. And because central banks now operated as agents to their finance ministries, secrecy was a crucial tool for their activities.

While this was largely accepted (or perhaps ignored) in the past, today, central banks have come under fire for bailing out foreign economies, widening their jurisdictional reach, and expanding their mandates to take on new activities and responsibilities.[17] In the GFC, while economic considerations certainly influenced decision-making, the interpersonal dynamics underlying cooperation shaped the crisis effort. Central banks took unprecedented risks in their crisis management approach, and although they did ultimately work, that they would work was unknown when these policies were first adopted.

At the same time, we cannot disregard the role that central banks can and have played in arresting financial crises and the need for them to act quickly in the guaranteed event of a future financial meltdown. When given the room and independence to take unprecedented actions, central banks have also proved that they are indispensable institutions. In many instances, their autonomy from governmental interference has been essential for monetary policymaking, allowing central banks to set appropriate targets and goals. And the confidence and privacy of their meetings has been an essential element to facilitating their actions, allowing for open debate, and for catalyzing experimentative governance when it is needed the most. In turn, as chapter 2 showed, the implications of central banks' failure to act can be ghastly.

But central banks today find themselves facing a legitimacy crisis across the world and on all points of the political spectrum. It is clear that this institutional setup needs a fundamental rethink. Their favoring of wealth and those who hold it shows that central bank neutrality is a myth.[18] As unelected powers, their lack of representation, accountability, and transparency has hindered public trust in the institution. But public support and trust is critical to affording central banks their authority and their independence.[19] This concern is even more pronounced when we factor in the expansion of central banks' toolkits, the increasingly broad interpretation of their mandates, and the new powers and responsibilities that central banks have assumed since the GFC.

The tensions between independent central banking and democratic principles pervade central banks' activities at the domestic and the international levels. The consequences of central bank policies do not only affect domestic publics but also those abroad, especially through these ad hoc governance frameworks and in the context of systemic crises.

A Global Financial Safety Net?

Bankers' Trust showed how, with a global governance system that time and again proves to be ill-equipped to deal with the most severe financial crises, central bankers' ad hockery, innovation, and experimentation have repeatedly saved the day. Indeed, when they have been unwilling or unable to pursue drastic firefighting strategies, as in the 1930s, disaster has ensued. We thus need these agencies and these agents—central bank leaders—to step up to the task, as both first- and last-resort responders, to any future crisis.

But while these ad hoc solutions have effectively managed financial pressures, they raise questions about the robustness and durability of the existing system of global financial governance and highlight serious inefficiencies in the use of time and resources outside of crisis conditions. Since the 1920s, and even more after 1945, states have invested tremendous amounts of time and resources toward building a more robust framework for global financial governance. The IMF was created for the very purpose of providing financial assistance to struggling economies and playing the role of international lender of last resort in the face of liquidity shortages.

However, as shown in chapters 3 and 4, these institutions have been ill equipped to play this role in the face of systemic pressures. During the 1960s sterling crises, there was a real risk that if the IMF stepped in to rescue Britain, it would no longer have the resources to arrest the inevitable dollar crises that did indeed follow. During the GFC, once again the Fund did not possess adequate resources to assist struggling states as the crisis spread across the world. Even more concerning was that in both periods, states actively sought to avoid going to these large international organizations for help and instead pursued alternative, quick, and low-cost financing from creditor central banks to avoid the costs of multilateral liquidity strategies.

This recurring pattern shines a light on the deep underlying fault lines of the current governance system in international monetary and financial affairs. Despite the huge amount of investment in creating international financial institutions, and systems and mechanisms to deal with financial crises, central bankers and monetary authorities regularly and decidedly opt to circumvent this system to go for ad hoc arrangements instead. This eagerness to shy away from the existing system, to avoid its costs, and because of its inadequacies, poses at least two significant problems for global financial governance moving forward.

First, the availability of ad hoc assurances at least for a few of the largest and richest, systemically important economies in global finance may serve to generate and reinforce a deeper underlying inertia preventing an *effective* reform of the system. Indeed, the GFC spurred a few important governance reforms in the Bretton Woods institutions in the last decade, but as scholars have argued, these reforms remain wanting.[20] Moreover, the scope of any sufficient and inequitable efforts remains at the mercy of the United States, on whom the world has come to rely, both in the institutional system as well as for ad hoc alternatives, such as the Fed swap program.[21]

A related and even more worrying problem is that this reliance on ad hoc policies in the absence of a robust governance system heightens the discretionary power of a few leaders in times of crisis. This leaves the stability and prosperity of national economies and the international financial system critically reliant on central bank leaders' personal preferences and personal relations when it is at its most vulnerable. As I showed in chapter 2, most frequently during the early years of the Great Depression, but also at other times in the earlier interwar years, and in the Bretton Woods era, the management of financial crises is not immune to the fickleness of human temperament.

The global financial governance system is always going to need a reliable and robust financial safety net that can be made available in times of need. But the record of the system working effectively in the face of financial crises is at best patchy. Instead, time and again, such a system is almost never adequate and therefore inherently unreliable. Even in the worst crises that were still resolved successfully enough, the most powerful central banks take the lead in playing the part of a global lender of last resort.

The standing swap lines were established precisely to remedy the stopgap nature of financial crisis management and may provide a more reliable, longstanding alternative that the Fed can scale up with ease, in the next crisis. As the rapid use and expansion of this program in March 2020 illustrates, the Fed's expansive liquidity arrangements once again proved to be an efficient response to the global health and accompanying financial crisis. For that reason, many scholars and experts on the topic posit that these instruments are likely to see continued use. However, historical experience suggests caution in making these bets, and the reasoning for this comes down to the particular preferences of central bank leaders.

The 1962 Fed swap network also evolved into a series of standing arrangements. While they were in place for several decades, they quickly fell out of use by the early 1970s, even during grave crises such as those of the 1970s. A few decades later, in a 1996 FOMC meeting, these lines were discontinued. During that meeting, Yellen observed that the Fed's swap network represented an "important symbol of [the Fed's] commitment to international cooperation." Her remarks during that meeting intimated that Alan Greenspan, then Fed chair, found them to be "by and large a legacy of times past and may have become something of an anachronism." During that meeting, William Joseph McDonough, then vice chair of the Fed, essentially articulated and illustrated the central themes of the argument made in this book:

> If we were to assume a world in which the swap network no longer existed, would any formal mechanism have to be created to replace it? My own working hypothesis on that would be "no." In my view, what would replace it is what in a way already replaces it. A good many of us spend a fair amount of our time—I spend essentially 10 percent of my time—attending BIS meetings. I don't do that because I like the Basle Hilton, I can assure you, but rather because of the close personal relationships that come from that activity. What that means is that if we have a problem with any of the people that the Chairman sees, say, at four meetings a year and I see at ten meetings a year, we are talking with someone we know very well. So what replaces the swap network is that personal relationship. It does not mean that we do them a favor or they do us a favor. What it does is to make it possible for two individuals representing their central banks to agree on what is in the mutual interest of their central banks and more importantly their countries.[22]

Yellen also suggested that Greenspan "look for an opportunity in Basle or elsewhere to discuss the future of these arrangements quietly with [the Fed's] central bank partners."[23] Greenspan, known for his free-market, anti-interventionist preferences, was not eager to keep these going, and under his Fed chairmanship, the midcentury RCAs were unilaterally dissolved. Even though ad hoc bilateral agreements that are reconstituted into standing arrangements ought to fill in some of the gaps in the financial governance framework, one cannot guarantee that they will remain standing lines. While today's standing arrangements seem more widely accepted, future Fed leaders may choose to follow in Greenspan's steps, if they too find them unfavorable.

Personality Is Policy

For long, technocratic governance has been praised and preferred for being purely scientific, and based in technical knowledge, science, and data, and consequently immune to the influences of messy politics and human temperament. But central bankers themselves are concerned about the impact on policymaking and cooperation when those who forged the last arrangements would have moved on to other things. Some even fear that a change of guard might hinder the ability of central banks to create them anew in the event of a future crisis, which raises alarm bells for the future of global finance and its governance. *Bankers' Trust* highlights the sensitivity of the financial system not only to the structures, interests, and ideas that frame policymaking but also to the people in charge.

The stories told in this book have mostly been success stories of how certain leaders were able to carry national economies through crises. But the experience of the Great Depression shows that this cannot be guaranteed if the "right" people are not in charge. This feeling is shared among bankers throughout the twentieth and twenty-first centuries, as I've shown in this book.

While this presents a sobering conclusion, it need not necessarily be that way, as this project demonstrates. But success stories abound, we know of no one formula for a successful and equitable response to systemic financial crises. For at least the last century, financial governance has relied far less on the financial governance system as we know it. Rather, the management of finance and the prevention of cataclysmic crises has taken the form, time and again, of ad hoc, stopgap arrangements created to manage the pressures that financial systems generate. The provision of these fixes ultimately lies in the hands of a few powerful people.

Notes

INTRODUCTION

1. Federal Reserve Archival System for Economic Research (FRASER), 1116.6.1, Norman to Strong, October 10, 1926.

2. FRASER, 1116.6, Strong to Norman, March 6, 1926.

3. FRASER, Strong to Pierre Jay, September 11, 1926, and previously, Jay to Strong, August 3, 1924.

4. FRASER, Strong to George L. Harrison, August 9, 1926.

5. Meyer 1970, 25.

6. Meyer 1970; Moreau 1991.

7. FRASER, 0320.115, Percy Jay Fuller, August 4, 1926.

8. Moreau 1991.

9. Turner 1996, 32.

10. Kindleberger 1973, 303.

11. Kindleberger 1973; Krasner 1976; Gilpin 1981; Gilpin 1987; Mearsheimer 1994.

12. Keohane 1984; Keohane and Nye 1977.

13. Eichengreen 1992; Simmons 1994; Webb 1995.

14. Aizenman and Pasricha 2010; McDowell 2012; Broz 2015.

15. Mitrany 1976; Haas 1964.

16. Granovetter 1973; Granovetter 1985; Haas 1992; Emirbayer 1997; McNamara 1998; Abdelal 2007; Chwieroth 2010; Nelson 2017.

17. With the notable exception of Morrison 2021.

18. Sociology, especially economic sociology and relational sociology, have evaluated the role of social ties in policymaking. See Granovetter 1973; Granovetter 1985; Emirbayer 1997; Emirbayer and Mische 1998; Zelizer 2000; Zelizer 2012; White 2002.

19. Keohane 2010; Avant, Finnemore, and Sell 2010.

20. North and Weingast 1989.

21. Friedman 1962; Siklos 2002, 21–26.

22. Katzenstein and Nelson 2013.

23. Mundell 1999; Morrison 2021.

24. Braun 2016; Beckert 2016.

25. Bagehot 1912.

26. For broader discussions on the origins and rationale for central banks and the political economy of financial governance, reform, and regulation, see Broz 1997; Bernhard, Broz, and Clark 2002; Obstfeld 2009a; Helleiner and Pagliari 2011; Borio, James, and Shin 2014; Frieden 2016.

27. Moessner and Allen 2010.

28. Nelson 2017; Copelovitch 2010; Vreeland 2003; Vreeland 2007.

29. Stone 2013.

30. Nelson and Katzenstein 2014, 362.

31. Keynes 1937, 214. Per Knight 1921 and Keynes 1937, the conceptual distinction between calculable risk, based in known probability distributions, and incalculable

uncertainty is where the "probable distribution of outcomes itself is unknown." Lockwood 2015, 727; Nelson and Katzenstein 2014.

32. Widmaier, Blyth, and Seabrooke 2007.

33. Blyth 2006; Nelson 2017; Kirshner 2015.

34. Keynes 1936, 162–63.

35. Haas 1992; McNamara 1998; Abdelal 2007; Nelson 2017; Chwieroth 2015.

36. Adolph 2013.

37. Seabrooke and Tsingou 2021.

38. Granovetter 1985, 486; Emirbayer and Mische 1998; Haas 1992.

39. Zelizer 2012, 148.

40. See Goddard 2009; McCourt 2016; Pouliot 2016; MacDonald 2018; and Jackson and Nexon 2019 on relational approaches to international politics. See Siklos 2002; Singleton 2011; Helleiner 2013; Bytheway and Metzler 2016; Johnson 2016; and Morrison 2021 on financial diplomacy.

41. Widmaier, Blyth, and Seabrooke 2007, 748.

42. Zelizer 2012, 148.

43. Volcker and Gyohten 1992. See also Johnson 2016 on how the transnational central bank community engages with one another.

44. Granovetter 1985, 486.

45. Collins quoted in Zelizer 2012, 8. See also White 2002.

46. Zelizer 2012, 145, 149.

47. Zelizer 2000.

48. FRASER, 1116.2.1, Strong to Norman, November 17, 1921.

49. Bank for International Settlements Archives (BISA), HAL.10 (F02), Edward Jay Epstein, "A Brave New Role for the BIS."

50. Silver 1989, 276.

51. Wheeler 2018, 59.

52. Mercer 2005, 95.

53. MacMillan 2003.

54. Dore 1983.

55. See Wheeler 2018 on a review of theories of trust in international relations and a discussion on the various means in which trust emerges. Also Larson 1997; Rathbun 2012; Jervis 1976; and Kydd 2001 on trust and trust formation.

56. Wheeler 2012; Wheeler 2018; Holmes 2018; Holmes and Yarhi-Milo 2017.

57. Gray 2013; Gray 2009.

58. FRASER, 1116.7.1, Strong to Norman, October 19, 1927; emphasis added.

59. On leaders' influence in central banking and crises, see Friedman 1962; Friedman and Schwartz 1963; Siklos 2002; Singleton 2011; Romer and Romer 2004. For international relations scholarship on leaders, see Saunders 2009; Lupton 2020; Horowitz 2018; Horowitz 2015; Fuhrmann and Horowitz 2015; Yarhi-Milo 2014; Krcmaric, Nelson, and Roberts 2020.

60. Author interview, anonymous.

61. Romer and Romer 2004.

62. Nelson 2017; Kertzer 2016; Lupton 2020; Yarhi-Milo 2014.

63. Krasner 1976; Kindleberger 1973.

64. See Strange 1971; Webb and Krasner 1989; Eichengreen and Flandreau 2009; Eichengreen, Mehl, and Chiţu 2019. Throughout this book, unless otherwise specified, "postwar" indicates the post-1945 period, "prewar" indicates the pre-1914 period, and "interwar" indicates the 1918–1938 years.

65. McDowell 2017.

66. Katzenstein 1977; Kapstein 1992; Kapstein 1994; Drezner 2007.

67. Kirshner 2015; Cohen 2015.

68. Aizenman and Pasricha 2010; McDowell 2012; Broz 2015.

69. Bernanke 2002.

70. Eichengreen 1992; Simmons 1994; Simmons 2001.

71. Keohane 1984; Keohane and Nye 1977.

72. Copelovitch 2010; Toniolo 2005; Borio, Toniolo, and Clement 2008.

73. Woods 2010; Helleiner 2014.

74. Keohane 2011; Kreps 2011.

75. Chwieroth 2010; Nelson 2014; Nelson 2017.

76. Adolph 2013; Chwieroth 2015; Marple 2021.

77. Kindleberger 1989; Kindleberger 1990; Kindleberger 1978.

78. Horowitz 2018, 185. See also Goddard 2009 on how political entrepreneurs can shape and produce structural change, from a lens of social network theory.

79. Broz 2015; Sahasrabuddhe 2024.

80. Johnson 2016 also illustrates the hierarchical nature of the transnational central bank community, with a focus on hierarchies in the transnational central bank communities in the West and Eastern Europe.

81. Carnegie and Carson 2020.

82. Brown 2014, 409.

83. Brown 2014.

84. Friedman 1962; Siklos 2002; Singleton 2011, 21–26.

85. Romer and Romer 2004.

86. Keating and Ruzicka 2014, 745.

87. Keating and Ruzicka 2014; Wheeler 2018.

88. Ku and Mitzen 2022, 800.

89. Gerring 2007.

90. Although the Depression continued through 1939, I do not address the post-1933 efforts as they present a distinct context to the pre-1933 years and are outside the scope of this project. The remilitarization of the Rhineland in March 1936 violated the Versailles and Locarno Treaties; states were now on the road to war.

91. Moss and Thomas 2021.

92. Frieden 2016, 45; Chinn and Frieden 2011.

93. Drezner 2014a; Drezner 2014b; Helleiner 2014, 35; FOMC 2008b.

94. Schedler 2007.

95. See Martin 2022 and Slobodian 2018 on the deep histories of political contestation in the origins of key global governance institutions and governing ideas.

96. Johnson 2016.

97. Ikenberry 2001; Cooley 2005; Lake 2009.

98. MacDonald 2018.

99. Essentially, central bankers tend to run in, and reinforce, elite networks that are propped up through ties to prestigious education backgrounds, past careers, wealth, race, and gender, not unlike other elitist organizations as studied in Mills 1956; Tsingou 2015; Rivera 2016.

100. McNamara 2002; Dietsch 2020; Best 2016; van 't Klooster 2020; Downey 2021; Monnet 2024; Moschella 2024.

101. Balls, Howat, and Stansbury 2018.

102. O'Driscoll, Jr. 2011; Perry 2020; Högenauer and Howarth 2019.

103. Smialek 2023; Greider 1989; Conti-Brown 2016.

104. Blinder 1998; Drazen 2002; Alesina and Tabellini 2007; Alesina and Tabellini 2008. For a discussion on the domestic politics of this institutional setup see Broz 2005; Tucker 2018.

105. See Farrell and Newman 2014 on the new interdependence approach on rule overlap across national jurisdictions.

106. Horowitz 2018, 249.

107. Clarke 1967.

1. STRONG MEN AND STRONG'S MEN

1. Clarke 1967.
2. Kirshner 2007; Poast 2015.
3. Mouré 2002, 50–51.
4. Kindleberger 1973.
5. Kindleberger 1973.
6. Eichengreen 1992.
7. Kindleberger 1973; Eichengreen 1992.
8. Simmons 1994, 30.
9. Eichengreen 1992.
10. Clarke 1967; Mouré 2002; Bytheway and Metzler 2016.
11. Berman 1998; Gourevitch 1986; Polanyi 1957. See also Eichengreen and Kakridis 2023 on the establishment and institutionalization of modern-day central bank practices in the interwar period.
12. Eichengreen 2019a, 34; Eichengreen 2019b.
13. MacMillan 2003.
14. Keynes 1920.
15. Fink 1991, 11.
16. Federal Reserve Archival System for Economic Research (FRASER), 797.04, Assistant Observer, James A. Logan, Jr., April–August 1922.
17. FRASER, 797.4, Strong to Logan, June 23, 1922.
18. Fink 1991, 17.
19. Eichengreen 1992.
20. Clarke 1967, 35.
21. Mouré 2002; Clarke 1967, 35.
22. Hawtrey 1922.
23. Sayers 1976, 162–63; Singleton 2011.
24. Eichengreen and Flandreau 2009.
25. Bytheway and Metzler 2016.
26. Boyle 1967.
27. Ahamed 2009.
28. Broz 1997.
29. Moreau 1991, 39. This ideological preference is recounted in Moreau's diary entry of July 20, 1926.
30. Bytheway and Metzler 2016, 65.
31. Bank of England Archives (BEA), Richard Sydney Sayers, Papers: Records of Interviews, 1969–1973, file ADM/33/25, Interview with R. N. Kershaw, March 27, 1969; and 1969–1973, file ADM/33/25, Interview with Lord Rennell, April 24, 1969.
32. FRASER, 210.1, Hamlin to Strong, January 9, 1917.
33. Sayers 1976 (appendices). NB: Only two of Norman's principles are listed here, as relevant to this discussion.
34. Turner 1996, 31.
35. FRASER, 1000.2, Strong's Diary, March 24, 28, and 30, 1916.
36. Mouré 2002.
37. FRASER, 1116.3.2, Norman to Strong, August 9, 1922. See also Mouré 2002.
38. FRASER, 1116.5.1, Norman to Strong, May 11, 1925.

39. FRASER, 1116.3.1, Strong to Norman, March 28, 1922.
40. FRASER, 1116.5.2, Norman to Strong, April 15 and May 11, 1925.
41. FRASER, 1116.5.1, Strong to Norman, April 27, 1925.
42. Mouré 2002, 155.
43. BEA, Overseas Department: Japan, OV16/106, Norman to Fukai, May 22, 1923; Fukai to Norman, May 29, 1923.
44. Sayers 1976, 339.
45. Eichengreen 1992; Sargent 1982.
46. Clarke 1967, 46.
47. Morrison 2021, 181.
48. Schacht 1956.
49. Weitz 1997.
50. LeBor 2013.
51. Moreau 1991.
52. BEA, ADM/33/24, Interview with Allan Sproul, October 21, 1969.
53. Mirwis 1987; Boyle 1967; Toniolo 2005.
54. LeBor 2013.
55. Schacht 1956, 179; Boyle 1967, 170.
56. Boyle 1967, 171.
57. Boyle 1967, 172–73.
58. Schacht 1956; Morrison 2021, 183.
59. Clay 1957, 212.
60. FRASER, 1116.4.2, Norman to Strong, January 7, 1924.
61. Meyer 1970, 11.
62. FRASER, 111.6.2.2, Norman to Havenstein, December 5, 1921.
63. FRASER, 1116.2.1, Strong to Norman, November 25, 1921.
64. FRASER, 1135.1, Office Correspondence, J. E. Crane to Mr. Case, December 8, 1921.
65. FRASER, 1116.3.1, Strong to Norman, February 2, 1922.
66. FRASER, 1135.1, Strong to Havenstein, February 2, 1922.
67. Schacht 1956, 185.
68. FRASER, 1116.3.1, Strong to Norman, March 28, 1922.
69. Boyle 1967, 168–69.
70. Clarke 1967, 47.
71. Schacht 1956, 190–91.
72. Clarke 1967, 58.
73. Clay 1957, 212.
74. Boyle 1967, 167.
75. FRASER, 1116.4.2, Norman to Strong, January 30, 1924.
76. FRASER, 1116.4.1, Strong to Norman, July 9, 1924.
77. Clarke 1967, 63.
78. Clarke 1967, 66.
79. Clarke 1967, 67–68.
80. Clarke 1967.
81. Sayers 1976, 183.
82. Clarke 1967, 111.
83. Schacht 1927, 206.
84. Chandler 1958, 285.
85. Chandler 1958.
86. FRASER, 1135.0, Telegram, Schacht to Strong, July 13, 1927.
87. Metzler 2006, 96.

88. Metzler 2006, 119–20.
89. Metzler 2006.
90. Bytheway and Metzler 2016, 94.
91. Kirshner 2007.
92. Smethurst 2001.
93. FRASER, 1116.1, Strong to Norman, March 27, 1917.
94. FRASER, 1330.1.1, Strong to Inoue, November 1, 1923.
95. Metzler 2006.
96. Pak 2013, 37.
97. Bytheway and Metzler 2016, 82.
98. FRASER, 1330.1, Speech by Eigo Fukai, "Mr. Benjamin Strong and the Restoration of the Gold Standard." October 23–24, 1924.
99. Bytheway and Metzler 2016, 83.
100. Metzler 2006, 128.
101. FRASER, 1000.4.2, Speech by Benjamin Strong at the Tokyo Ginko Club, May 24, 1920.
102. FRASER, 1330.1.1, Strong to Inoue, November 17, 1921.
103. Pak 2013; Metzler 2006.
104. Eichengreen 1992; Eichengreen and Temin 2000.
105. Inoue and de Bunsen 1931; Bytheway 2014; Bytheway and Metzler 2016; Kirshner 2007.
106. FRASER, 1330.1.1, Strong to Inoue, November 1, 1923.
107. FRASER, 1330.1.1, Strong to Inoue, November 1, 1923.
108. FRASER, 1330.1.1, Inoue to Strong, December 13, 1923.
109. Pak 2013, 177.
110. FRASER, 1330.1.1, Telegram, Inoue to Strong, January 31, 1924.
111. FRASER, 1330.1.1, Telegram, Inoue to Strong, January 23, 1924.
112. BEA, Overseas Department: Japan, OV16/107, Norman to Inoue, October 30, 1924.
113. FRASER, 1330.1.1, Strong to Inoue, October 28, 1924.
114. Bytheway and Metzler 2016; Metzler 2006.
115. FRASER, I330.1.1, Strong to Inoue, May 10, 1927.
116. Moggridge 1972; Eichengreen 1992; Morrison 2021.
117. Keynes 1923; Morrison 2021.
118. Clarke 1967, 73–74.
119. Morrison 2021, 193.
120. FRASER, 1116.4.1, Norman to Strong, October 16, 1924; Clarke 1967, 80.
121. FRASER, 1116.4.1, Strong to Norman, November 4, 1924.
122. FRASER, 1116.4.1, Strong to Norman, November 4, 1924.
123. FRASER, 1116.2.1, Strong to Norman, February 8, 1921.
124. FRASER, 1116.4.1, Norman to Strong, October 16, 1924.
125. FRASER, 1116.4.2, Norman to Strong, October 8, 1923.
126. FRASER, 1116.4.1, Strong to Norman, November 18, 1924.
127. FRASER, 1116.2.1, Strong to Norman, November 17, 1921.
128. FRASER, 1116.5.2, Norman to Strong, January 18, 1925.
129. Morrison 2021.
130. Clarke 1967.
131. FRASER, 1116.5.1, Strong to Norman, April 15, 1925.
132. FRASER, 1116.5.2, Norman to Strong, April 8, 1925.
133. Bytheway and Metzler 2016.
134. The National Archives, n.d.

135. Bytheway 2014, 112.

136. BEA, Richard Sydney Sayers, Papers, ADM/33/25, Interview with R. N. Kershaw, March 27, 1969.

137. Clavin 2013.

138. Meyer 1970.

139. Ahamed 2009, 68.

140. Ahamed 2009, 267.

141. BEA, ADM/33/24, Interview with Mr. I. Rooth, May 17, 1968.

142. Turner 1996, 32.

143. BEA, ADM/33/32, Interview with Jacques Leon Reuff, May 8, 1969.

144. BEA, ADM/33/24, Interview with Allan Sproul, October 21, 1969.

145. BEA, ADM/33/32, Interview with Robert Lacour-Gayet, May 9, 1969.

146. Moreau 1991, 51.

147. Moreau 1991, 53.

148. Strong to Harrison, August 1926, quoted in Mouré 2002, 157.

149. Mouré 2002, 166.

150. Moreau 1991; Mouré 2002.

151. Strong to Pierre Jay, quoted in Chandler 1958, 350.

152. Moreau 1991, 54.

153. Martin 2022, 113.

154. Meyer 1970; Moreau 1991.

155. Meyer 1970, 41; Moreau 1991; Mouré 2002, 158–59.

156. Kindleberger 1973, 303.

157. Meyer 1970, 64–68.

158. Pittaluga and Seghezza 2012, 599.

159. Pauly 1996; Clavin 2013; Martin 2022.

160. FRASER, 1007.1, Strong to Harrison, May 15, 1926.

161. Rosenberg 1999.

162. Martin 2022, 93.

163. Meyer 1970, 74–75.

164. See Rosenberg 1999 on Germany's preference for strong controls. I am grateful to Jamie Martin for highlighting this point on the political dispute between Germany and Poland on the Polish corridor.

165. Columbia University Rare Book and Manuscript Library (RBML), Harrison Papers, Box 21, Binder 46, Memorandum of Conversation with Governor Norman, April 11, 1927.

166. Allen 2020, 65.

167. Turner 1996, 38; Moreau 1991.

168. Meyer 1970, 76.

169. Kindleberger 1973, 303; Meyer 1970.

170. FRASER, 0320.227, Strong to Deputy Governor James Herbert Case, February 20, 1927.

171. RBML, Harrison Papers, Box 34, Harrison to Case and Strong, March 29, 1927.

172. RBML, Harrison Papers, Box 21, Binder 45, Memorandum of Conversation with Governor Norman, April 11, 1927.

173. BEA, Norman Diaries, ADM34/16, March 31, 1927.

174. Clay 1957, 259.

175. Allen 2020, 59.

176. RBML, Harrison Papers, Box 21, Binder 45, Memorandum of Conversation with Governor Norman, April 11, 1927.

177. Allen 2020, 62.

178. Allen 2020.

179. RBML, Harrison Papers, Box 21, Binder 45, Memorandum of Conversation with Governor Norman, April 12, 1927.

180. RBML, Harrison Papers, Box 21, Binder 45, Memorandum of Conversation with Governor Norman, April 11, 1927.

181. RBML, Harrison Papers, Box 21, Binder 45, Memorandum of Conversation at Bank of France, April 11, 1927.

182. Moreau 1991.

183. Turner 1996, 38.

184. RBML, Harrison Papers, Box 13, Binder 27, Strong to Moreau, June 23, 1927; Clay 1957; Boyle 1967.

185. FRASER, 1000.9, Strong Papers. "Memorandum Re.: Discussions with the Bank of France," May 27, 1928, 1.

186. FRASER, 1000.9, Strong Papers. "Memorandum," 5.

187. Boyle 1967, 237.

188. FRASER, Foreign Countries: Trip to Europe, 1928, "Postscript to Memorandum Re.: Discussions with the Bank of France," May 27, 1928, 1000.9, Strong Papers; "anything of that sort" refers to the prospect of overcoming personal disagreements with Moreau.

189. Moreau 1991, 246.

190. Boyle 1967, 238.

2. THINGS FALL APART

1. Clarke 1967, 33.

2. Kindleberger 1973.

3. Bernanke 2000, 11.

4. Friedman and Schwartz 1963, 412.

5. Wheelock 1992, 4.

6. Meltzer 2003.

7. Discount rates are distinct from interest rates. The discount rate is that charged to commercial banks or depository institutions for overnight loans from Federal Reserve Banks. They are not affected by market demand and supply nor by interest rates but are determined by the central bank. Interest rates are those charged by the lender on loans and are affected by market dynamics.

8. Federal Reserve Archival System for Economic Research (FRASER), Allan Meltzer Papers, The Discount Rate Controversy Between the Federal Reserve Board and the Federal Reserve Bank of New York, Box 1246. See also Meltzer 2003; Calomiris and Wheelock 1997; Romer and Romer 2013.

9. Bernanke 1983.

10. Kindleberger 1973; Eichengreen and Temin 2000, 186.

11. Eichengreen and Temin 2000, 2.

12. Eichengreen and Temin 2000, 28.

13. Kindleberger 1973, 30.

14. FRASER, 1116.2.2, Norman to Strong, September 15, 1921.

15. FRASER, 1116.2.1, Strong to Norman, November 17, 1921.

16. Palyi 1972, 143; Eichengreen 1992.

17. Boyle 1967, 239.

18. *The New York Times* 1928.

19. Chandler 1958; Bytheway and Metzler 2016, 32.

20. Of course, the BIS in Basel did not exist in Strong's lifetime, but Harrison's active avoidance of international central bank meetings in Basel, which in important ways

emulated the Long Island meeting of 1927, was a stark departure from Strong's international activism.

21. Boyle 1967, 239.

22. Clingan 2010, 9, 55.

23. Bank of England Archive (BEA), OV/34 79; Clingan 2010.

24. Sayers 1976, 344.

25. Sayers 1976, 455, 464; Clavin 1992; Mouré 1992, 274.

26. Chandler 1971.

27. Chandler 1958, 42.

28. Wicker 1966; Chandler 1971.

29. Chandler 1958, 465.

30. Clarke 1967, 41.

31. BEA, ADM/33/24, Richard Sayers Papers, Interview with Allan Sproul, October 21, 1969.

32. Clement 2023. See also Baffi 2002 on the first two years of the BIS and its role in systematizing and institutionalizing central bank cooperation.

33. Clay 1957, 269.

34. Eichengreen 1992.

35. Clay 1957, 366.

36. Eichengreen 1992, 260; Mouré 1992, 274.

37. Hungary also faced a similar crisis; however, I do not consider that case study in this book.

38. Eichengreen 1992.

39. Bennett 1962.

40. Horn 2022.

41. Eichengreen 1992.

42. BEA, OV32/7, Overseas Department: FRBNY—Confidential Cables, FRBNY Telegram to Norman, May 29, 1931.

43. Bank for International Settlements Archive (BISA), 7.18.2.MCG.1.20191217-2174.1 Credit-Anstalt crisis, Personal Harrison to McGarrah, May 26, 1931.

44. BISA, 7.18.2.MCG.1.20191217-2174.1 Credit-Anstalt crisis, Personal McGarrah to Harrison, May 26, 1931.

45. Horn 2022.

46. BEA, OV32/7, Overseas Department: FRBNY—Confidential Cables, Telegram to Harrison, June 3, 1931.

47. BISA, 7.18.2.MCG.1.20191217-2174.1 Credit-Anstalt crisis, "Telephone Message Received," Gates McGarrah, June 1, 1931.

48. Pak 2013.

49. BISA, 7.18.2.MCG.1.20191217-2174.1 Credit-Anstalt crisis, "Telephone Message Received," Gates McGarrah, June 1, 1931.

50. Clement 2023.

51. BISA, 7.16.3.RBL.B1, Harrison to McGarrah, April 24, 1931.

52. Meltzer 2003, 344.

53. BEA, Overseas Department: Germany: Reichsbank, OV34/79, Sir Horace Rumbold to Arthur Henderson, MP, March 12, 1930.

54. Boyle 1967, 260.

55. Columbia University Rare Book and Manuscript Library (RBML), Harrison Papers, Box 9, Binder 20, Norman to Harrison, June 2, 1931. Norman references his correspondence with Stewart in this communication with Harrison. Emphasis added.

56. BEA, Overseas Department: FRBNY—Confidential Cables, OV32/7, Harrison to Norman, June 1; Norman to Harrison, June 2, 1931.

57. BEA, Overseas Department: FRBNY—Confidential Cables, OV32/7, Harrison to Norman, June 1; Norman to Harrison, June 2, 1931.

58. RBML Harrison Papers, Box 21, Binder 45, Telephone Conversation with Norman, July 1, 1931.

59. Ahamed 2009.

60. BEA, Overseas Department: Germany, OV34/8, Telephone call Norman and Luther, June 22, 1931.

61. Horn 2022.

62. RBML, Harrison Papers, Box 21, Binder 45, Telephone Conversation with McGarrah, December 21, 1931.

63. BEA, OV32/7, Norman Phone Call with Harrison, July 9, 1931.

64. RBML, Harrison Papers, Box 21, Binder 45, Telephone Conversation with McGarrah, July 14, 1931; Conversation with Norman, July 14, 1931; Box 14, Binder 29, Harrison to Moret, Copy of Cable to Luther, November 17, 1931.

65. BISA, 7.16.3.RBL.B1, Harrison's Office Correspondence "Germany; Meeting of BIS Directors at Basle," July 14, 1931.

66. BISA, 7.16.3.RBL.B1, Harrison's Office Correspondence "Germany; Meeting of BIS Directors at Basle," July 21, 1931.

67. Horn 2022.

68. Singleton 2011, 105.

69. BEA, Overseas Department: Germany, OV34/8, H. A. Siepmann Note, June 23, 1931.

70. Clay 1957; James 1984.

71. BEA, Overseas Department: FRBNY—Confidential Cables, OV32/7 Harrison to Norman, July 8, 1931.

72. Eichengreen 1992, 277; Mouré 2002, 194.

73. RBML, Harrison Papers, Box 21, Binder 45, Conversation with Lacour-Gayet, July 11, 1931.

74. RBML, Harrison Papers, Box 21, Binder 45, Conversation with Lacour-Gayet, July 11, 1931.

75. RBML, Harrison Papers, Box 21, Binder 45, Conversation with Lacour-Gayet, July 11, 1931.

76. Eichengreen 1992.

77. Sayers 1976.

78. BEA, G1, 456, Siepmann conversation with Moret, August 5, 1931.

79. Mouré 2002, 202.

80. See BEA, ADM33, Papers of Richard Sydney Sayers Relating to the Composition of His History of the Bank of England. See files ADM33/24-27 and 31-31 for Sayers's interviews, especially regarding Norman, Norman's relationship with Harvey and deputies, and also with other key associates at this time.

81. Boyle 1967, 296.

82. BEA, G1, 456 Harvey to Norman, August 10, 1931.

83. Eich 2022; Ahamed 2009.

84. RBML, Harrison Box 21, Binder 45, Telephone conversation with Lacour-Gayet, August 8, 1931.

85. BEA, G1, 457 record of comms with French and US, US and French Credits to UK, August 25, 1931.

86. RBML, Harrison Box 21, Binder 45, Telephone conversation with Lacour-Gayet, August 25, 1931.

87. BEA, Governor's File: Netherlands—Financial Crisis 1931, and French and American Credits to United Kingdom (UK) Government, G1/457 Harvey to Norman, August 31, 1931; Daily Express News clipping, September 1, 1931.

88. RBML, Harrison Papers, Box 21, Binder 45, Conversation with Harvey, September 16, 1931.

89. RBML, Harrison Papers, Box 21, Binder 45, Telephone calls with Harvey and Norman, September 16–17.

90. RBML, Harrison Papers, Box 21, Binder 45, Telephone conversation with Harvey, September 17, 1931.

91. BEA, ADM/33/27, Interview with Mr. P. S. Beale, October 18, 1972; RBML, Harrison Papers, Box 21, Binder 45, Conversation with Harvey, September 19, 1931.

92. BEA, Richard Sayers Papers, ADM/33/27, Interview with Mr. P. S. Beale, October 18, 1972.

93. Ahamed 2009.

94. Eichengreen 1992.

95. RBML, Harrison Papers, Box 21, Binder 45, Conversation with Norman and Harvey, October 2, 1931.

96. Schacht 1956.

97. Clarke 1973, 41.

98. Meltzer 2003, 344.

99. BEA, ADM/33/24, Interview with Mr. H. Schacht, August 20, 1968.

100. Clavin 1992, 291.

101. Clavin 1992; Clavin 1996.

102. Mouré 2002.

103. Mouré 1992.

104. Clavin 1992, 287; Clavin 1996; Mouré 2002.

105. RBML, Box 21, Binder 46; Harrison and Norman Telephone, May 26, 1933.

106. Clavin 1992; Eichengreen 1992, 321; Mouré 2002.

107. RBML, Box 21, Binder 46; Harrison and Lacour-Gayet, Telephone, May 26, 1933; and Harrison and US Secretary of State, Henry Stimson, Telephone, June 2, 1932.

108. Hull 1948, 260.

109. Edwards 2017, 10.

110. Lindley 1933.

111. Edwards 2017.

112. Roosevelt 1938, 264–65.

113. Hull 1948, 262.

114. Papers Relating to the Foreign Relations of the United States (FRUS), 1931–35, Vol. 1 (Washington, DC: State Department, 1933), 673–74.

115. Hull 1948, 267.

116. Clavin 1996, 121.

117. Clavin 1996, 121.

118. This arrangement was later formalized in 1934.

119. BEA, G1, 415 Schacht papers, November 11, 1933.

120. Friedman 1962; Bernanke 2002.

121. Friedman and Schwartz 1963, 298.

122. Friedman and Schwartz 1963, 411; James 2013.

3. SPRINGTIME FOR BRETTON WOODS?

1. Singleton 2011, 154.

2. Borio, Toniolo, and Clement 2008, 4.

3. James 1996.

4. James 1996; Ruggie 1982; Best 2004; Helleiner 1994.

5. Coombs 1976, 32.

6. Note that these were not the only available arrangements to prop up the Bretton Woods system in the 1960s. See James 1996; Toniolo 2005; Borio, Toniolo, and Clement 2008; Bordo, Monnet, and Naef 2019 on the Gold Pool; and various IMF arrangements.

7. Allen 2013, 85–86.

8. McDowell 2017, 42.

9. Borio, Toniolo, and Clement 2008, 4.

10. Toniolo 2005, 352.

11. Toniolo 2005; Kaplan 1989.

12. Kaplan 1989, vi.

13. Cardwell 2011; P. B. 1952; Schenk 2010; Bordo, MacDonald, and Oliver 2009.

14. Borio, Toniolo, and Clement 2008, 82.

15. Borio, Toniolo, and Clement 2008.

16. Toma 1986; Singleton 2011.

17. Einzig 1960, 240.

18. Toniolo 2005.

19. Gavin 2004.

20. James 1996.

21. Toniolo 2005, 353.

22. Kindleberger 1973; Kindleberger 1987.

23. James 1996.

24. James 1996; Toniolo 2005.

25. Per Jacobsson quoted in James 1996, 162.

26. James 1996.

27. Singleton 2011, 147; Borio, Toniolo, and Clement 2008.

28. Federal Reserve Archival System for Economic Research (FRASER), Letter, Charles Coombs to Allan Sproul, Coombs 1964.

29. LeBor 2013, xvii.

30. Helleiner 1994.

31. Triffin 1961; Triffin 1978, 2.

32. Bank for International Settlement Archive (BISA), GILB9, *Papers: Milton Gilbert*. These initial measures in 1961 were precursors to the "Basel Group Arrangements" offered to the Bank of England in 1966 and 1968.

33. Coombs 1976, 32.

34. Bank of England Archive (BEA), Economic Intelligence Department, Balance of Payments Estimates, EID3/352, Bank Bulletin—Basel Arrangements, September 20, 1961.

35. Coombs 1976, 31; Toniolo 2005.

36. Coombs 1976, 33.

37. Coombs 1976, 28.

38. LeBor 2013, 188.

39. Coombs 1976, 33.

40. Kaplan 1989, 210.

41. Bank for International Settlements 1980.

42. Coombs 1976, 31.

43. Schweizerische Nationalbank 2007, 149.

44. Schweizerische Nationalbank 2007, 148–49. Department III is the Banking Operations department, the SNB entity tasked with open market operations.

45. Schweizerische Nationalbank 2007, 151.

46. Meltzer 2003. He suggests that Coombs used the March 1961 Basel meeting as an opportunity to approve swap lines with Iklé and Bridge.

47. Coombs 1976.

48. Coombs 1976, 36.
49. Schweizerische Nationalbank 2007, 154.
50. Coombs 1976, 37.
51. From Swiss National Bank Archives in Schweizerische Nationalbank 2007.
52. Coombs 1976.
53. McCauley and Schenk 2020, 9.
54. See, for instance, BEA, Overseas Department: Sterling Balances: Central Bank Assistance and Coombs's Scheme, OV44/34, Roosa to Cobbold, March 17, 1961.
55. Coombs 1976, 38.
56. BEA, Economic Intelligence Department, Balance of Payments Estimates, EID3/352, Bank Bulletin—Basel Arrangements, September 20, 1961.
57. BEA, Overseas Department, OV44/34, "I.M.F. and Central Bank Co-operation," May 2, 1961.
58. BISA, HAL.10 (F02), "The Role of the BIS in the International Monetary System Seen in a Historical Setting."
59. BEA, Overseas Department: Sterling Balances: Central Bank Assistance and Coombs's Scheme, OV44/34, M. Parsons, "Notes of Conversations in Basel on 10/11th April," April 14, 1961.
60. Speech by Louis Rasminsky, 1973, in Bank for International Settlements 1980.
61. Coombs 1976, 26.
62. BEA, Economic Intelligence Department, Balance of Payments Estimates, EID3/352, note on revisions September 1, 1961 Draft: "Basel Co-operation" (no date, author unknown).
63. BISA, HAL.10 (F02), History Lectures, 1929–1986, Edward Jay Epstein, "A Brave New Role for the BIS," *BIS Press Service*.
64. BEA, Overseas Department: Sterling Balances: Central Bank Assistance and Coombs's Scheme, OV44/34, M. Parsons, "Notes of Conversations in Basel on 10/11th April," April 14, 1961.
65. BEA, Overseas Department: Sterling Balances: Central Bank Assistance and Coombs's Scheme, OV44/35, "Governor's Note," June 11, 1961.
66. BEA, Overseas Department: Sterling Balances: Central Bank Assistance and Coombs's Scheme, OV44/35, Lord Cromer, "B.I.S. 'Experts' Meeting," December 20, 1961. Emphasis added.
67. BEA, Economic Intelligence Department, Balance of Payments Estimates, EID3/352, Draft, "Basle [Basel] Co-operation," September 1, 1961.
68. BEA, Economic Intelligence Department, Balance of Payments Estimates, EID3/352, "Basle [Basel] Guidance" (no date specified).
69. BEA, Central Bank Assistant: General, 7A229/9, "Basel Arrangements: Reporting to B.I.S.," November 27, 1964.
70. Coombs 1976, 37.
71. Volcker and Gyohten 1992, 77.
72. Coombs 1976, 28.
73. Bordo, Humpage, and Schwartz 2015.
74. BEA, Cashier's Department: Gold and Foreign Exchange Files, C43/368, Bridge to Parsons on Switzerland, December 15, 1959; Coombs 1976.
75. Coombs 1976, 74.
76. Coombs 1976.
77. Coombs 1976, 74–75.
78. Coombs 1976, 75–76.
79. Bremner 2004, 167.
80. McDowell 2017.

81. BEA, Cashier's Department: Gold and Foreign Exchange Files, C43/742, Note of Meeting between Cromer and Brunet, May 8, 1962.

82. Gilbert 1980, 132.

83. McCauley and Schenk 2020, 9.

84. FRASER, Box 26, Folder 3, Joint Economic Committee Hearings, January 19, 1962.

85. FRASER, Box 24, Folder 8, Joint Economic Committee Hearings, August 1962.

86. FOMC 1962a.

87. Coombs 1976, 28–29.

88. Volcker and Gyohten 1992, 77.

89. BISA, DEA.12 (F35), "Note of Meeting of the Study Group on the Creation of Reserve Assets," Rome, October 26–30, 1964.

90. Coombs 1976, 91.

91. Coombs 1976; Bordo, Humpage, and Schwartz 2015.

92. BISA, DEA.12 (F36), "Comments by U.S. Representatives on Compatibility of the Various Proposals with the Evolution of the Existing System," January 27, 1965.

93. Letter, Charles Coombs to Allan Sproul, Coombs 1964. Online Archival Collections, St. Louis Fed.

94. Toniolo 2005, 388.

95. BEA Cashier's Department: Gold and Foreign Exchange Files, C43/742, Rickett to Stevens, March 30, 1962.

96. McCauley and Schenk 2020.

97. BEA, Cashier's Department: Gold and Foreign Exchange Files, C43/742, Memo, J. M. Stevens, April 27, 1962.

98. BEA, Overseas Department: Sterling and Sterling Area, OV44/35 R. Bridge, "Coombs Scheme," October 11, 1961.

99. BEA, Cashier's Department: Gold and Foreign Exchange Files, C43/742, Bridge to Parsons, March 9, 1962.

100. BEA, Overseas Department: Sterling and Sterling Area, OV44/35, H. Mynors, December 22, 1961.

101. FOMC 1962a; Coombs 1976.

102. FOMC 1962a.

103. Coombs 1976, 78.

104. BEA, Overseas Department: Sterling and Sterling Area, OV44/35, "Notes of B.I.S Meeting 12th June 1961," June 13, 1961.

105. Coombs 1976, 79.

106. BEA, Cashier's Department: Gold and Foreign Exchange Files, C43/742, Bridge to Parsons, April 5, 1962.

107. FOMC 1962b; Coombs 1976.

108. Schweizerische Nationalbank 2007, 153.

109. Capie 2010, 165.

110. Iklé memoirs, SNB.

111. BEA, Overseas Department: Sterling and Sterling Area, OV44/34, Parsons to Iklé, March 16, 1961.

112. BEA, Overseas Department: Sterling Balances: Central Bank Assistance and Coombs's Scheme, OV44/35, Lord Cromer, "Meeting of 'Experts' in Basel Saturday the 7th April 1962," April 10, 1962.

113. BEA, Overseas Department: Sterling Balances: Central Bank Assistance and Coombs's Scheme, OV44/35, Roy Bridge, "American Ideas for Strengthening the International Exchange Structure," April 12, 1962.

114. BEA, Overseas Department: Sterling Balances: Central Bank Assistance and Coombs's Scheme, OV44/35, Roy Bridge, "American Ideas for Strengthening the International Exchange Structure," April 12, 1962.

115. Fforde 1992, 567.
116. Schenk 2010, 124.
117. Capie 2010, 227.
118. Capie 2010, 225.
119. Coombs 1976, 111.
120. Capie 2010.
121. Coombs 1976; Meltzer 2003; Schenk 2010.
122. BEA, Overseas Department: Sterling and Sterling Area: Sterling Policy, OV44/125, Governor's Note, August 3, 1965.
123. Schenk 2010, 162.
124. Quoted in Schenk 2010, 162.
125. Coombs 1976, 86; Toniolo 2005.
126. Toniolo 2005, 395.
127. Toniolo 2005; Schenk 2010.
128. Quoted in Schenk 2010, 172.
129. Gavin 2004; Schenk 2010.
130. BEA, Economic Intelligence Department, Papers Concerning Work for Official Inquiries, EID 1/24, Cooke and Bull, "A History of the Sterling Crisis," 1967, 52.
131. BEA, Overseas Department: Sterling and Sterling Area: Sterling Crisis, OV44/124, Bridge to O'Brien, "For Treasury Meeting 5 p.m. Friday, 15 July," July 15, 1966.
132. BEA, Overseas Department: Sterling and Sterling Area: Sterling Crisis, OV 44/123, McMahon to Cromer/O'Brien, "Economic Policy," March 18, 1966.
133. Schenk 2010, 177.
134. Capie 2010; Coombs 1976; Fforde 1992; Schenk 2010; Toniolo 2005. See also elsewhere in this chapter the references to Bank of England communications from collections at the Bank of England Archive.
135. Capie 2010, 227.
136. Gavin 2004.
137. Garber 1993; Helleiner 1994; James 1996; Bordo and Eichengreen 1993; Bordo 2017.
138. Frieden 2006; Eichengreen 2019a.
139. Kindleberger 1978.

4. THIS TIME IS DIFFERENT?

1. Irwin 2013, 11.
2. Helleiner 2014; Henning 2015.
3. Obstfeld, Shambaugh, and Taylor 2009, 9.
4. Irwin 2013, 8.
5. Oatley 2015.
6. Drezner 2014b, 2.
7. Singleton 2011, 18.
8. Irwin 2013, 6.
9. Tooze 2018, 167.
10. Federal Reserve Board Press Release 2007.
11. Baker 2013; Irwin 2013, 133.
12. Baker 2013.
13. Bernanke 2009; Ball 2018.
14. Darling 2011.
15. Drezner 2014b; Drezner 2014a.
16. Drezner 2014b, 1.
17. Helleiner 2014, 35; FOMC 2008b.
18. Obstfeld, Shambaugh, and Taylor 2009.
19. Bernanke 2015, 36. Also Bernanke, interview.

20. Bernanke 2015, 410.
21. Bertuch-Samuels and Ramlogan 2007.
22. Moessner and Allen 2010.
23. FOMC 2008b, 10.
24. FOMC 2008b.
25. Lockwood 2016, 727. See also Nelson and Katzenstein 2014.
26. FOMC 2007b, 189.
27. FOMC 2007c, 110.
28. FOMC 2007a, 36.
29. Dudley 2012.
30. Aizenman and Pasricha 2010; McDowell 2012; Broz 2015.
31. Sahasrabuddhe 2019; Marple 2021.
32. Moessner and Allen 2010; Prasad 2014.
33. Samuelson 2008.
34. Irwin 2013, 12.
35. Interview with Benjamin Bernanke, Chair of the Board of Governors of the Federal Reserve System (2006–2014). Interview by Aditi Sahasrabuddhe. Brookings Institute, Washington DC, August 29, 2019. See also Bernanke 2015.
36. Bernanke 2015.
37. King 2004.
38. Irwin 2013, 112.
39. Irwin 2013.
40. Bernanke 2015.
41. Tabuchi 2013.
42. Author interviews, anonymous.
43. Irwin 2013.
44. Bernanke, interview.
45. Interview with Mervyn King, Governor of the Bank of England (2003–2013). Interview by Aditi Sahasrabuddhe. NYU Law School, New York, December 17, 2018.
46. Interview with Donald Kohn, Vice Chair of the Board of Governors of the Federal Reserve System (2006–2010). Interview by Aditi Sahasrabuddhe. Phone call, May 30, 2018. For a discussion on political constraints on the Fed's independence, see Binder and Spindel 2017.
47. Interview with Masaaki Shirakawa, Governor of the Bank of Japan (2008–2013). Interview by Aditi Sahasrabuddhe. The Millennium Hilton, New York City, December 5, 2019.
48. Interview with Charlie Bean, Deputy Governor of the Bank of England for Monetary Policy (2008–2014). Interview by Aditi Sahasrabuddhe. 32 Lincoln's Inn Fields, London School of Economics, October 18, 2018.
49. Author interviews, anonymous.
50. Bean, Bernanke, King, Shirakawa, and Trichet interviews.
51. Bernanke, interview.
52. Author interviews, anonymous.
53. Simmons 2006; Keohane 1984; Oye 1986.
54. Author interview, anonymous.
55. Haas 1992.
56. Author interviews, anonymous.
57. Kohn, interview. Bernanke similarly emphasized the importance of working within the Fed's legal and political constraints.
58. FOMC 2007c; FOMC 2008b; FOMC 2010.
59. Bean, interview.

60. Interview with Jean-Claude Trichet, President of the European Central Bank (2003 to 2011). Interview by Aditi Sahasrabuddhe. Skype, March 30, 2020.

61. Author interview, anonymous.

62. Bean, interview.

63. Mercer 2005, 95.

64. Park 2011.

65. Sahasrabuddhe 2019.

66. Prasad 2014.

67. Author interviews, anonymous.

68. Matthijs 2022.

69. Author interview, anonymous.

70. On this point, see also Irwin 2013.

71. Author interviews, anonymous.

72. Shirakawa, interview.

73. Bernanke, interview.

74. Bernanke 2002.

75. Author interview, anonymous.

76. Author interviews, anonymous.

77. Shirakawa, interview.

78. Aizenman and Pasricha 2010; Broz 2015; McDowell 2012.

79. Wessel 2009.

80. FOMC 2007a; FOMC 2008b.

81. FOMC 2007c, 128.

82. Tooze 2018, 90.

83. Author interview, anonymous.

84. Bernanke 2015.

85. King, interview.

86. Kohn, interview.

87. Interview with Paul Tucker, Deputy Governor of the Bank of England for Financial Stability (2009–2013). Interview by Aditi Sahasrabuddhe. The Delaunay, Aldwych, London, December 18, 2018.

88. FOMC 2008c; FOMC 2008a.

89. Shirakawa 2021, 155.

90. Trichet, interview.

91. Shirakawa 2021, 155. Also, Kohn, Shirakawa, interviews.

92. Irwin 2013.

93. King, interview.

94. Author interview, anonymous.

95. Bernanke 2015, 183.

96. Author interviews, anonymous.

97. These data are retrieved from the Federal Reserve's disclosures starting in December 1, 2007, to February 1, 2010, available at https://www.federalreserve.gov/regreform/reform-swaplines.htm; Interviews, anonymous.

98. Grim 2009.

99. O'Driscoll, Jr. 2011.

100. Perry 2020.

101. Baker 2013.

102. FOMC 2010.

103. Irwin 2013, 154; Tooze 2018, 212.

104. FOMC 2007a.

105. Bernanke 2015; Bernanke, interview.

106. Author interviews, anonymous.
107. Bernanke 2015; Bernanke interview.
108. Author interview, anonymous.
109. Author interviews, anonymous.
110. FOMC 2010.
111. FOMC 2010.
112. FOMC 2010, 4.
113. FOMC 2010, 5.
114. Shirakawa, interview.
115. King, interview.
116. Bernanke 2015, 151.
117. Bernanke, Geithner, and Paulson 2019, 81; Bernanke 2015, 164.
118. Author interview, anonymous.
119. Kohn 2010; Volcker and Gyohten 1992.
120. FOMC 2008b.
121. Sahasrabuddhe 2019; Marple 2021.
122. Vaughn 2020.
123. Government Accountability Office 2011; Broz 2015. See Bodea and Hicks 2015 and Garriga and Rodriguez 2020 on the disciplining effect of CBI on inflation.
124. Sahasrabuddhe 2019.
125. FOMC 2008b.
126. FOMC 2008b, 42.
127. FOMC 2008b, 39.
128. FOMC 2008b, 10.
129. FOMC 2008b, 17, 39.
130. Author interviews, anonymous.
131. Author interviews, anonymous.
132. Bernanke, interview.
133. Author interviews, anonymous.
134. Author interview, anonymous.
135. Author interview, anonymous.
136. Author interview, anonymous.
137. FOMC 2008b, 23.
138. FOMC 2008b.
139. Bernanke, interview.
140. Benediktsdóttir, Eggertsson, and Þórarinsson 2017.
141. Ingves 2022.
142. Freeman 2009.
143. Hilmarsson 2022, 28.
144. Author interview, anonymous.
145. Ingves 2022.
146. Ingves 2022.
147. Hilmarsson 2022, 27.
148. Author interviews with Icelandic officials, anonymous.
149. Author interviews with ECB and Iceland officials, anonymous.
150. Hilmarsson 2022.
151. Ingves 2022.
152. FOMC 2008b, 42.
153. FOMC 2008b.
154. Sahasrabuddhe 2019.
155. Author interview, anonymous.

156. Tucker 2022.

157. Author interviews, anonymous. NB: not Bernanke or Subbarao.

158. Interview with Duvvuri Subbarao, Governor of the Reserve Bank of India (2008–2013). Interview by Aditi Sahasrabuddhe. WhatsApp Call, May 13, 2020.

159. Author interview, anonymous.

160. Subbarao, interview.

161. Author interview, anonymous. See also Subbarao 2016.

162. Shirakawa, interview.

163. Subbarao, interview.

164. Shirakawa, interview; Subbarao, interview; interviews, anonymous.

165. Shirakawa, interview.

166. Author interview, anonymous. Note that I have not spoken to Geithner or Bernanke specifically about Indonesia's swap request or had the chance to evaluate their side of this interaction.

167. Like India, Indonesia also secured a swap line from the Bank of Japan during the GFC.

168. Author interview, anonymous.

169. All quotes in this discussion and what follow below are sourced from FOMC 2009, 30–53. Emphases added.

170. FOMC 2013.

CONCLUSION

1. Ortlieb 2020.

2. Tett 2020.

3. Leonard 2020.

4. Wiggins et al. 2023.

5. Author interview, anonymous.

6. Culpepper 2011.

7. Pop, Fleming, and Politi 2022.

8. Toniolo 2005, 584.

9. Sheets, Truman, and Lowery 2018.

10. Kirshner 2019.

11. Park 2011.

12. Meyer 1970.

13. Aizenman, Ito, and Pasricha 2022.

14. Best 2016; van 't Klooster 2020.

15. Fleming and Klagge 2010; Obstfeld 2009a; Sheets, Truman, and Lowery 2018; Baker 2013; Jacobs and King 2016.

16. Sayers 1976, 75.

17. O'Driscoll, Jr. 2011; Perry 2020; Högenauer and Howarth 2019.

18. Tooze 2020; Sahasrabuddhe 2021.

19. Allen and Sahasrabuddhe 2022; Högenauer and Howarth 2019.

20. Woods 2014; Woods 2010.

21. McDowell 2017.

22. FOMC 1996, 107.

23. FOMC 1996.

References

Abdelal, Rawi. 2007. *Capital Rules: The Construction of Global Finance*. Cambridge, MA: Harvard University Press.

Adolph, Christopher. 2013. *Bankers, Bureaucrats, and Central Bank Politics: The Myth of Neutrality*. New York: Cambridge University Press.

Ahamed, Liaquat. 2009. *Lords of Finance: The Bankers Who Broke the World*. New York: Penguin.

Aizenman, Joshua, Hiro Ito, and Gurnain Kaur Pasricha. 2022. "Central Bank Swap Arrangements in the COVID-19 Crisis." *Journal of International Money and Finance* 122: 102555.

Aizenman, Joshua, and Gurnain Kaur Pasricha. 2010. "Selective Swap Arrangements and the Global Financial Crisis: Analysis and Interpretation." *International Review of Economics & Finance* 19 (3): 353–65.

Alesina, Alberto, and Guido Tabellini. 2007. "Bureaucrats or Politicians? Part I: A Single Policy Task." *American Economic Review* 97 (1): 3–179.

Alesina, Alberto, and Guido Tabellini. 2008. "Bureaucrats or Politicians? Part II: Multiple Policy Tasks." *Journal of Public Economics* 92 (3): 426–47.

Allen, Michael O., and Aditi Sahasrabuddhe. 2022. "Crisis, Intervention, and the Politics of Central Bank Independence." Nashville, TN: International Studies Association Annual Meeting.

Allen, William A. 2013. *International Liquidity and the Financial Crisis*. Cambridge: Cambridge University Press.

Allen, William A. 2020. "Poland, the International Monetary System and the Bank of England, 1921–1939." *Narodowy Bank Polski* (Working Paper No. 328). https://static.nbp.pl/publikacje/materialy-i-studia/328_en.pdf.

Avant, Deborah D., Martha Finnemore, and Susan K. Sell. 2010. *Who Governs the Globe?* New York: Cambridge University Press.

Baffi, Paolo. 2002. *The Origins of Central Bank Cooperation: The Establishment of the Bank for International Settlements*. Rome: Editori Laterza.

Bagehot, Walter. 1912. *Lombard Street: A Description of the Money Market*. New York: Scribner.

Baker, Colleen M. 2013. "The Federal Reserve's Use of International Swap Lines." *SSRN Electronic Journal*. http://www.ssrn.com/abstract=2226708. Accessed January 9, 2022.

Ball, Laurence M. 2018. *The Fed and Lehman Brothers: Setting the Record Straight on a Financial Disaster*. Cambridge: Cambridge University Press.

Balls, Ed, James Howat, and Anna Stansbury. 2018. *Central Bank Independence Revisited: After the Financial Crisis, What Should a Model Central Bank Look Like?* Working Paper. Cambridge, MA: Harvard Kennedy School. https://www.hks.harvard.edu/sites/default/files/centers/mrcbg/working.papers/x87_final.pdf.

Bank for International Settlements. 1980. *Personal Recollections and Opinions: Published on the Occasion of the Fiftieth Anniversary, 1930—1980*. Basel: Bank for International Settlements.

Beckert, Jens. 2016. *Imagined Futures: Fictional Expectations and Capitalist Dynamics*. Cambridge, MA: Harvard University Press.

Benediktsdóttir, Sigríður, Gauti B. Eggertsson, and Eggert Þórarinsson. 2017. "The Rise, the Fall, and the Resurrection of Iceland." *National Bureau of Economic Research Working Paper Series*, Working Paper (24005). http://www.nber.org/papers/w24005.

Bennett, Edward W. 1962. *Germany and the Diplomacy of the Financial Crisis, 1931*. Cambridge, MA: Harvard University Press.

Berman, Sheri. 1998. *The Social Democratic Moment: Ideas and Politics in the Making of Interwar Europe*. Cambridge, MA: Harvard University Press.

Bernanke, Ben S. 1983. "Nonmonetary Effects of the Financial Crisis in the Propagation of the Great Depression." *American Economic Review* 73 (3): 257–76. http://www.jstor.org/stable/1808111. Accessed September 21, 2023.

Bernanke, Ben S. 2000. *Essays on the Great Depression*. Princeton, NJ: Princeton University Press.

Bernanke, Ben S. 2002. "Remarks by Governor Ben S. Bernanke, on Milton Friedman's Ninetieth Birthday." Speech presented at the Conference to Honor Milton Friedman, University of Chicago. https://www.federalreserve.gov/boarddocs/speeches/2002/20021108/default.htm. Accessed June 5, 2021.

Bernanke, Ben S. 2009. "Reflections on a Year of Crisis." Speech by Chairman of the Federal Reserve Board. Presented at the Federal Reserve Bank of Kansas City's Annual Economic Symposium, Jackson Hole, WY. https://www.federalreserve.gov/newsevents/speech/bernanke20090821a.htm.

Bernanke, Ben S. 2015. *The Courage to Act: A Memoir of a Crisis and Its Aftermath*. New York: Norton.

Bernanke, Ben S., Timothy F. Geithner, and Henry M. Paulson. 2019. *Firefighting: The Financial Crisis and Its Lessons*. New York: Penguin.

Bernhard, William, J. Lawrence Broz, and William Roberts Clark. 2002. "The Political Economy of Monetary Institutions." *International Organization* 56 (4): 693–723. https://www.cambridge.org/core/article/political-economy-of-monetary-institutions/E00927FDABFC822F713E18A033B2FCAC.

Bertuch-Samuels, Axel, and Parmeshwar Ramlogan. 2007. "Finance and Development." *Finance and Development* 44 (1). https://www.imf.org/external/pubs/ft/fandd/2007/03/bertuch.htm. Accessed April 20, 2020.

Best, Jacqueline. 2004. "Hollowing out Keynesian Norms: How the Search for a Technical Fix Undermined the Bretton Woods Regime." *Review of International Studies* 30 (3): 383–404.

Best, Jacqueline. 2016. "Rethinking Central Bank Accountability in Uncertain Times." *Ethics & International Affairs* 30 (2): 215–32.

Binder, Sarah, and Mark Spindel. 2017. *The Myth of Independence*. Princeton, NJ: Princeton University Press.

Blinder, Alan S. 1998. *Central Banking in Theory and Practice*. Boston: MIT Press.

Blyth, Mark. 2006. "Great Punctuations: Prediction, Randomness, and the Evolution of Comparative Political Science." *American Political Science Review* 100 (4): 493–98.

Bodea, Cristina, and Raymond Hicks. 2015. "Price Stability and Central Bank Independence: Discipline, Credibility, and Democratic Institutions." *International Organization* 69 (1): 35–61. http://www.jstor.org/stable/43283290. Accessed January 15, 2024.

Bordo, Michael D. 2017. "The Operation and Demise of the Bretton Woods System: 1958 to 1971." *National Bureau of Economic Research Working Paper Series* (Working Paper 23189). https://www.nber.org/system/files/working_papers/w23189/w23189.pdf.

Bordo, Michael D., and Barry Eichengreen. 1993. *A Retrospective on the Bretton Woods System: Lessons for International Monetary Reform*. National Bureau of Economic Research Project Report. Chicago: University of Chicago Press.

Bordo, Michael D., Owen F. Humpage, and Anna J. Schwartz. 2015. "The Evolution of the Federal Reserve Swap Lines since 1962." *IMF Economic Review* 63 (2): 353–72.

Bordo, Michael D., Ronald MacDonald, and Michael J. Oliver. 2009. *Sterling in Crisis: 1964–1967*. SSRN Scholarly Paper. https://papers.ssrn.com/abstract=1329275. Accessed March 19, 2021.

Bordo, Michael, Eric Monnet, and Alain Naef. 2019. "The Gold Pool (1961–1968) and the Fall of the Bretton Woods System: Lessons for Central Bank Cooperation." *Journal of Economic History* 79 (4): 1027–59.

Borio, C. E. V., Gianni Toniolo, and Piet Clement, eds. 2008. *Past and Future of Central Bank Cooperation*. Cambridge: Cambridge University Press.

Borio, Claudio, Harold James, and Hyun Song Shin. 2014. "The International Monetary and Financial System: A Capital Account Historical Perspective." *Federal Reserve Bank of Dallas, Globalization and Monetary Policy Institute Working Papers* (204). https://www.dallasfed.org/institute/~/media/documents/institute/wpapers/2014/0204.pdf. Accessed September 9, 2023.

Boyle, Andrew. 1967. *Montagu Norman: A Biography*. London: Cassell.

Braun, Benjamin. 2016. "Speaking to the People? Money, Trust, and Central Bank Legitimacy in the Age of Quantitative Easing." *Review of International Political Economy* 23 (6): 1064–92.

Bremner, Robert P. 2004. *Chairman of the Fed William McChesney Martin, Jr., and the Creation of the Modern American Financial System*. New Haven, CT: Yale University Press.

Brown, Jonathan N. 2014. "The Sound of Silence." *Conflict Management and Peace Science* 31 (4): 406–31.

Broz, J. Lawrence. 1997. *The International Origins of the Federal Reserve System*. Ithaca, NY: Cornell University Press.

Broz, J. Lawrence. 2005. "Congressional Politics of International Financial Rescues." *American Journal of Political Science* 49 (3): 479–96.

Broz, J. Lawrence. 2015. "The Politics of Rescuing the World's Financial System: The Federal Reserve as a Global Lender of Last Resort." *Korean Journal of International Studies* 13 (2): 323–51.

Bytheway, Simon James. 2014. *Investing Japan: Foreign Capital, Monetary Standards, and Economic Development, 1859–2011*. Cambridge, MA: Harvard University Asia Center.

Bytheway, Simon James, and Mark Metzler. 2016. *Central Banks and Gold: How Tokyo, London, and New York Shaped the Modern World*. Ithaca, NY: Cornell University Press.

Calomiris, Charles, and David Wheelock. 1997. *Was the Great Depression a Watershed for American Monetary Policy?* Cambridge, MA: National Bureau of Economic Research. http://www.nber.org/papers/w5963.pdf. Accessed February 6, 2021.

Capie, Forrest. 2010. *The Bank of England: 1950s to 1979*. New York: Cambridge University Press.

Cardwell, Curt, ed. 2011. "The British Sterling-Dollar Crisis of 1949–1950." In *NSC 68 and the Political Economy of the Early Cold War*, 128–59. Cambridge: Cambridge University Press.

Carnegie, Allison, and Austin Carson. 2020. *Secrets in Global Governance: Disclosure Dilemmas and the Challenge of International Cooperation*. Cambridge: Cambridge University Press.

Chandler, Lester V. 1958. *Benjamin Strong, Central Banker*. Washington, DC: Brookings Institution.

Chandler, Lester V. 1971. *American Monetary Policy, 1928–1941*. New York: Harper & Row.

Chinn, Menzie David, and Jeffry A. Frieden. 2011. *Lost Decades: The Making of America's Debt Crisis and the Long Recovery*. New York: Norton.

Chwieroth, Jeffrey M. 2010. *Capital Ideas: The IMF and the Rise of Financial Liberalization*. Princeton, NJ: Princeton University Press.

Chwieroth, Jeffrey M. 2015. "Professional Ties That Bind: How Normative Orientations Shape IMF Conditionality." *Review of International Political Economy* 22 (4): 757–87.

Clarke, Stephen V. O. 1967. "Central Bank Cooperation 1924–1931." *Federal Reserve Bank of New York*, 234. https://fraser.stlouisfed.org/files/docs/meltzer/clacen67.pdf.

Clarke, Stephen V. O. 1973. *The Reconstruction of the International Monetary System: The Attempts of 1922 and 1933*. Princeton, NJ: International Finance Section, Princeton University.

Clavin, Patricia. 1992. "'The Fetishes of So-Called International Bankers': Central Bank Co-operation for the World Economic Conference, 1932–3." *Contemporary European History* 1 (3): 281–311. http://www.jstor.org.proxy.library.cornell.edu/stable/20081451. Accessed February 8, 2021.

Clavin, Patricia. 1996. *The Failure of Economic Diplomacy: Britain, Germany, France and the United States, 1931–36*. London: Macmillan.

Clavin, Patricia. 2013. *Securing the World Economy: The Reinvention of the League of Nations, 1920–1946*. Oxford: Oxford University Press.

Clay, Henry. 1957. *Lord Norman*. London: Macmillan.

Clement, Piet. 2023. "Institutionalizing Central Bank Cooperation: The Norman-Schacht Vision and Early Experience of the Bank for International Settlements, 1929–1933." In *The Spread of the Modern Central Bank and Global Cooperation, 1919–1939*, edited by Barry J. Eichengreen and Andreas Kakridis, 80–102. Cambridge: Cambridge University Press.

Clingan, C. Edmund. 2010. *The Lives of Hans Luther, 1879–1962: German Chancellor, Reichsbank President, and Hitler's Ambassador*. Lanham, MD: Lexington Books.

Cohen, Benjamin J. 2015. *Currency Power: Understanding Monetary Rivalry*. Princeton, NJ: Princeton University Press.

Conti-Brown, Peter. 2016. *The Power and Independence of the Federal Reserve*. Princeton, NJ: Princeton University Press.

Cooley, Alexander. 2005. *Logics of Hierarchy: The Organization of Empires, States, and Military Occupations*. Ithaca, NY: Cornell University Press.

Coombs, Charles A. 1976. *The Arena of International Finance*. New York: Wiley.

Copelovitch, Mark S. 2010. *The International Monetary Fund in the Global Economy: Banks, Bonds, and Bailouts*. Cambridge: Cambridge University Press.

Corsetti, Giancarlo, Paolo Pesenti, and Nouriel Roubini. 1999. "What Caused the Asian Currency and Financial Crisis? Federal Reserve Bank of New York." https://www.newyorkfed.org/medialibrary/media/research/economists/pesenti/whatjapwor.pdf.

Culpepper, Pepper D. 2011. *Quiet Politics and Business Power: Corporate Control in Europe and Japan*. Cambridge: Cambridge University Press.

Darling, Alistair. 2011. *Back from the Brink*. London: Atlantic.

Dietsch, Peter. 2020. "Independent Agencies, Distribution, and Legitimacy: The Case of Central Banks." *American Political Science Review* 114 (2): 591–95.

Dore, Ronald. 1983. "Goodwill and the Spirit of Market Capitalism." *British Journal of Sociology* 34 (4): 459–82.

Downey, Leah. 2021. "Delegation in Democracy: A Temporal Analysis." *Journal of Political Philosophy* 29 (3): 305–29.

Drazen, Allan. 2002. "Central Bank Independence, Democracy, and Dollarization." *Journal of Applied Economics* 5 (1): 1–17.

Drezner, Daniel W. 2007. *All Politics Is Global: Explaining International Regulatory Regimes*. Princeton, NJ: Princeton University Press.

Drezner, Daniel W. 2014a. "The System Worked: Global Economic Governance during the Great Recession." *World Politics* 66 (1): 123–64.

Drezner, Daniel W. 2014b. *The System Worked: How the World Stopped Another Great Depression*. New York: Oxford University Press.

Dudley, William C. 2012. "Dollar-Swaps Protect U.S. Markets." *Wall Street Journal*. https://online.wsj.com/article/SB10001424052970204720204577130960867648528.html. Accessed February 11, 2022.

Edwards, Sebastian. 2017. *The London Monetary and Economic Conference of 1933 and the End of the Great Depression: A "Change of Regime" Analysis*. Cambridge, MA: National Bureau of Economic Research. http://www.nber.org/papers/w23204.pdf. Accessed August 13, 2023.

Eich, Stefan. 2022. *The Currency of Politics: The Political Theory of Money from Aristotle to Keynes*. Princeton, NJ: Princeton University Press.

Eichengreen, Barry J. 1992. *Golden Fetters: The Gold Standard and the Great Depression, 1919–1939*. New York: Oxford University Press.

Eichengreen, Barry J. 2019a. *Globalizing Capital: A History of the International Monetary System*, 3rd ed. Princeton, NJ: Princeton University Press.

Eichengreen, Barry J. 2019b. "The Specter of Versailles: The Conference That Ended World War I Was Followed by an Inward Turn That Has Parallels Today." *Finance and Development*. https://www.imf.org/en/Publications/fandd/issues/2019/06/specter-of-versailles-eichengreen.

Eichengreen, Barry, and Marc Flandreau. 2009. "The Rise and Fall of the Dollar (or When Did the Dollar Replace Sterling as the Leading Reserve Currency?)." *European Review of Economic History* 13 (3): 377–411.

Eichengreen, Barry J., and Andreas Kakridis, eds. 2023. *The Spread of the Modern Central Bank and Global Cooperation, 1919–1939*. Cambridge: Cambridge University Press.

Eichengreen, Barry J., and Peter Temin. 2000. "The Gold Standard and the Great Depression." *Contemporary European History* 9 (2): 183–207. http://www.jstor.org/stable/20081742.

Eichengreen, Barry, Arnaud Mehl, and Livia Chiţu. 2019. "Mars or Mercury? The Geopolitics of International Currency Choice." *Economic Policy* 34 (98): 315–63.

Einzig, Paul. 1960. *In the Centre of Things: The Autobiography of Paul Einzig*. London: Hutchinson.

Emirbayer, Mustafa. 1997. "Manifesto for a Relational Sociology." *American Journal of Sociology* 103 (2): 281–317.

Emirbayer, Mustafa, and Ann Mische. 1998. "What Is Agency?" *American Journal of Sociology* 103 (4): 962–1023.

Evans, Peter B. 1995. *Embedded Autonomy States and Industrial Transformation*. Princeton, NJ: Princeton University Press.

Farrell, Henry, and Abraham L. Newman. 2014. "Domestic Institutions beyond the Nation-State: Charting the New Interdependence Approach." *World Politics* 66 (2): 331–63.

Federal Reserve Board Press Release. 2007. "Federal Reserve and Other Central Banks Announce Measures Designed to Address Elevated Pressures in Short-Term Funding Markets." *Board of Governors of the Federal Reserve System*. https://www.federalreserve.gov/newsevents/pressreleases/monetary20071212a.htm. Accessed July 6, 2020.

Fforde, John. 1992. *The Bank of England and Public Policy, 1941–1958*. Cambridge: Cambridge University Press.

Fink, Carole. 1991. "Beyond Revisionism: The Genoa Conference of 1922." In *Genoa, Rapallo, and European Reconstruction in 1922*. Washington, DC: German Historical Institute.

Fleming, Michael J., and Nicholas Klagge. 2010. "The Federal Reserve's Foreign Exchange Swap Lines." *Current Issues in Economics and Finance* 16 (4). https://www.newyorkfed.org/medialibrary/media/research/current_issues/ci16-4.pdf.

FOMC. 1962a. *FOMC Historical Meeting Minutes, March 27, 1962*. Washington, DC: Board of Governors of the Federal Reserve System. https://www.federalreserve.gov/monetarypolicy/files/fomchistmin19620327.pdf. Accessed April 6, 2019.

FOMC. 1962b. *FOMC Historical Meeting Minutes, May 29, 1962*. Washington, DC: Board of Governors of the Federal Reserve System. https://www.federalreserve.gov/monetarypolicy/files/fomchistmin19620529.pdf. Accessed March 3, 2016.

FOMC. 1982a. *Meeting of the Federal Open Market Committee, August 24, 1982*. Washington, DC: Board of Governors of the Federal Reserve System. https://www.federalreserve.gov/monetarypolicy/files/FOMC19820824meeting.pdf. Accessed May 6, 2024.

FOMC. 1982b. *Meeting of the Federal Open Market Committee June 30–July 1, 1982*. Washington, DC: Board of Governors of the Federal Reserve System. https://www.federalreserve.gov/monetarypolicy/files/FOMC19820701meeting.pdf. Accessed February 14, 2024.

FOMC. 1994. *Meeting of the Federal Open Market Committee March 22, 1994*. Washington, DC: Board of Governors of the Federal Reserve System. https://www.federalreserve.gov/monetarypolicy/files/FOMC19940322meeting.pdf. Accessed May 6, 2024.

FOMC. 1996. *Meeting of the Federal Open Market Committee July 2–3, 1996*. Washington, DC: Board of Governors of the Federal Reserve System. https://www.federalreserve.gov/monetarypolicy/files/FOMC19960703meeting.pdf. Accessed March 3, 2016.

FOMC. 2007a. *Conference Call of the Federal Open Market Committee on December 6, 2007. Federal Reserve Bank, FOMC: Transcripts and Other Historical Materials, 2008, Washington, DC*. Washington, DC: Board of Governors of the Federal Reserve System. https://www.federalreserve.gov/monetarypolicy/files/FOMC20071206confcall.pdf. Accessed April 9, 2019.

FOMC. 2007b. *Meeting of the Federal Open Market Committee on June 27–28, 2007*. Washington, DC: Board of Governors of the Federal Reserve System. https://www.federalreserve.gov/monetarypolicy/files/FOMC20070628meeting.pdf. Accessed April 9, 2016.

FOMC. 2007c. *Meeting of the Federal Open Market Committee on September 18, 2007, Federal Reserve Bank, FOMC: Transcripts and Other Historical Materials, 2008, Washington, DC*. Washington, DC: Board of Governors of the Federal Reserve System. https://www.federalreserve.gov/monetarypolicy/files/FOMC20070918meeting.pdf. Accessed March 3, 2016.

FOMC. 2008a. *Conference Call of the Federal Open Market Committee on September 29, 2008*. Washington, DC: Board of Governors of the Federal Reserve System. https://www.federalreserve.gov/monetarypolicy/files/FOMC20080929confcall.pdf. Accessed April 1, 2020.

FOMC. 2008b. *Meeting of the Federal Open Market Committee on October 28–29, 2008. Federal Reserve Bank, FOMC: Transcripts and Other Historical Materials, 2008, Washington, DC*. Washington, DC: Board of Governors of the Federal Reserve System. https://www.federalreserve.gov/monetarypolicy/files/FOMC20081029meeting.pdf. Accessed March 3, 2016.

FOMC. 2008c. *Meeting of the Federal Open Market Committee on September 16, 2008. Federal Reserve Bank, FOMC: Transcripts and Other Historical Materials, 2008, Washington, DC*. Washington, DC: Board of Governors of the Federal Reserve System.

https://www.federalreserve.gov/monetarypolicy/files/FOMC20080916meeting.pdf. Accessed April 1, 2020.

FOMC. 2009. *Meeting of the Federal Open Market Committee on November 3–4, 2009. Federal Reserve Bank, FOMC: Transcripts and Other Historical Materials, 2009, Washington, DC.* Washington, DC: Board of Governors of the Federal Reserve System. https://www.federalreserve.gov/monetarypolicy/files/FOMC20091104meeting.pdf. Accessed January 4, 2019.

FOMC. 2010. *Conference Call of the Federal Open Market Committee on May 9, 2010.* Washington, DC: Board of Governors of the Federal Reserve System. https://www.federalreserve.gov/monetarypolicy/files/FOMC20100509confcall.pdf. Accessed March 3, 2016.

FOMC. 2013. *Meeting of the Federal Open Market Committee on October 29–30, 2013.* Washington, DC: Board of Governors of the Federal Reserve System. https://www.federalreserve.gov/monetarypolicy/files/FOMC20131030meeting.pdf. Accessed August 19, 2023.

Freeman, Colin. 2009. "Former Iceland Bank Governor David Oddsson Defends Role in Meltdown." *Telegraph*. https://www.telegraph.co.uk/finance/newsbysector/banksandfinance/5231082/Former-Iceland-bank-governor-David-Oddsson-defends-role-in-meltdown.html. Accessed April 20, 2020.

Frieden, Jeffry A. 2006. *Global Capitalism: Its Fall and Rise in the Twentieth Century.* New York: Norton.

Frieden, Jeffry. 2016. "The Governance of International Finance." *Annual Review of Political Science* 19 (1): 33–48.

Friedman, Milton. 1962. *Capitalism and Freedom*. Chicago: Chicago University Press.

Friedman, Milton, and Anna J. Schwartz. 1963. *A Monetary History of the United States, 1867–1960*. Princeton, NJ: Princeton University Press.

Fuhrmann, Matthew, and Michael C. Horowitz. 2015. "When Leaders Matter: Rebel Experience and Nuclear Proliferation." *Journal of Politics* 77 (1): 72–87.

Garber, Peter M. 1993. "The Collapse of the Bretton Woods Fixed Exchange Rate System." In *A Retrospective on the Bretton Woods System: Lessons for International Monetary Reform*, 461–94. Chicago: Chicago University Press. https://www.nber.org/books-and-chapters/retrospective-bretton-woods-system-lessons-international-monetary-reform/collapse-bretton-woods-fixed-exchange-rate-system. Accessed January 10, 2022.

Garriga, Ana Carolina, and Cesar M. Rodriguez. 2020. "More Effective Than We Thought: Central Bank Independence and Inflation in Developing Countries." *Economic Modelling* 85: 87–105.

Gavin, Francis J. 2004. *Gold, Dollars, and Power: The Politics of International Monetary Relations, 1958–1971*. Chapel Hill: University of North Carolina Press.

Gerring, John. 2007. *Case Study Research: Principles and Practices*. Cambridge: Cambridge University Press.

Gilbert, Milton. 1980. *Quest for World Monetary Order: The Gold-Dollar System and Its Aftermath*. New York: Wiley.

Gilpin, Robert. 1981. *War and Change in World Politics*. Cambridge: Cambridge University Press.

Gilpin, Robert. 1987. *The Political Economy of International Relations*. Princeton, NJ: Princeton University Press.

Goddard, Stacie E. 2009. "Brokering Change: Networks and Entrepreneurs in International Politics." *International Theory* 1 (2): 249–81.

Gourevitch, Peter Alexis. 1986. *Politics in Hard Times: Comparative Responses to International Economic Crises*. Ithaca, NY: Cornell University Press.

Government Accountability Office, United States. 2011. *The Federal Reserve System: Opportunities Exist to Strengthen Policies and Processing for Managing Emergency Assistance*. GAO-11-696, July 21. Washington DC. https://www.gao.gov/new.items/d11696.pdf.

Granovetter, Mark. 1973. "The Strength of Weak Ties." *American Journal of Sociology* 78 (6): 1360–80.

Granovetter, Mark. 1985. "Economic Action and Social Structure: The Problem of Embeddedness." *American Journal of Sociology* 91 (3): 481–510.

Gray, Julia. 2009. "International Organization as a Seal of Approval: European Union Accession and Investor Risk." *American Journal of Political Science* 53 (4): 931–49.

Gray, Julia. 2013. *The Company States Keep: International Economic Organizations and Investor Perceptions*. Cambridge: Cambridge University Press.

Greider, William. 1989. *Secrets of the Temple: How the Federal Reserve Runs the Country*. New York: Simon and Schuster.

Grim, Ryan. 2009. "Bernanke: 'I Don't Know' Which Foreign Banks Got Half Trillion U.S. Dollars" (VIDEO) | *HuffPost*. https://www.huffpost.com/entry/bernanke-i-dont-know-whic_n_244302. Accessed March 8, 2020.

Haas, Ernst B. 1964. *Beyond the Nation-State: Functionalism and International Organization*. Stanford, CA: Stanford University Press.

Haas, Peter M. 1992. "Introduction: Epistemic Communities and International Policy Coordination." *International Organization* 46 (1): 1–35.

Hawtrey, R. G. 1922. "The Genoa Resolutions on Currency." *Economic Journal* 32 (127): 290–304.

Helleiner, Eric. 1994. *States and the Reemergence of Global Finance: From Bretton Woods to the 1990s*. Ithaca, NY: Cornell University Press.

Helleiner, Eric. 2013. "Financial Officials as Diplomats: Evolving Issues, Actors, and Techniques since the 1920s." *The Oxford Handbook of Modern Diplomacy*. Oxford: Oxford University Press.

Helleiner, Eric. 2014. *The Status Quo Crisis: Global Financial Governance after the 2008 Financial Meltdown*. Oxford: Oxford University Press.

Helleiner, Eric, and Stefano Pagliari. 2011. "The End of an Era in International Financial Regulation? A Postcrisis Research Agenda." *International Organization* 65 (1): 169–200.

Henning, C. Randall. 2015. "The Global Liquidity Safety Net: Institutional Cooperation on Precautionary Facilities and Central Bank Swaps." *New Thinking and the New G20 Series* (Paper No. 5). The Centre for International Governance Innovation. https://www.cigionline.org/static/documents/new_thinking_g20_no5_web.pdf.

Hilmarsson, Hilmar Þór. 2022. "The Collapse of the Icelandic Banking System and the (Dis)Honest and/or (In)Competent Response of the International Community." *Regional Formation and Development Studies* 16 (2): 24–32.

Högenauer, Anna-Lena, and David Howarth. 2019. "The Democratic Deficit and European Central Bank Crisis Monetary Policies." Edited by Diane Fromage, Paul Dermine, Phedon Nicolaides, and Klaus Tuori. *Maastricht Journal of European and Comparative Law* 26 (1): 81–93.

Holmes, Marcus. 2018. *Face-to-Face Diplomacy: Social Neuroscience and International Relations*. Cambridge: Cambridge University Press.

Holmes, Marcus, and Keren Yarhi-Milo. 2017. "The Psychological Logic of Peace Summits: How Empathy Shapes Outcomes of Diplomatic Negotiations." *International Studies Quarterly* 61 (1): 107–22.

Horn, Martin. 2022. *J. P. Morgan & Co. and the Crisis of Capitalism: From the Wall Street Crash to World War II*. Cambridge: Cambridge University Press.

Horowitz, Michael. 2015. *Why Leaders Fight*. New York: Cambridge University Press.

Horowitz, Michael. 2018. "Leaders, Leadership, and International Security." In *The Oxford Handbook of International Security*. Oxford: Oxford University Press.

Hull, Cordell. 1948. *The Memoirs of Cordell Hull*. New York: Macmillan.

Ikenberry, G. John. 2001. *After Victory: Institutions, Strategic Restraint, and the Rebuilding of Order after Major Wars*. Princeton, NJ: Princeton University Press.

Ingves, Stefan. 2022. Lessons Learned Oral History Project Interview, Yale Program on Financial Stability. Interview by Maryann Haggerty and Carly Mott. Zoom. https://ypfsresourcelibrary.blob.core.windows.net/fcic/YPFS/LL_Ingves_Trans_2023-08-01_ready.pdf.

Inoue, Junnosuke, and E. H. de Bunsen. 1931. *Problems of the Japanese Exchange, 1914–1926*. Translated by E. H. de Bunsen. London: Macmillan.

Irwin, Neil. 2013. *The Alchemists: Three Central Bankers and a World on Fire*. New York: Penguin.

Jackson, Patrick Thaddeus, and Daniel H. Nexon. 2019. "Reclaiming the Social: Relationalism in Anglophone International Studies." *Cambridge Review of International Affairs* 32 (5): 582–600.

Jacobs, Lawrence R., and Desmond King. 2016. *Fed Power: How Finance Wins*. New York: Oxford University Press.

James, Harold. 1984. "The Causes of the German Banking Crisis of 1931." *Economic History Review* 37 (1): 68–87.

James, Harold. 1996. *International Monetary Cooperation since Bretton Woods*. Washington, DC: International Monetary Fund.

James, Harold. 2013. "International Cooperation and Central Banks." *Center for International Governance Innovation* 1 (October): 31. https://www.cigionline.org/static/documents/vol.1.pdf.

Jervis, Robert. 1976. *Perception and Misperception in International Politics*. Princeton, NJ: Princeton University Press.

Johnson, Juliet. 2016. *Priests of Prosperity: How Central Bankers Transformed the Postcommunist World*. Ithaca, NY: Cornell University Press.

Kahler, Miles. 1998. *Capital Flows and Financial Crises*. Ithaca, NY: Cornell University Press.

Kaplan, Jacob J. 1989. *The European Payments Union: Financial Diplomacy in the 1950s*. Oxford: Clarendon.

Kapstein, Ethan B. 1992. "Between Power and Purpose: Central Bankers and the Politics of Regulatory Convergence." *International Organization* 46 (1): 265–87.

Kapstein, Ethan B. 1994. *Governing the Global Economy: International Finance and the State*. Cambridge, MA: Harvard University Press.

Katzenstein, Peter J., ed. 1977. *Between Power and Plenty: Foreign Economic Policies of Advanced Industrial States*. Madison: University of Wisconsin Press.

Katzenstein, Peter J., and Stephen C. Nelson. 2013. "Reading the Right Signals and Reading the Signals Right: IPE and the Financial Crisis of 2008." *Review of International Political Economy* 20 (5): 1101–31.

Keating, Vincent Charles, and Jan Ruzicka. 2014. "Trusting Relationships in International Politics: No Need to Hedge." *Review of International Studies* 40 (4): 753–70.

Keohane, Nannerl O. 2010. *Thinking about Leadership*. Princeton, NJ: Princeton University Press.

Keohane, Robert O. 1984. *After Hegemony: Cooperation and Discord in the World Political Economy*. Princeton, NJ: Princeton University Press.

Keohane, Robert O. 2011. "Global Governance and Legitimacy." *Review of International Political Economy* 18 (1): 99–109.

Keohane, Robert O., and Joseph S. Nye. 1977. *Power and Interdependence: World Politics in Transition*. New York: Little, Brown.

Kertzer, Joshua D. 2016. *Resolve in International Politics*. Princeton, NJ: Princeton University Press.

Keynes, John Maynard. 1920. *The Economic Consequences of the Peace*. London: Harcourt, Brace and Howe.

Keynes, John Maynard. 1923. *A Tract on Monetary Reform*. London: Macmillan.

Keynes, John Maynard. 1936. *The General Theory of Employment, Interest and Money*. London: Harcourt, Brace.

Keynes, John Maynard. 1937. *The Collected Writings of John Maynard Keynes: Volume 14: The General Theory and after: Part II. Defence and Development*. Edited by Elizabeth Johnson and Donald Moggridge. London: Royal Economic Society.

Kindleberger, Charles P. 1973. *The World in Depression, 1929–1939*. Berkeley: University of California Press.

Kindleberger, Charles P. 1978. *Manias, Panics, and Crashes: A History of Financial Crises*. New York: Basic Books.

Kindleberger, Charles P. 1987. *Marshall Plan Days*. Boston: Allen & Unwin.

Kindleberger, Charles P. 1989. *Economic Laws and Economic History*. Cambridge: Cambridge University Press.

Kindleberger, Charles P. 1990. *Historical Economics: Art or Science?* Berkeley: University of California Press.

King, Mervyn. 2004. Comments on "Risk and Uncertainty in Monetary Policy" by Alan Greenspan, AEA Annual Conference, 2004. *Bank of England*: 10. https://www.bankofengland.co.uk/-/media/boe/files/speech/2004/comments-made-on-3-january-by-mervyn-king.pdf.

Kirshner, Jonathan. 2007. *Appeasing Bankers: Financial Caution on the Road to War*. Princeton, NJ: Princeton University Press.

Kirshner, Jonathan. 2015. "The Economic Sins of Modern IR Theory and the Classical Realist Alternative." *World Politics* 67 (1): 155–83.

Kirshner, Jonathan. 2019. "The Fire Last Time." *Los Angeles Review of Books*. https://lareviewofbooks.org/article/the-fire-last-time/. Accessed August 27, 2022.

van 't Klooster, Jens. 2020. "The Ethics of Delegating Monetary Policy." *Journal of Politics* 82 (2): 587–99.

Knight, Frank H. 1921. *Risk, Uncertainty and Profit*. Boston: Houghton Mifflin.

Kohn, Donald. 2010. Federal Reserve Board Oral History Project: Interview with Donald L. Kohn. Interview by David H. Small, David E. Lindsey, and James Clouse. https://www.federalreserve.gov/aboutthefed/files/donald-l-kohn-interview-20100527.pdf.

Krasner, Stephen D. 1976. "State Power and the Structure of International Trade." *World Politics* 28 (3): 317–47.

Krcmaric, Daniel, Stephen C. Nelson, and Andrew Roberts. 2020. "Studying Leaders and Elites: The Personal Biography Approach." *Annual Review of Political Science* 23 (1): 133–51.

Kreps, Sarah. 2011. *Coalitions of Convenience: United States Military Interventions after the Cold War*. New York: Oxford University Press.

Ku, Minseon, and Jennifer Mitzen. 2022. "The Dark Matter of World Politics: System Trust, Summits, and State Personhood." *International Organization* 76 (4): 799–829.

Kydd, Andrew. 2001. "Trust Building, Trust Breaking: The Dilemma of NATO Enlargement." *International Organization* 55 (4): 801–28.

Lake, David A. 2009. *Hierarchy in International Relations*. Ithaca, NY: Cornell University Press.

Larson, Deborah Welch. 1997. *Anatomy of Mistrust: U.S.-Soviet Relations during the Cold War.* Ithaca, NY: Cornell University Press.

LeBor, Adam. 2013. *Tower of Basel: The Shadowy History of the Secret Bank That Runs the World.* New York: Public Affairs.

Leonard, Christopher. 2020. "How Jay Powell's Coronavirus Response Is Changing the Fed Forever." *Time.* https://time.com/5851870/federal-reserve-coronavirus/. Accessed August 19, 2023.

Lindley, Ernest Kidder. 1933. *The Roosevelt Revolution, First Phase.* New York: Viking.

Lockwood, Erin. 2015. "Predicting the Unpredictable: Value-at-Risk, Performativity, and the Politics of Financial Uncertainty." *Review of International Political Economy* 22 (4): 719–56.

Lockwood, Erin. 2016. *The Global Politics of Central Banking: A View from Political Science.* Report. Mario Einaudi Center for International Studies. https://ecommons.cornell.edu/handle/1813/55059. Accessed March 7, 2022.

Lupton, Danielle L. 2020. *Reputation for Resolve: How Leaders Signal Determination in International Politics.* Ithaca, NY: Cornell University Press.

MacDonald, Paul K. 2018. "Embedded Authority: A Relational Network Approach to Hierarchy in World Politics." *Review of International Studies* 44 (1): 128–50.

MacMillan, Margaret. 2003. *Paris 1919: Six Months That Changed the World.* New York: Random House.

Marple, Tim. 2021. "The Social Management of Complex Uncertainty: Central Bank Similarity and Crisis Liquidity Swaps at the Federal Reserve." *Review of International Organizations* 16 (2): 377–401.

Martin, Jamie. 2022. *The Meddlers: Sovereignty, Empire, and the Birth of Global Economic Governance.* Cambridge, MA: Harvard University Press.

Matthijs, Matthias. 2022. "Hegemonic Leadership Is What States Make of It: Reading Kindleberger in Washington and Berlin." *Review of International Political Economy* 29 (2): 371–98.

McCauley, Robert N., and Catherine R. Schenk. 2020. "Central Bank Swaps Then and Now: Swaps and Dollar Liquidity in the 1960s." *Working Paper, BIS* (No. 851): 47. https://www.bis.org/publ/work851.pdf.

McCourt, David M. 2016. "Practice Theory and Relationalism as the New Constructivism." *International Studies Quarterly* 60 (3): 475–85.

McDowell, Daniel. 2012. "The US as 'Sovereign International Last-Resort Lender': The Fed's Currency Swap Programme during the Great Panic of 2007–09." *New Political Economy* 17 (2): 157–78.

McDowell, Daniel. 2017. *Brother, Can You Spare a Billion? The United States, the IMF, and the International Lender of Last Resort.* New York: Oxford University Press.

McNamara, Kathleen R. 1998. *The Currency of Ideas: Monetary Politics in the European Union.* Ithaca, NY: Cornell University Press.

McNamara, Kathleen. 2002. "Rational Fictions: Central Bank Independence and the Social Logic of Delegation." *West European Politics* 25 (1): 47–76.

Mearsheimer, John J. 1994. "The False Promise of International Institutions." *International Security* 19 (3): 5–49.

Meltzer, Allan H. 2003. *A History of the Federal Reserve, Volume 1: 1913–1951.* Chicago: University of Chicago Press.

Mercer, Jonathan. 2005. "Rationality and Psychology in International Politics." *International Organization* 59 (1): 77–106.

Metzler, Mark. 2006. *Lever of Empire: The International Gold Standard and the Crisis of Liberalism in Prewar Japan (Twentieth-Century Japan).* Berkeley: University of California Press.

Meyer, Richard Hemmig. 1970. *Bankers' Diplomacy: Monetary Stabilization in the Twenties*. New York: Columbia University Press.

Mills, C. Wright. 1956. *The Power Elite*. New York: Oxford University Press.

Mirwis, Arnold T. 1987. "Carl Jung and Lord Montagu Norman: A Failed Consultation." *American Imago* 44 (2): 159–69.

Mitrany, David. 1976. *The Functional Theory of Politics*. London: London School of Economics and Political Science.

Moessner, Richhild, and William A. Allen. 2010. "Options for Meeting the Demand for International Liquidity during Financial Crises." *BIS Quarterly Review* (September). https://www.bis.org/publ/qtrpdf/r_qt1009g.pdf.

Moggridge, D. E. 1972. *British Monetary Policy, 1924–1931: The Norman Conquest of $4.86*. Cambridge: Cambridge University Press.

Monnet, Eric. 2024. *Balance of Power: Central Banks and the Fate of Democracies*. Translated by Steven Randall. Chicago: Chicago University Press.

Moreau, Emile. 1991. *The Golden Franc: Memoirs of a Governor of the Bank of France: The Stabilization of the Franc (1926–1928)*. Boulder, CO: Westview.

Morrison, James Ashley. 2021. *England's Cross of Gold: Keynes, Churchill, and the Governance of Economic Beliefs*. Ithaca, NY: Cornell University Press.

Moschella, Manuela. 2024. *Unexpected Revolutionaries: How Central Banks Made and Unmade Economic Orthodoxy*. Ithaca, NY: Cornell University Press.

Moss, Michael S., and David Thomas. 2021. *Archival Silences: Missing, Lost, and Uncreated Archives*. Abingdon, UK: Routledge.

Mouré, Kenneth. 1992. "The Limits to Central Bank Co-operation, 1916–36." *Contemporary European History* 1 (3): 259–79.

Mouré, Kenneth. 2002. *The Gold Standard Illusion: France, the Bank of France, and the International Gold Standard, 1914–1939*. Oxford: Oxford University Press.

Mundell, R. A. 1999. "A Reconsideration of the Twentieth Century." Speech presented at the Nobel Prize Lecture, Aula Magna, Stockholm University. https://www.nobelprize.org/prizes/economic-sciences/1999/mundell/lecture/.

Nelson, Stephen C. 2014. "Playing Favorites: How Shared Beliefs Shape the IMF's Lending Decisions." *International Organization* 68 (2): 297–328.

Nelson, Stephen C. 2017. *The Currency of Confidence: How Economic Beliefs Shape the IMF's Relationship with Its Borrowers*. Ithaca, NY: Cornell University Press.

Nelson, Stephen C., and Peter J. Katzenstein. 2014. "Uncertainty, Risk, and the Financial Crisis of 2008." *International Organization* 68 (2): 361–92.

North, Douglass C., and Barry R. Weingast. 1989. "Constitutions and Commitment: The Evolution of Institutions Governing Public Choice in Seventeenth-Century England." *Journal of Economic History* 49 (4): 803–32.

Oatley, Thomas H. 2015. *A Political Economy of American Hegemony: Buildups, Booms, and Busts*. Cambridge: Cambridge University Press.

Obstfeld, Maurice. 2009a. "Lender of Last Resort and Global Liquidity." *Development Outreach* 11 (3): 43–46.

Obstfeld, Maurice. 2009b. "Lenders of Last Resort in a Globalized World." Institute for Monetary and Economic Studies, Bank of Japan, Tokyo, Discussion Paper No. 2009-E-18. https://www.imes.boj.or.jp/research/papers/english/09-E-18.pdf. Accessed April 20, 2020.

Obstfeld, Maurice, Jay C. Shambaugh, and Alan M. Taylor. 2009. "Financial Instability, Reserves, and Central Bank Swap Lines in the Panic of 2008." *American Economic Review* 99 (2): 480–86.

O'Driscoll, Jr., Gerald P. 2011. "The Federal Reserve's Covert Bailout of Europe." *Wall Street Journal*. https://online.wsj.com/article/SB10001424052970204464404577118682763082876.html. Accessed January 9, 2022.

Ortlieb, Pierre. 2020. "Fed Should Bring Back Dollar Swap Lines." *OMFIF*. https://www.omfif.org/2020/03/fed-should-bring-back-dollar-swap-lines/. Accessed April 15, 2020.

Oye, Kenneth A., ed. 1986. *Cooperation under Anarchy*. Princeton, NJ: Princeton University Press.

P. B. 1952. "The Sterling Crisis." *World Today* 8 (4): 140–48.

Pak, Susie J. 2013. *Gentlemen Bankers: The World of J. P. Morgan*. Cambridge, MA: Harvard University Press.

Palyi, Melchior. 1972. *The Twilight of Gold 1914–1936: Myths and Realities*. Chicago: Henry Regnert.

Park, Yung Chul. 2011. "The Role of Macroprudential Policy for Financial Stability in East Asia's Emerging Economies." *SSRN Electronic Journal*. http://www.ssrn.com/abstract=1853243. Accessed April 20, 2020.

Pauly, Louis W. 1996. "The League of Nations and the Foreshadowing of the International Monetary Fund." *Essays in International Finance* 201: 1–52.

Perry, Alexander R. 2020. "The Federal Reserve's Questionable Legal Basis for Foreign Central Bank Liquidity Swaps." *Columbia Law Review* 120 (3): 729–68.

Pittaluga, Giovanni B., and Elena Seghezza. 2012. "The Role of 'Rentiers' in the Stabilization Processes of the 1920s." *European Review of Economic History* 16 (2): 188–210.

Poast, Paul. 2015. "Central Banks at War." *International Organization* 69 (1): 63–95.

Polanyi, Karl. 1957. *The Great Transformation*. Boston: Beacon.

Pop, Valentina, Sam Fleming, and James Politi. 2022. "Weaponisation of Finance: How the West Unleashed 'Shock and Awe' on Russia." *Financial Times*. https://www.ft.com/content/5b397d6b-bde4-4a8c-b9a4-080485d6c64a. Accessed September 8, 2023.

Pouliot, Vincent. 2016. *International Pecking Orders: The Politics and Practice of Multilateral Diplomacy*. Cambridge: Cambridge University Press.

Prasad, Eswar. 2014. *The Dollar Trap: How the U.S. Dollar Tightened Its Grip on Global Finance*. Princeton, NJ: Princeton University Press.

Rathbun, Brian C. 2012. *Trust in International Cooperation: International Security Institutions, Domestic Politics and American Multilateralism*. Cambridge: Cambridge University Press.

Rivera, Lauren A. 2016. *Pedigree: How Elite Students Get Elite Jobs*. Princeton, NJ: Princeton University Press.

Rodrik, Dani. 2014. "When Ideas Trump Interests: Preferences, Worldviews, and Policy Innovations." *Journal of Economic Perspectives* 28 (1): 189–208.

Romer, Christina D., and David H. Romer. 2004. "Choosing the Federal Reserve Chair: Lessons from History." *Journal of Economic Perspectives* 18 (1): 129–62.

Romer, Christina D., and David H. Romer. 2013. "The Missing Transmission Mechanism in the Monetary Explanation of the Great Depression." *American Economic Review* 103 (3): 66–72.

Roosevelt, Franklin D. 1938. *The Public Papers and Addresses of Franklin Delano Roosevelt*, vol. 1. New York: Random House.

Rosenberg, Emily S. 1999. *Financial Missionaries to the World: The Politics and Culture of Dollar Diplomacy, 1900–1930*. Cambridge, MA: Harvard University Press.

Ruggie, John Gerard. 1982. "International Regimes, Transactions, and Change: Embedded Liberalism in the Postwar Economic Order." *International Organization* 36 (2): 379–415.

Sahasrabuddhe, Aditi. 2019. "Drawing the Line: The Politics of Federal Currency Swaps in the Global Financial Crisis." *Review of International Political Economy* 26 (3): 461–89.

Sahasrabuddhe, Aditi. 2021. "Legitimacy Gap." *Phenomenal World*. https://www.phenomenalworld.org/analysis/legitimacy-gap/. Accessed August 1, 2022.

Sahasrabuddhe, Aditi. 2024. "Central Bankers in Crisis: Interpersonal Trust, Cooperation, and the Creation of the Fed Swap Network during the 2008 Global Financial Crisis." *International Studies Quarterly* 68 (2).

Samuelson, Robert J. 2008. "The NEWSWEEK 50: Bernanke, Trichet, Shirakawa." *Newsweek*. https://www.newsweek.com/newsweek-50-bernanke-trichet-shirakawa-83099. Accessed August 26, 2022.

Sargent, Thomas J., ed. 1982. "The Ends of Four Big Inflations." In *Rational Expectations and Inflation*, 38–110. Princeton, NJ: Princeton University Press.

Saunders, Elizabeth N. 2009. "Transformative Choices: Leaders and the Origins of Intervention Strategy." *International Security* 34 (2): 119–61.

Sayers, R. S. 1976. *The Bank of England, 1891–1944*. Cambridge: Cambridge University Press.

Schacht, Hjalmar Horace Greeley. 1927. *The Stabilization of the Mark*. New York: Adelphi.

Schacht, Hjalmar Horace Greeley. 1956. *Confessions of "the Old Wizard": The Autobiography of Hjalmar Horace Greeley Schacht*. Boston: Houghton Mifflin.

Schedler, Andreas. 2007. "Mapping Contingency." In *Political Contingency*, edited by Ian Shapiro and Sonu Bedi, 54–78. New York: New York University Press.

Schenk, Catherine R. 2010. *The Decline of Sterling: Managing the Retreat of an International Currency, 1945–1992*. Cambridge: Cambridge University Press.

Schweizerische Nationalbank. 2007. *The Swiss National Bank, 1907–2007*. Zurich: Swiss National Bank.

Seabrooke, Leonard, and Eleni Tsingou. 2021. "Revolving Doors in International Financial Governance." *Global Networks* 21 (2): 294–319.

Sheets, Nathan, Edwin Truman, and Clay Lowery. 2018. "The Federal Reserve's Swap Lines: Lender of Last Resort on a Global Scale." In *Responding to the Global Financial Crisis: What We Did and Why We Did It*. Hutchins Center on Fiscal & Monetary Policy at Brookings and Yale School of Management Program of Financial Stability. https://www.brookings.edu/wp-content/uploads/2018/08/14-B-International-Swaps-Prelim-Disc-Draft-2018.09.11.pdf.

Shirakawa, Masaaki. 2021. *Tumultuous Times: Central Banking in an Era of Crisis*. New Haven, CT: Yale Program on Financial Stability Series.

Siklos, Pierre L. 2002. *The Changing Face of Central Banking: Evolutionary Trends since World War II*. Cambridge: Cambridge University Press.

Silver, Allan. 1989. "Friendship and Trust as Moral Ideals: An Historical Approach." *European Journal of Sociology* 30 (2): 274–97.

Simmons, Beth A. 1994. *Who Adjusts? Domestic Sources of Foreign Economic Policy during the Interwar Years*. Princeton, NJ: Princeton University Press.

Simmons, Beth A. 2001. "The International Politics of Harmonization: The Case of Capital Market Regulation." *International Organization* 55 (3): 589–620.

Simmons, Beth A. 2006. "The Future of Central Bank Cooperation." In *Celebrating 75 Years of the Bank for International Settlements, 1930–2005*, vol. 200. BIS Working Paper. https://www.bis.org/publ/work200.pdf.

Singleton, John. 2011. *Central Banking in the Twentieth Century*. Cambridge: Cambridge University Press.

Slobodian, Quinn. 2018. *Globalists: The End of Empire and the Birth of Neoliberalism*. Cambridge, MA: Harvard University Press.

Smethurst, Richard J. 2001. "Internationalism in Interwar Japanese Financial Politics." In *Japan in the World, the World in Japan: Fifty Years of Japanese Studies at Michigan*, edited by The University of Michigan Center for Japanese Studies, 197–204. Ann Arbor: University of Michigan Press.

Smialek, Jeanna. 2023. *Limitless: The Federal Reserve Takes on a New Age of Crisis*. New York: Penguin Random House.

Stone, Randall W. 2013. "Informal Governance in International Organizations: Introduction to the Special Issue." *Review of International Organizations* 8 (2): 121–36.

Strange, Susan. 1971. "The Politics of International Currencies." *World Politics* 23 (2): 215–31.

Subbarao, Duvvuri. 2016. *Who Moved My Interest Rate? Leading the Reserve Bank of India through Five Turbulent Years*. Gurgaon, India: Penguin.

Tabuchi, Hiroko. 2013. "At Odds with the Government, Japan's Central Bank Chief Offers an Early Exit." *New York Times*. https://www.nytimes.com/2013/02/06/business/global/japanese-central-bank-chief-to-step-down-early.html. Accessed September 21, 2020.

Tett, Gillian. 2020. "Coronavirus Trade Disruption Could Start a 'Dash for Cash.'" https://www.ft.com/content/28df6fe4-6467-11ea-b3f3-fe4680ea68b5. Accessed April 15, 2020.

The National Archives. n.d. "Economic Slump." The National Archives, Kew, Surrey TW9 4DU. https://www.nationalarchives.gov.uk/cabinetpapers/themes/economic-slump.htm. Accessed June 25, 2022.

The New York Times. 1928. "Benjamin Strong, Banker, Dies at 56." http://timesmachine.nytimes.comhttp://timesmachine.nytimes.com/timesmachine/1928/10/17/118344900.html. Accessed August 28, 2022.

Toma, Eugenia Froedge. 1986. *Central Bankers, Bureaucratic Incentives, and Monetary Policy*. Dordrecht: Springer.

Toniolo, Gianni. 2005. *Central Bank Cooperation at the Bank for International Settlements, 1930–1973*. New York: Cambridge University Press.

Tooze, J. Adam. 2018. *Crashed: How a Decade of Financial Crises Changed the World*. New York: Viking.

Tooze, J. Adam. 2020. "The Death of the Central Bank Myth." *Foreign Policy*. https://foreignpolicy.com/2020/05/13/european-central-bank-myth-monetary-policy-german-court-ruling/. Accessed August 1, 2022.

Triffin, Robert. 1961. *Gold and the Dollar Crisis: The Future of Convertibility*, rev. ed. New Haven, CT: Yale University Press.

Triffin, Robert. 1978. "Gold and the Dollar Crisis: Yesterday and Tomorrow." International Finance Section, Department of Economics. Princeton, NJ: Princeton University (No. 132): 40.

Tsingou, Eleni. 2015. "Club Governance and the Making of Global Financial Rules." *Review of International Political Economy* 22 (2): 225–56.

Tucker, Paul M. W. 2018. *Unelected Power: The Quest for Legitimacy in Central Banking and the Regulatory State*. Princeton, NJ: Princeton University Press.

Tucker, Paul M. W. 2022. *Global Discord: Values and Power in a Fractured World Order*. Princeton, NJ: Princeton University Press.

Turner, Arthur. 1996. "Anglo-French Financial Relations in the 1920s." *European History Quarterly* 26 (1): 31.

Vaughn, Abigail. 2020. "Ties That Bind: The Geopolitics of Bilateral Currency Swaps." The Political Economy of International Organization Annual Conference. https://www.peio.me/wp-content/uploads/2020/01/PEIO13_paper_138.pdf.

Volcker, Paul A., and Toyoo Gyohten. 1992. *Changing Fortunes: The World's Money and the Threat to American Leadership*. New York: Times Books.

Vreeland, James Raymond. 2003. "Why Do Governments and the IMF Enter into Agreements? Statistically Selected Cases." *International Political Science Review* 24 (3): 321–43.

Vreeland, James Raymond. 2007. *The International Monetary Fund: Politics of Conditional Lending*. New York: Routledge.

Webb, Michael C. 1995. *The Political Economy of Policy Coordination: International Adjustment since 1945*. Ithaca, NY: Cornell University Press.

Webb, Michael C., and Stephen D. Krasner. 1989. "Hegemonic Stability Theory: An Empirical Assessment." *Review of International Studies* 15 (2): 183–98.

Weitz, John. 1997. *Hitler's Banker: Hjalmar Horace Greeley Schacht*. Boston: Little, Brown.

Wessel, David. 2009. *In Fed We Trust: Ben Bernanke's War on the Great Panic*. New York: Crown.

Wheeler, Nicholas J. 2012. "Trust-Building in International Relations." *Peace Prints: South Asian Journal of Peacebuilding* 4 (2): 13.

Wheeler, Nicholas J. 2018. *Trusting Enemies: Interpersonal Relationships in International Conflict*. Oxford: Oxford University Press.

Wheelock, David C. 1992. "Monetary Policy in the Great Depression: What the Fed Did, and Why." *Review* 74 (2). https://research.stlouisfed.org/publications/review/1992/03/01/monetary-policy-in-the-great-depression-what-the-fed-did-and-why.

White, Harrison C. 2002. *Markets from Networks: Socioeconomic Models of Production*. Princeton, NJ: Princeton University Press.

Wicker, Elmus R. 1966. *Federal Reserve Monetary Policy, 1917–1933*. New York: Random House.

Widmaier, Wesley W., Mark Blyth, and Leonard Seabrooke. 2007. "Exogenous Shocks or Endogenous Constructions? The Meanings of Wars and Crises." *International Studies Quarterly* 51 (4): 747–59.

Wiggins, Rosalind, Benjamin Hoffner, Greg Feldberg, and Andrew Metrick. 2023. "Central Bank Foreign Currency Swaps and Repo Facilities Survey." *Journal of Financial Crisis* 5 (1): 25–222. https://elischolar.library.yale.edu/cgi/viewcontent.cgi?article=1480&context=journal-of-financial-crises.

Woods, Ngaire. 2010. "Global Governance after the Financial Crisis: A New Multilateralism or the Last Gasp of the Great Powers?" *Global Policy* 1 (1): 51–63.

Woods, Ngaire. 2014. *The Globalizers: The IMF, the World Bank, and Their Borrowers*. Ithaca, NY: Cornell University Press.

Yarhi-Milo, Keren. 2014. *Knowing the Adversary: Leaders, Intelligence, and Assessment of Intentions in International Relations*. Princeton, NJ: Princeton University Press.

Yeager, Leland B. 1962. *In Search of a Monetary Constitution*. Cambridge, MA: Harvard University Press.

Zelizer, Viviana A. 2000. "The Purchase of Intimacy." *Law & Social Inquiry* 25 (3): 817–48.

Zelizer, Viviana A. 2012. "How I Became a Relational Economic Sociologist and What Does That Mean?" *Politics & Society* 40 (2): 145–74.

Index

Figures and tables are indicated by "f" and "t" following page numbers.

www.ingramcontent.com/pod-product-compliance
Lightning Source LLC
Chambersburg PA
CBHW021826080126
37932CB00008B/114/J
9781501782589